OPEN TARGET

OPEN TARGET

WHERE AMERICA IS VULNERABLE TO ATTACK

Clark Kent Ervin

palgrave
macmillan

OPEN TARGET
Copyright © Clark Kent Ervin, 2006.

First published 2006 by
PALGRAVE MACMILLAN™
175 Fifth Avenue, New York, N.Y. 10010 and
Houndmills, Basingstoke, Hampshire, England RG21 6XS.
Companies and representatives throughout the world.

PALGRAVE MACMILLAN IS THE GLOBAL ACADEMIC IMPRINT OF THE PALGRAVE MACMILLAN division of St. Martin's Press, LLC and of Palgrave Macmillan Ltd. Macmillan® is a registered trademark in the United States, United Kingdom and other countries. Palgrave is a registered trademark in the European Union and other countries.

ISBN-13: 978-1-4039-7288-5
ISBN-10: 1-4039-7288-5

Library of Congress Cataloging-in-Publication Data
Ervin, Clark Kent, 1959–
    Open target : where America is vulnerable to attack / by Clark Kent Ervin.
      p.   cm.
    ISBN 1-4039-7288-5 (alk. paper)
    1. Civil defense—United States.   2. United States—Defenses.   I. Title.
UA 927.E78   2006
363.350973—dc22

                                                                           2005058669

A catalogue record for this book is available from the British Library.

Design by Letra Libre, Inc.

First edition: May 2006
10 9 8 7 6 5 4 3 2 1
Printed in the United States of America.

CONTENTS

ACKNOWLEDGMENTS

Like all authors, I have many people to thank for helping me to make the idea of this book a reality. Unlike most authors, I suppose that I should start by thanking Serendipity. It is through serendipity that I met my extraordinary agent, Eric Lupfer, at the William Morris Agency. Eric was an enthusiastic and indefatigable champion of me and this work. In addition to ably representing me in contract negotiations, he also went above and beyond the call of duty by providing invaluable editorial advice and wise counsel.

I am grateful, too, to my superb editor at Palgrave Macmillan, Airie Stuart. From the beginning, she believed in the importance of this book and she worked tirelessly to help me improve it. Her penetrating questions and insightful comments throughout the process were indispensable to making *Open Target* the book that it now is.

I am grateful to my wife, Carolyn Harris. She, too, was a perceptive and insightful reader of each draft, and her suggestions improved the book immeasurably. Her unfailing love and unflagging support will always mean the world to me.

My heartfelt thanks to Walter Isaacson and the Aspen Institute, which he so ably heads, for providing me a professional home during the course of researching and writing this book. The Institute's focus on enlightened dialogue, timeless values, and nonpartisan inquiry could not be more compelling and necessary today.

During my time as the Inspector General of the State Department, I came to know and admire the ability of two senior inspectors, Doug Ellice and Ken McKune, experts in consular affairs and counterterrorism, respectively. Each of them read early drafts of the Border Security section and gave me the benefit of their long experience and unparalleled expertise. I am grateful to Wrede Petersmeyer and Tyler Allard for their help with my research.

I dedicate this book to the men and women with whom I was privileged to work for all too short a time at the Department of Homeland Security's Office of Inspector General. As you will see from reading these pages, during my time as Inspector General of the department, I had my share of failures. For one thing, I failed to convince the department's leaders that there were serious gaps in America's security that implementing the recommendations my team and I devised could help to close. For another, I failed to convince two key senators that I deserved their support and that of their colleagues. As a consequence, I was never confirmed for the job, and, as a consequence, my tenure in office was far briefer than I had hoped or expected it to be.

But, if I failed in two significant respects, I succeeded beyond my imagining in one other. Given the department's historic and critically important mission—doing everything possible to prevent another terror attack on American soil—I was determined to recruit the best and brightest people I could find to serve with me as my senior management team. In Rick Skinner, my deputy (and now successor); Rick Reback (Counsel to the Inspector General); Bob Ashbaugh (the Assistant Inspector General for Inspections, who along with his staff did outstanding work in examining many of the border issues I discuss in chapter 3); Dick Berman (the Assistant Inspector General for Audits, who is mentioned periodically in several chapters); Frank Deffer (the Assistant Inspector General for Information Technology, who with his team produced groundbreaking reports on intelligence matters and various cyber vulnerabilities); Lisa Redman (the Assistant Inspector General for Investigations, who led a peerless group of criminal investigators superbly); Ed Cincinnati (the Assistant Inspector General for Administrative Services, who made our own office run effectively, efficiently, and economically); Tamara Faulkner (my skilled Congressional and Media Affairs liaison); and my three able Executive Assistants (Jennifer Price, Pat Wallis, and Sandra Penny), I found and got the very best. These pages do not, and, indeed, could not, do justice to their contributions. This management team was supported by a stellar staff of nearly 500 auditors, inspectors, investigators, lawyers, and administrative personnel who collectively made the Department of Homeland Security's Office of Inspector General the very best in the business.

The primary purpose of *Open Target*, as its name implies, is to alert the American people to the mortal dangers we face, in the hope that they collectively will *force* our leaders to make homeland security the priority that it is now only claimed to be. If, as a result of this book, the public also comes to appreciate the work of my former colleagues in particular, and the vital role that the institution of Inspector General plays in our constitutional scheme of government by holding our leaders to account, it will be an immensely important added benefit.

Clark Kent Ervin
Washington, D.C.
December 2005

PROLOGUE

February 27, 2003. It was a historic day. The Senate committee with jurisdiction over the newly created Department of Homeland Security assembled promptly at 10 o'clock that morning to consider my nomination by the President as the department's very first Inspector General. As I sat in the back of the black sedan that had been dispatched to take me down the snow-strewn streets of Washington and up to Capitol Hill, I read over my opening statement. It was not as if I needed to. By that point, I'd all but memorized it, so I had no trouble getting the words out when my turn to speak finally came an hour or so later.

" . . . I am humbled, gratified, and excited by the prospect, if confirmed, of serving as the first Inspector General of the newest cabinet department, representing . . . the largest reorganization of the federal government in more than half a century, and charged with a mission of paramount importance—protecting our homeland against terrorist attack. . . . It is no exaggeration to say that the fate of our nation depends upon the degree to which the department succeeds in accomplishing its mission. And, in seeking to accomplish a mission such as this, the department cannot afford to waste one minute or one dollar. The Inspector General will play a key role. . . . I pledge to each of you to be independent, objective, thorough, apolitical, and, when need be, critical of the department's programs and operations. . . ."[1]

Those five words—independent, objective, thorough, apolitical, and critical—would later prove to be my undoing, not because I said them, but because I meant them.

I waited for nearly two years for the Senate to confirm me, but the committee chairman who had seemed so supportive of me that snowy February morning kept my nomination suspended in limbo for the next 650 days. The White House that asked me to take the job eventually abandoned me.

Meanwhile, my efforts to call attention to the gaps in our security were derided, dismissed, and ignored by the men whose job it was to close those gaps. And,

Osama bin Laden is still out there somewhere with this chilling message, "It's only a matter of time. [Attacks] are in the planning stages, and you will see them in the heart of your land as soon as planning is complete."[2]

It is an exaggeration to say that America is as vulnerable to a terrorist attack today as it was on the wintry day, three years ago now, that the committee met to consider my nomination, but it is not much of an exaggeration. There is still a big gap between how much more secure we can be and how secure we really are. As long as the "vulnerability gap" remains as wide as it is today, America remains an open target.

INTRODUCTION

The job of Inspector General of the Department of Homeland Security was not one that I asked for, and when it was offered to me, I was of two minds about whether to take it. I'd come to Washington at the beginning of the administration of George W. Bush from Texas, where I'd served as the Assistant Secretary of State for the first four years of his tenure as governor, and, for the final two years of his term, as a Deputy Attorney General. By the time of his election to the statehouse, I'd known the President for quite some time; I'd been an aide in his father's White House, and Bush had campaigned for me during my run for Congress in the early 1990s.

When I returned to Washington in January 2001, it was the thrill of a lifetime. A man I counted as a friend had risen through the ranks of politics to become the President of the United States, and I, a longtime foreign policy and international relations devotee, was to be interviewed for a top job in the State Department. I was being interviewed for this job by the Secretary of State himself. And, to top it all off, the Secretary of State was the legendary Colin Powell, a longtime hero of mine.

I went to that interview prepared to talk about other jobs, but Powell surprised me by saying that, while I appeared to be well qualified for the other slots, too, the ideal job for me was that of Inspector General. "You're a lawyer. You've got managerial experience from your time in state government. And, I think that you're a man of integrity. You're someone who can maintain your personal loyalty to the President, the Republican Party, and me, but at the same time, be an independent and aggressive watchdog over the department and its operations."

The notion of being the Inspector General intrigued me—I would lead a team of inspectors, auditors, and investigators to help me examine the operations of our embassies and consulates throughout the world. Our mission would be to weed out waste, fraud, and mismanagement, and to ensure that our diplomats around the globe were faithfully carrying out the foreign policy of the United States. We would make recommendations to help the Department of State become as effective, efficient, and economical as possible. Knowing that I would have the full support of the Secretary of State made the prospect of taking on the job even more attractive.

I knew that I would have no trouble keeping my politics separate from the demands of my job. The President was a friend, I agreed with his policies (well, most of them anyway), and I wanted him and his new administration to succeed. But my guiding principle was that, in the event of conflict, friendship and partisanship would have to give way to doing what was right. After all, ultimately, I was to be accountable not to the President, but to the American people.

Eventually, the lengthy background check process that all senior presidential nominees must endure was completed by White House lawyers and Federal Bureau of Investigation (FBI) investigators. I was unanimously approved by the Senate shortly thereafter.

A month or so later, Secretary Powell swore me into office in an elaborate ceremony before a throng of my family, friends, and colleagues in the ornate Benjamin Franklin Diplomatic Reception Room on the top floor of the State Department. At the time, I found his words to be inspiring and eloquent. In retrospect, I find them also to be eerily prescient and, even, foreboding: "[I]f our foreign policy is to be sustained and if it is to be successful around the world, it has to have the trust of the American people. . . . The work of the Inspector General . . . contributes invariably to building that crucial public trust . . . Clark, . . . I am counting on you to be absolutely independent, absolutely vigorous, absolutely objective, and absolutely candid. I want you to always tell me what I like hearing and what I don't like to hear . . . I will take action on the things you and your team bring us. That is my obligation as Secretary of State, and it's Clark's obligation to make sure I hear it straight. He is the kind of young man who will do that . . . and that's why President Bush and I are so pleased that he has been willing to take on this new responsibility—this new job for the American people." The Secretary of State wanted the facts, however unpleasant they might be to hear. The Secretary of Homeland Security, I would soon learn, wanted spin. The Secretary of State would work to fix the problems I brought to his attention. The Secretary of Homeland Security would deny that there were problems to fix.

Four days after my swearing-in ceremony, terror struck the homeland, killing nearly 3,000 Americans. The President and both parties in Congress resolved that the homeland would never be attacked again.

Inevitably, there were proposals to reorganize the government to better detect, deter, and defend against terrorism. Responsibility for homeland security was diffused among a multitude of agencies. Indeed, it is said that in the immediate aftermath of the attacks, there wasn't a conference room in the entire White House complex big enough to accommodate representatives from all the agencies with a stake in the fight.

It was not just a question of there being too many players, however. It soon became clear in the aftermath of the attacks that at least part of the reason for the government's inability to prevent them was that the key agencies were stove-piped and compartmentalized. Each agency jealously guarded the intelligence it possessed, and each refused to share with the others information that might be mutually useful in protecting the homeland.

Logic led me to agree with those, such as one of my soon-to-be antagonists, Democratic Senator Joe Lieberman, who were pushing to put all of the homeland security–related functions across government into one agency. It seemed to make sense, intuitively, that putting all the players on one team would make them more likely to play against the opposing team—Al Qaeda and its offshoots and imitators—and not each other.

On the other hand, the conservative in me recoiled against the very notion of bigger government, and the cynic in me doubted that reorganizing the government would make much difference. The pessimist in me worried that even *trying* to reorganize the government might wind up making things even worse. By that point, I knew enough about government to know that things seldom work out as they are intended to, and I knew enough about life to know that things rarely turn out to be as simple as they seem to be. After all, it wasn't until the Goldwater-Nichols Act of 1986, forty years after the creation of the Department of Defense, that the four armed services began to operate more or less cooperatively, and, more or less as originally intended. Unlike, say, the Transportation Security Administration (TSA), the Secret Service, the Immigration and Naturalization Service (INS), and the Federal Emergency Management Agency (FEMA), disparate agencies that were ultimately merged into the Department of Homeland Security, the Army, the Navy, the Air Force, and the Marines all did pretty much the same thing.

For a time, the President and his congressional allies managed to hold off those pushing for a new department. Chiefly, they were able to point to the appointment of the then widely respected former Governor of Pennsylvania, Tom Ridge, to the newly created post of White House Homeland Security Adviser. Just as the National Security Adviser coordinates the various departments and agencies involved in foreign relations and international affairs, the Homeland Security Adviser was charged with coordinating the various agencies involved to one degree or another in securing the homeland.

By the fall of 2002, however, the political pressure to reorganize the government became irresistible. Ridge's power, it soon became clear, was limited. He could try to sweet-talk or strong-arm the various agencies into doing his bidding, but, ultimately, each could continue to do as it pleased. Each agency had its own budget, its own legal authority, and its own constituency on Capitol Hill. Only a new agency headed by a Cabinet Secretary would have the political, legal, and financial clout to take the scattered pieces of homeland security and put them together into a whole greater than the sum of its parts.

Bowing to political reality, the President reversed course and enthusiastically embraced the notion of a Department of Homeland Security as the year began to draw to a close. Other names were bandied about from time to time, but most political handicappers were convinced that the job of Secretary would be Tom Ridge's to turn down. Even after the White House threw its considerable weight behind the idea, it still took some back and forth in Congress for all sides to agree on the precise terms of legislation. I watched the process unfold from my perch at the State Department, having no idea that I would soon be asked to play a key role in this massive new counterterrorism agency.

Late one blustery October afternoon, as I sat at my desk in my office admiring the majestic view of the Washington Monument, my phone buzzed. "Clark, the White House personnel office is on the line," my assistant said. "I wonder what that's about," I thought to myself. From time to time, I'd received calls asking for my recommendations for this job or that, and I expected the purpose of this call to be no different.

"Yes, this is Clark Ervin."

"Mr. Ervin, this is Julie Lapeyre from the White House Personnel Office. I'm calling to ask whether you'd consider coming in to talk to us about something. As you know, it's all but certain now that this much-talked-about new Department of Homeland Security will become a reality. We're going to need an Inspector General. It's going to be a huge agency, with a huge budget, and, therefore, a huge potential for waste, fraud, abuse, and mismanagement. And, since its job will be to prevent another 9/11, it's going to be the most important agency in the whole federal government. From everything we've heard, you've done a great job at the State Department. You've been thorough, aggressive, and fair, all at the same time. Would you consider at least talking to us about this?"

Well, I was, in a word, conflicted. In part, I was reluctant to leave the State Department because I'd arrived only a little over a year earlier. I was only beginning to make progress in moving the Office of Inspector General in what I considered to be the right direction. I was reinvigorating the process of inspecting our embassies and consulates abroad. My team and I had done exciting and important things, such as determining whether our government had played any role in the brief overthrow of the leftist Chavez government in Venezuela (we could find no evidence that it had), and whether Ahmad Chalabi (the anti–Saddam Hussein Iraqi exile and activist favored by Vice President Dick Cheney and Secretary of Defense Donald Rumsfeld, who arguably did more than any other single person to convince the United States to go to war to topple the regime) had properly accounted for millions of dollars of aid for his "Iraqi National Congress Foundation" (he hadn't always). Finally, I was already playing a role in homeland security by examining what changes needed to be made to our visa procedures to make it harder for terrorists to gain entry into the United States.

That said, when I received the call to serve at a new Department of Homeland Security, I felt that I had no choice but to consider it. What could be more important than securing the nation against the possibility of another terrorist attack? If I could play an even bigger part in helping to carry out that most important mission, I owed it to my country to sign up. Powell's words were reassuring. "You've done a great job here, and we'd miss you. But, while we need you here, Tom Ridge is *really* going to need you there. He's going to have a huge challenge on his hands, and he's going to need somebody like you to help him get a handle on things. And, by the way, you'll like him. He's a very good man." Before long, I found myself with the same title, but a whole new job.

The Department of Homeland Security (DHS) became a reality on January 24, 2003, and I was among the handful of senior leaders who were at work on that historic day. The various pre-existing agencies that were to form the core of the department would not be merged, and its various new components were not to be created until March 1, but the Secretary and his top leadership team needed a few weeks of lead time to lay the groundwork. I considered it to be a hopeful sign that an Inspector General had been selected and installed so early in the process, and that I'd been included in all of the planning meetings leading up to the department's first day.

The memory of the terror attacks was still fresh, and a sense of urgency about getting the department up and running as quickly as possible pervaded Washington. To facilitate this, the Homeland Security Act contained a provision permitting certain officials to serve at the new agency from day one in an "acting" capacity. Having been nominated by the President and confirmed by the Senate already as Inspector General of the State Department, I was allowed by this provision to serve as Acting Inspector General of the Homeland Security Department until I was formally nominated and approved by the Senate again.

The very first order of business was to assemble a management team to help me to discharge the responsibilities of Inspector General. Of course, I wanted to attract the best and brightest leaders the federal Inspector General community had to offer to serve beside me. There were two logical places to start my search.

First, I'd come to know, respect and admire every single member of the management team I had assembled at the State Department's Office of Inspector General. But, I realized that I couldn't take every single one of them with me to DHS. That would not be fair to State OIG, which had begun to move in the right direction after years of drift and dysfunction, and it would not be reflective of the diversity of the various bits and pieces of Offices of Inspector General I would be inheriting from colleagues who had previously overseen what was to become part of the Department of Homeland Security.

In the end, I managed to persuade several of my colleagues at State to join me at the new department—Dick Berman, the Assistant Inspector General for Audits; Frank Deffer, the Assistant Inspector General for Information Technology; Hal Fuller, the Assistant Inspector General for Administrative Services; and Rick Reback, Counsel to the Inspector General.

Dick Berman was a forty-year government veteran, having served for years at the Government Accountability Office, Congress' investigative arm, and in various other Offices of Inspector General. He was extraordinarily smart, adept at demystifying the arcane worlds of auditing and accounting and explaining them in terms that math-challenged laymen like me could easily understand, an indefatigable worker, and unfailingly gracious, even-tempered, and unflappable to boot. I had hoped that he would agree to come with me, but I had already resigned myself to his saying no. I knew that he was already several years past eligibility for retirement, and I found it hard to believe that he would be willing to pack up and move to a whole new agency so close to the end of his long government career. But, the challenge of starting a new office, and having a much bigger staff to supervise (not only in Washington, but in more than 20 field offices throughout the country), not to mention the importance of the department's mission, convinced him to make the move.

I had spotted a "keeper" in Frank Deffer early on in my time at the State Department. Secretary Powell took a special interest in information technology issues. Given the importance that the Secretary placed on information technology, and the degree to which it was essential to carrying out the mission of the department effectively, I decided early on in my tenure as State Department Inspector General to set up a separate unit within my office to focus on nothing but evaluating information technology issues. Frank was serving as an IT-focused auditor in Dick's shop when I arrived at State in the spring of 2001, and I soon asked him to head a separate unit to examine the department's various IT initiatives.

If IT issues were important at State, they would be hugely important at DHS, I knew. The Department of Homeland Security would be inheriting hundreds, if not thousands, of different systems, some of which, doubtless, would be duplicative of each other, and dysfunctional to one degree or another. Inventorying these systems, pruning the ones that did not work or were redundant, and making the rest of them interoperable would be an immense challenge. Making all of these systems secure from internal compromise or external attack would be an even greater challenge. If terrorists could penetrate or disable the computer systems of the nation's chief anti-terrorism agency, there was no telling what havoc they could wreak on the millions of systems maintained by private citizens and businesses.

Like Dick, Hal Fuller had been in government for decades. He had served as a Foreign Service Officer in locales throughout the world, before finally settling in Washington in the Office of Inspector General to focus on inspecting our global network of embassies and consulates. After many years of traveling from one diplomatic outpost to another, Hal came to me one day asking to try something different. I was not at all pleased with how our internal administrative services unit, which handled our budget, accounting, human resources, and facilities needs, was functioning, and so I asked Hal to try his hand at running it. He proved in the space of a few short months to be a gifted administrator, and the office started to hum like a well-oiled machine. Like Dick, he, too, was past retirement eligibility, so I was surprised but delighted that he, too, agreed to join me at DHS. (Within a few months, Hal was forced to retire to care for his ailing wife. I found an ideal replacement for him in Ed Cincinnati, a longtime Justice Department administrator whose exceptional administrative skills were rivaled only by his grace and good humor.)

Rick Reback had proved to be absolutely indispensable to me at State as Counsel to the Inspector General. In that job, Rick was responsible for giving me legal advice about all manner of issues. He and his small staff would review each and every inspection, audit, and investigative report to ensure that every sentence could withstand legal challenge and that classified and otherwise sensitive information was appropriately handled. He worked with the Department of Justice to defend us from occasional lawsuits, and he was constantly at work negotiating with other State Department offices for access to witnesses and documents and defending us from challenges to our legal authority. Rick was the very antithesis of the lawyer's stereotype. He spoke and wrote plain English. He was invariably polite and easygoing, even in the tensest situations. He defused conflict, instead of encouraging it. I breathed a sigh of relief when Rick agreed to join me at DHS. A difficult job would be that much more difficult without him at my side helping me to navigate what I was sure would be treacherous legal shoals.

That left three other key slots to fill—Deputy Inspector General, the number two slot in the office; Assistant Inspector General for Investigations; and Assistant Inspector General for Inspections, Evaluations, and Special Reviews, and I needed to look outside the State Department to broaden the management ranks and to reflect the diversity of the new department.

The total size of the Office of Inspector General would be 459, consisting of 200 people from FEMA's OIG, 195 from Treasury's, 45 from Transportation's, 15 from Justice's, and two employee slots each from the Agriculture Department and the General Services Administration. Since FEMA would be supplying the largest contingent, it seemed logical to turn to FEMA's then Acting Inspector General, Rick Skinner, for the job of Deputy Inspector General of DHS.

Like Hal and Dick, Rick Skinner had served for decades in the federal government. He had served in senior capacities in several other Offices of Inspector General, including those for the State Department and the Commerce Department. I knew that this kind of broad-based experience would be invaluable to me, and I was also drawn to Rick's low-key and pleasant personality. Admirably, he appeared to place a premium on treating his employees respectfully and courteously, and he seemed to know everything there was to know about every single one of them. Finally, knowing that I was more of a policy wonk at heart than a nuts-and-bolts, day-to-day administrator, Rick's facility and fondness for the relatively mundane budgetary, personnel, facilities, and other administrative-type matters would serve to complement my set of skills and interests nicely. Rick readily agreed to serve as my number two.

The Inspector General is required by law to have an Assistant Inspector General for Investigations to help him or her investigate allegations of criminal and serious non-criminal misconduct on the part of department employees, contractors, and grantees. This would be an especially critical position at DHS, given the size of its workforce and budget, the large amounts of money in contracts and grants that it would be awarding, and the prospect of intense turf battles with other law enforcement agencies within the department. For this ultra-sensitive slot, I picked a tough, no nonsense, super-organized veteran of the Treasury Department, Lisa Redman. I had found that the Office of Investigations was the one unit at State OIG that I failed to make as productive and cohesive as I had hoped. I was confident that Lisa had the gumption and administrative ability to make the Office of Investigations at DHS OIG run smoothly.

Finally, there was the Assistant Inspector General for Inspections, Evaluations, and Special Reviews spot to fill. The work of an Inspector General's audit team is governed by a stringent set of standards called the "Yellow Book." Much like those in a law review article or a scientific paper, every word in an audit report must be supported by documented sources, and every assertion must be checked and re-checked for accuracy. The upside is that audit reports can be taken to the proverbial bank as a definitive account of whatever program or operation is being evaluated. The downside is that, by the time an audit report is released, its contents may be so dated that it ceases to be useful for policymakers. I knew that there would be lots of hot button, "breaking news-type" issues at the Department of Homeland Security that would require the Inspector General to do a quick review and to make "Johnny on the spot" recommendations for immediate action by the department and Congress. So, it was critical that I find someone to lead a team to do just that.

Bob Ashbaugh was a veteran Justice Department lawyer, who at the time had served for a number of years as the number two man in the Justice Department's Office of Inspector General. Out of the blue, Bob stopped by my office one day and offered to be of help. He said that he had a great interest in homeland security related matters, and that Justice's Inspector General was willing to let him spend as much time as I thought was needed to help me get my office up and running. I told Bob that I really needed an "AIG" for Inspections, and I asked him to help me look for one. After a couple of weeks, he came in one day to volunteer for the job himself. I could hardly believe that he would be willing to give up the prestigious rank of Deputy Inspector General to serve one rank below as an Assistant Inspector General, but I was overjoyed by the prospect of having someone of his rank, caliber, and experience at the helm of this critically important slot. Rounding out the team was my very able young Executive Assistant, Jennifer Price, whom I brought with me from State, and the gracious and efficient Pat Wallis from FEMA.

As Inspector General of DHS, it was my job to examine and evaluate the programs and operations of the department to determine whether it was protecting the American people from the prospect of another terror attack as effectively, efficiently, and economically as possible. As the days, weeks, and months went by, what I would find would test my faith in the leadership of our nation. Time and again, to my growing disillusionment and dismay, I found that our leaders were not taking the threat of terrorism seriously. As I will show in detail in the chapters that follow, they were not doing everything in their power to detect, deter, and defend against another attack. Worse still, I found that the leadership of the Department of Homeland Security seemed to care more about protecting their reputations than protecting the country.

For example, when I sent an undercover team of investigators[*] to airports around the nation to test screeners' ability to conceal guns, knives, and bombs, they found that it was far easier to sneak these deadly weapons through the checkpoints than it should have been. The then head of TSA's (Jim Loy) reaction was that we were needlessly making his agency look bad and making a mountain out of the proverbial molehill.

When we pointed out flaws in port inspectors' procedures and radiation detection devices that allowed the very same shipment of depleted uranium to be smuggled into the country undetected *twice,* the top officials in the Customs and Border Protection bureau essentially shrugged their shoulders, even though enough weapons-grade uranium could cause a nuclear catastrophe, killing hundreds of thousands of people.

When we pointed out that the Department of Homeland Security was to take the lead on consolidating the various terrorist watch lists, Tom Ridge insisted that this was the FBI's responsibility. When we pointed out that the Department of Homeland Security was intended to be the central clearinghouse for all information concerning threats against the homeland, he in-

---

[*] I use the term "investigators" here colloquially. In fact, the team members were auditors.

sisted that that was the responsibility of the Central Intelligence Agency (CIA). Instead of connecting the dots, the Secretary of Homeland Security was passing the buck.

When we found multiple instances of DHS border inspectors' knowingly admitting foreigners with stolen passports, the department said that we found too few instances of this security gap to worry about it, even though it took only nineteen terrorists to pull off the deadliest attack in our history.

Throughout my time at DHS, I also found examples of waste, mismanagement, and inefficiency. Millions of dollars were spent on programs that did not work. Contractors were allowed time and again to take the taxpayer for a ride. While, to be sure, waste, mismanagement, and inefficiency are endemic in government, the Department of Homeland Security is not just *any* government agency. Every dollar misspent by the Department of Homeland Security is a dollar less that could be spent to make America safer.

My pointing out the security gaps that I was finding did not make me popular in the Department of Homeland Security. In fact, I quickly became a pariah. Before too long, I was dropped from the list of invitees to policy and strategy meetings with the Secretary and his top leadership team. Though a Republican and a longtime friend of and aide to the President, I was seen by the Secretary and his top aides as a traitor and turncoat. After one congressional hearing, when I spoke up to contradict misleading testimony from the TSA chief, one of his legislative assistants was heard to say afterwards, "Why is he so tough? I thought he was one of us." Though I had sworn an oath before God and to the American people to be objective and apolitical, I was castigated for not being a team player. "Are you *my* Inspector General?" Ridge thundered one day when he summoned me to his office to complain about our report on gaps in visa security. "No, I'm not, sir. I'm the American people's Inspector General. You and I both work for them."

Though I had a legal obligation to report my findings not just to the Secretary, but also to Congress—Republicans and Democrats alike—I was chided within the department for doing so, and urged by the Secretary himself to keep Congress in the dark. Though I felt a moral obligation to keep the public as informed as possible about the nation's vulnerabilities and what their government was doing (or *not* doing) to address them, I was pilloried by my colleagues in the department for being a showboat and a media hound. A national news magazine quoted one senior official as saying of me, "He doesn't miss many opportunities for glory."[1]

I made a couple of powerful enemies on Capitol Hill, too. In fact, but for them, I'd still be on the job today, continuing to point out from the inside where our nation remains vulnerable to terrorist attack and trying to get the Department of Homeland Security to live up to the promise of its name.

There was no time limit on my ability to serve as Acting Inspector General of the department. According to the law, I could at all times exercise the full powers and authority of the job as if I had been confirmed, but for symbolic reasons, it was important for me to be confirmed by the Senate in my new capacity. Senate confirmation would show that I had not only the President's confidence, but also that of Republicans and Democrats alike in Congress.

Furthermore, the political aide who had been sent by the White House to the department to ensure that all appointees toed the Administration line, Libby Camp, and her allies in the White House Office of Legislative Affairs, which guides nominees through the byzantine confirmation process, were insisting that I not testify before Congress unless and until I was confirmed. They argued that it was a longstanding matter of policy that nominees not testify before being confirmed for their positions, and that some senators might choose not to approve my nomination simply because I had testified prematurely. Senators certainly guard their prerogatives jealously, and none is taken more seriously than their power to approve or reject presidential nominees.

All of this was true, I countered, but it was also all beside the point. I explained that the drafters of the Homeland Security Act had anticipated this very conflict and had resolved it in favor of giving those in an acting capacity the full powers of the office, including the power to testify before Congress. Knowing how long and capricious the confirmation process can be, the lawmakers who crafted the law wanted to empower acting officials to hit the ground running. Otherwise, the time they could be spending to protect the homeland would be spent trying to satisfy the whims of this Senator or that.

It didn't help that I'd known Libby for years. We'd worked together in Texas government—I as Assistant Secretary of State, and she as the secretary and scheduler of the then Secretary of State and soon-to-be White House Counsel, Alberto Gonzales. It also didn't help that I knew Gonzales. I called his office to get his support for my interpretation of the Homeland Security Act. I could get only his deputy, David Leitch, on the line. Leitch said that I was right about the law—there was no legal limitation on my ability to testify—but *whether* I should testify was a matter of policy for the White House Legislative Affairs Office to decide, bringing me back to square one.

I suspected that the *real* reason for the reluctance to let me testify was the fear that I would tell the truth and show how and where department leaders were failing to protect the homeland. In any event, being able to testify before Congress was yet another reason why it was important for me to be confirmed for DHS Inspector General as quickly as possible.

The only problem was that the Republican chairman of the key Senate oversight committee, Susan Collins of Maine, and the senior Democrat on the panel, Joe Lieberman of Connecticut, were blocking their colleagues on the committee from voting on my nomination and sending it to the Senate floor for the consideration of the full body. This was puzzling to me and disturbing in the extreme. My confirmation hearing had gone exceedingly well. Lieberman did not show up for the hearing, but Collins was welcoming and gracious. She and her colleagues—Republicans and Democrats alike—were complimentary and they appeared to like my answers to their questions. But, subsequent to the hearing, Collins' staff called to say that a former State Department staffer was raising objections to my nomination. The complainant said that during my time at the State Department she had asked my office to examine allegations of wrongdoing in a program in the Middle East, and I had declined to do so.

I explained to the staff that the wrongdoing in question was alleged against an entity over which I had no jurisdiction. As the Inspector General of the State Department, I was authorized to look into allegations of wrongdoing only on the part of State Department officials or wrongdoing in connection with only State Department programs. In this instance, the complainant was not a State Department employee at the time, the alleged wrongdoers were not State Department employees, and the program in question was not a State Department program, but one run by an international organization. I explained this for hours and hours and weeks and weeks, both in lengthy face-to-face meetings and telephone conversations with Collins' and Lieberman's staffs and in correspondence with the senators themselves, but, all to no avail.

After having been on the job for over a year, I finally got a meeting with Collins to discuss the matter directly with her. She gave me ten minutes to explain myself, and then when I tried to answer her questions, she stormed out of the room. I repeatedly tried to get a meeting with Lieberman, but he never once agreed to see me. In desperation, I eventually asked Secretary Powell to call him to vouch for my integrity. Powell reported back that Lieberman claimed to be unaware of his staff's objections to my nomination and he promised to look into it.

The bottom line is that the chairman and ranking member of the top Senate oversight committee over the Homeland Security Committee held up my nomination for nearly two full years. I was, then, fighting a pitched battle on two fronts. On the one hand, I was fighting inside the department to uncover and expose the security gaps in its programs and operations, which terrorists could exploit to strike the homeland again, and in so doing, making myself more and more controversial and unpopular with each passing day. And, on the other, I was fighting with the two Senators, who should have been my biggest allies, to keep my job.

Up until the end of my first year in office, I at least had the support of the White House. Indeed, at the end of 2003, the President took the extraordinary step of giving me a "recess appointment." A recess appointment is a parliamentary maneuver that enables presidents to bypass the Senate to install their nominees over the Senate's objections. The catch is that the appointments may be made only when the Senate is out of session, and they last only until the end of the congressional term during which they are made. So, as a practical matter, the appointment bought me one more year to try to convince Collins and Lieberman to release their chokehold. At least I was then free to testify before Congress as the duly authorized, though not confirmed, Inspector General of the department.

And testify I did, pointing out gaps in visa security, port security, and aviation security. Report after report was issued, pointing out how the department was failing to protect the American people from terrorism. Needless to say, by the end of the year, I'd so alienated the few friends I had left in the White House that no one would help me in my continuing efforts to get Senate confirmation. Without this, I'd have to leave office the minute the congressional session adjourned; the whole of the year 2004 was a race against the clock. It turned out to be a losing race in the end. In the early morning hours of December 8, the term of the 108th Congress was gaveled to a close. A few hours later I was in my office, packing up my boxes and preparing to head home.

As I did so, I could only think of the ironies of the situation. I hadn't asked for this job, but I had taken it on and done my best. Perhaps *that* was the problem; perhaps I would have had the White House's and the senators' support if I hadn't done the job I'd been asked to do.

Why would Collins and Lieberman, of all people, oppose my nomination? I was a Republican, yes, but not a fire-breathing, ultra-right-wing conservative. My politics and Collins' were almost exactly the same, and so if any Republican would oppose me she would be among the least likely suspects. Like me, she prided herself on not being an ideologue, but on reaching out whenever possible to the other side of the aisle.

As for Lieberman, he too was the very model of bipartisanship, and, as a centrist Democrat, his politics likewise were hard to distinguish from mine. On top of that, he was noted for his courtesy and graciousness. It was astounding to me that he, of all people, would oppose my nomination without at least giving me the courtesy of a face-to-face opportunity to plead my case.

My nomination was being held up, ostensibly, because I wasn't aggressive enough in the exercise of my jurisdiction as State Department Inspector General, when the rap on me at DHS was that I was *too* aggressive.

To add insult to injury, neither senator ever introduced legislation to give the State Department Inspector General the explicit authority and the express obligation to investigate the alleged wrongdoing they professed to care so much about.

Most of all, I couldn't help but wonder why the two Senators with the most authority over homeland security issues would block the confirmation of someone who was pressing the administration and the Congress to address these very issues.

As I packed my bags and said my goodbyes to my loyal and able staff that day, I could only shake my head at the strange ways of Washington. Doing your job can ruin your career. Tom Ridge and his leadership team had not done their jobs, but *I* was going and *they* were staying. Remembering author Edward Abbey's stirring admonition to public servants provided some comfort: "A patriot must always be ready to defend his country against his government."[2]

But it really wasn't about me. I'd get another job and have another career, but what about the country? I knew where the gaps were in America's security and exactly how terrorists could exploit them to attack the homeland again. I'd tried to share this crucially important information with the leaders charged with doing something about it, but they put almost as much time and energy into fighting me as they did in fighting the terrorists.

I spend my time today assessing the state of homeland security from the outside. I am often asked whether America is safer today than we were when we were attacked. The answer to that question, in my judgment, is yes.

For example, we are notably safer in certain aspects of aviation. Cockpit doors are hardened. Some pilots are armed. The number of air marshals protecting flights has been significantly increased. The perimeters and interiors of airports are better protected and more closely monitored for suspicious activity. Screeners are better trained and more keenly aware of their role as the last line of defense before would-be terrorists board airplanes.

There have been improvements in other aspects of security, too. For example, it is significantly harder for terrorists to exploit the visa issuance process and port-of-entry inspection procedures. The law enforcement and intelligence communities are sharing information to a greater degree than ever before. A greater percentage of money to protect against terrorist attacks is being allocated to those states, localities, police and fire departments, and emergency medical personnel whose communities are most at risk.

The bad news is that whether we're safer today than we were five years ago isn't the key question. The key questions are: Are we as safe as we need to be? Are we as safe as we can be? and, Are we as safe as we think we are? In my judgment, the answer to all of these questions, regrettably, is no.

This was made plain enough for all to see in the catastrophic aftermath of Hurricane Katrina. If we were so woefully unprepared for an utterly foreseeable natural disaster, how prepared could we be for another surprise attack by terrorists? Clearly, the Homeland Security Department has served to make us only marginally safer, and, in the age of terror, "marginally" safer is not safe enough.

If Katrina was a big wake-up call, so were the London bombings in the summer of 2005. For that matter, 9/11 itself should have been the *mother* of all wake-up calls. Yet, in the absence of another attack, and before Katrina struck, our leaders were beginning to grow complacent again. When, for example, a stray plane wandered to within three miles of the White House, the President of the United States, who happened at the time to be out for a bike ride, was not told about the incident by his Secret Service bodyguards until nearly an hour after it was over; however, the scare was taken seriously enough by others in Washington that day that the White House and the Capitol were immediately evacuated. To this day, the official administration position continues to be that the Commander-in-Chief's security detail was right not to interrupt his exercise regimen at a time when the capital might once again have been under attack. Could anything better illustrate the danger that America was already going back to sleep?

The London bombings in the summer of 2005 spurred intensified security measures at mass transit stations throughout the United States for a few weeks after the attacks, but those attacks soon faded from the headlines, and the nation went back to business as usual. Katrina faded from the headlines eventually, and in time it will fade from memory, too. When it does, we will revert to our pattern—as soon as the storm passes, the sense of threat passes, too.

Lacking a sense of threat, we correspondingly lack a sense of urgency about taking the additional necessary steps to make ourselves as secure as we can be against the near certainty of another attempted attack.

My fear is that it will take another attack—perhaps one even worse than 9/11—to teach the American people and our government leaders what Al Qaeda already knows—that there are still gaps in our defenses that terrorists can easily exploit. My fear is that only after yet another attack will we be shaken from our complacency, and only then will our leaders be forced to close the security gaps that have yet to be closed. My hope is that an informed and alarmed nation will be motivated enough to force our leaders to plug these gaps *before* terror strikes again. This book is intended to be that motivation.

WHERE ARE WE TODAY?

Even in the area in which the most time, attention, and resources have been invested—aviation security—serious vulnerabilities remain. A few months after I was forced to step down as Inspector General, the team of undercover investigators I had sent out two years earlier to test airport security reported that they had repeated their tests and still were able to sneak guns, knives, and bombs past screeners all too often. Obviously, our recommendations for improvement had been all but ignored.

About 33 million people in our country use mass transit each day to commute to and from work, school, worship, or play. To date, terrorists have not attacked our nation's railways, subways, and bus systems, but we all know too well the scale of death and destruction that would result if they were to do so. The bombings in London, those in Madrid the preceding year, and the serious scare in New York in the fall of 2005 should have been wake-up calls for us here, alerting us to our vulnerability to this kind of attack. Yet relatively little has been done since on a sustained basis to secure this key transportation sector against the possibility of terrorist attack.

Government investigations, academic studies, think tank thought pieces, and media reports continue to warn of the possibility of a terrorist attack with a weapon of mass destruction, but the nation's efforts to prevent terrorists from smuggling a nuclear bomb into the United States aboard the thousands of cargo containers arriving at our seaports each day remain poorly managed and dependent on insufficient and ineffective radiation detection equipment. There are thousands of "loose nukes" in former Soviet countries that could be obtained by Al Qaeda and their sympathizers to launch a catastrophic attack on our homeland.

While it is harder than it has ever been for a known or suspected terrorist to get a visa to enter our country or to use a lost, stolen, or fake passport to do so, it is far from impossible, as I will explain in detail later. Furthermore, this is to say nothing of the ease with which terrorists can bypass inspection at official checkpoints at airports, seaports, and land crossings altogether by sneaking into the country. The millions of illegal aliens who continue to make their way into the United States from all over the world are the living, breathing, walking, and talking proof of just how easy it is. Indeed, the former Deputy Secretary of the Department of Homeland Security, Jim Loy, worried aloud in his final appearance before Congress that terrorists might already have sneaked into America among the throngs streaming across our porous border with Mexico each year.[3]

Our intelligence and law enforcement agencies are sharing information and cooperating with each other as never before, and yet bottlenecks, institutional resistance, bureaucratic bungling, and technological challenges to collecting, analyzing, and then using information that could detect and foil another terrorist attack remain. Later, I will show that DHS today is such a minor player in the intelligence community that it would probably be the last to know if another agency picked up indications of an impending terror attack.

The "first responder community" is better funded, better trained, and better coordinated than at any other time in our history, but, as the response to Katrina shows, it still has far to go before it can respond as effectively and efficiently as it might have to someday in order to minimize the death, destruction, and recovery time from any future terrorist attack. When disaster struck the Gulf Coast late in the summer of 2005, there were no evacuation plans, no designated shelters, and no prepositioned stocks of food, water, and medicine. There was no clear chain of command, and key actors couldn't communicate with each other. If terrorists had targeted the New Orleans levees rather than Mother Nature, the response would have been just as bungled and slow, and the results would have been at least as disastrous.

IS THE DEPARTMENT OF HOMELAND SECURITY
PART OF THE SOLUTION OR PART OF THE PROBLEM?

The nation's hopes for detecting, deterring, and defending against any future terrorist attack largely rest on the effectiveness of the Department of Homeland Security. The creation of DHS constituted the largest and most complex reorganization of our government in more than half a century. Twenty-two different agencies, as disparate as the Transportation Security Administration, the Immigration and Naturalization Service, the Federal Emergency Management Agency, and the Coast Guard, were merged into one mega-department, creating the third-largest cabinet agency, with a workforce of 180,000 and a budget in excess of $30 billion.[4]

By any measure, the department has proved to be less than the sum of its parts. It is a huge amalgam of pre-existing agencies that were involved to one degree or another in homeland security–related matters, but it lacks the cohesion and coherence that the term "department" implies. Part of the reason why the department's finances are a mess is that the Chief Financial Officer doesn't have authority over the components' Chief Financial Officers. Part of the reason why the department's contracting practices are so lax is that the Chief Procurement Officer doesn't have authority over the components' procurement officers. Some of the information technology challenges the department continues to have stem from the fact that the department's Chief Information Officer doesn't have authority over the components' information chiefs. When Michael Chertoff succeeded Tom Ridge, he announced plans to conduct a top-to-bottom review of every aspect of the department, including its organizational structure. I had hoped that among his first orders of business would have been giving the CFO, CPO, and CIO the authority to do these jobs. But this relatively simple fix was conspicuously missing from the package of executive decisions and proposals for legislative action he announced in July 2005.

"Homeland security," too, is something of a misnomer in that only some of what the department does has anything to do with homeland security. For example, when Coast Guard crews rescue mariners in distress, that has nothing to do with homeland security. When Customs inspectors at international airports search incoming passengers' baggage for drugs, Cuban cigars, and historical artifacts, that has nothing to do with homeland security. Likewise, other agencies continue to play key roles in homeland security matters. For example, as noted above and to be explained in detail later, the FBI and the CIA play key intelligence and law enforcement roles with regard to homeland security. Similarly, the Health and Human Services Department, the Agriculture Department, and the Centers for Disease Control are all at least as involved in the nation's efforts to guard against bio-terror and agricultural terrorism as the Department of Homeland Security is.

DHS was quickly and haphazardly patched and stitched together in order to "do something, quick!" without worrying all that much about whether the something done would do much good. If the homeland is not secure, creating a department will secure it, the thinking went, but each of the agencies brought together to form DHS was itself dysfunctional to one degree or another, and, in the pell-mell rush to combine them, there was simply no time to correct these dysfunctions. The dysfunctions compound one another in a pathological symbiosis, making bad matters even worse; today, the Department of Homeland Security remains essentially a collection of variously dysfunctional components held together tenuously by little more than a common name, logo, and mission statement.

Perversely, then, creating the Department of Homeland Security has actually worked *against* the imperative of securing the homeland. People have come to believe that the fact that we have not been attacked again, and the fact that the Department of Homeland Security was created in response to the first attack, prove that the department has succeeded in securing the homeland. Of course, given the manifold security gaps that remain, the department has really done no such thing. Rather than having created a department to secure the homeland, we have attempted to secure the homeland simply by the act of creating a department.

I had hoped that a new DHS leadership team would recognize that equating the absence of another attack with the creation of the Department of Homeland Security is a false and even dangerous syllogism. Ominously, however, in his very first appearance before a congressional committee as the new chief of Homeland Security, Secretary Michael Chertoff observed, "Tom Ridge, Jim Loy, Asa Hutchinson, and the other pioneers of the Department of Homeland Security have done great work in building the department from the ground up, while at the same time protecting the homeland on a daily basis. Of all their many accomplishments, one stands out—over the two years that the department has been in existence, there has not been a major terrorist attack here on American soil. That is a record of accomplishment that seemed unlikely—if not impossible—in the immediate aftermath of 9/11."[5]

Just as the Maginot Line gave the French a false sense of security, and, when put to the test, proved to be no match for Hitler's bloodthirsty legions, so the Department of Homeland Security has given America the false sense that the homeland is secure when, in fact, it remains far more vulnerable than it has to be. The people chosen to lead the department may be under the comforting illusion that its very existence is our sure defense against terrorism, but the terrorists know better. In claiming that the homeland is more secure than it really is, and in attributing that security largely to an ill-conceived, hastily constructed, and poorly performing government bureaucracy, we are only deceiving ourselves.

All of this raises obvious, urgent questions: Why are we deceiving ourselves about how secure we are? Why are the terrorists more determined to strike us than we are to stop them from striking us?

TURNING A BLIND EYE TO HISTORY AND PUTTING OFF THE FUTURE

Many cultures in the world are driven by history. They are spurred to action by their Technicolor-vivid memory of historical events, however distant, and their fierce determination to right old wrongs and to address old grievances. The Middle East, especially, is a boiling cauldron of ancient enmities that dominate national agendas and animate daily life, ranging from the Palestinian rejectionists who struggle to the death to destroy the "Zionist entity" that stole their homeland a half century ago, to fundamentalist militants in Morocco dedicated to overthrowing the Spanish government and reclaiming their beloved Al-Andalus, from which the Moors were expelled half a millennium ago.

By way of contrast, America is a relatively new nation, and we Americans think in much shorter time frames. We are very much people of the moment. To be sure, this has generally been a good thing, and a key ingredient in the mix of traits and tendencies that have made our country the unmatched political, economic, and military success that it has become. The weight of history can drag a nation down and keep it forever bound in a paralyzing political straightjacket of its own making.

Add to the mix our complementary tendency to put off planning for the future until the future is upon us. Other peoples, by way of contrast, are driven by a vision of the future; they have an idealized view of what their nation should be like and then they plan in meticulous detail how to realize that vision. Soviet Russia and Maoist China had elaborate five- and ten-year plans with specific goals and timetables for everything from farm output and factory production to family size.

By not obsessing about the future and trying to plan too meticulously for it, we have likewise helped ourselves in the great game of nations, at least as a general rule. Too detailed, rigorous, mechanical, and centrally directed a plan can rob a nation of the dynamism, creativity, spontaneity, and flexibility it needs to respond and adapt to ever changing internal and external events and circumstances.

In the struggle against this still new threat of terrorism here at home, our immediacy-focused culture has worked against us, however. The farther we get without another terrorist attack, the more we forget having been attacked. The more we forget that attack, the more we begin to lose the fear, rage, unity, and sense of purpose that can motivate us to do everything in our power to see to it that we are never attacked again. In addition, our devil-may-care attitude toward planning for the future leads us to drag our feet on implementing countermeasures and building up defenses that could protect us from another attack someday.

UNACCOUNTABLE GOVERNMENT

Another part of the answer lies in the fact that the executive branch of our government is run by largely unaccountable short-term political appointees and career bureaucrats. If, as the old saying goes, war is too important to leave to the generals, the "war on terror" here at home is too important to leave to the civilians who pay no price when their performance fails to measure up to their pronouncements, promises, and press releases. The average tenure of presidential appointees is about eighteen months, and irrespective of how well they actually do their jobs, when they leave, Cabinet secretaries and other senior officials can command high private sector salaries and lucrative consulting arrangements, not to mention high speaking fees, lavish book contracts, and remunerative and prestigious board seats. FEMA's disastrous response to Katrina further demonstrates the danger of placing political cronies rather than experienced professionals in key government positions. Poor performers in the civil service can rarely, if ever, be fired, and their compensation increases with their longevity.

As for the legislative branch, pork-barrel spending, turf wars over jurisdiction, partisan bickering, and regional rivalries are, to put it mildly, not unknown. So many congressional committees (about 88) assert some oversight authority over the Department of Homeland Security that, as a practical matter, none of them oversees it effectively. Though their performance in office is often wanting, campaigns are so costly nowadays and jurisdictional lines are drawn so artfully that incumbents can rarely be beaten at the polls, whatever their legislative record.

THE "NO NEWS IS GOOD NEWS" SYNDROME

To use an enigmatic phrase that riddle-prone Secretary of Defense Rumsfeld might, we don't know what we don't know, but we still have a tendency to think we do. As far as threats to the homeland are concerned, our knowledge is limited. Our intelligence and law enforcement agencies pick up information from terrorists and their sympathizers all the time. Indeed, the volume of such information is overwhelming, which is a problem in itself. For example, on September 10, 2001, the National Security Agency—which eavesdrops on global telecommunications for threats against the United States— recorded one militant telling another that "zero hour is tomorrow," but the message was neither translated nor its significance grasped until the day *after* the attacks.

However, we can't always tell how reliable any of this information is, and, in any event, it's impossible by definition to know what information is out there that we're *not* picking up. The extent to which we're under threat will always be, to some degree, then, a big question mark.

It's part of human nature to assume over time that what hasn't happened in a good long while probably won't happen again, or at least anytime soon. The old saw "lightening doesn't strike twice" may well be true—but it's certainly easier to assume that it's true and not worry about it, the fewer lightning storms you have been through.

THE FALSE DISTINCTION

Much of the answer can be traced to a false dichotomy that is implicit in our leaders' thinking. Perhaps the clearest illustration of what I mean came out of nowhere in the middle of an otherwise uneventful congressional hearing. In January 2005, my old antagonists, Chairman Collins and Senator Lieberman, had called a panel of outside experts to testify as to what they thought the newly nominated Secretary of Homeland Security, Michael Chertoff, should do to turn the floundering department around. New Mexico Republican Senator Pete Domenici was making the inarguable and commendable point that homeland security money should be allocated on the basis of risk and not pork-barrel politics. What he went on to say caught my attention as I sat in the back of the packed hearing room observing the proceedings: "We cannot cover every risk that people dream up. If we did, we would spend more on *this* than the defense of our nation."[6]

That was *it* in a nutshell. The false distinction between securing the homeland and defending the nation is exactly what's wrong with our approach to homeland security today. I wanted to shout, "Senators, securing the homeland *is* defending the nation!" In fact, securing the homeland is the most important and fundamental part of defending the nation. If the homeland is insecure, the nation is undefended.

This naïve and dangerous distinction is not drawn at only one end of Pennsylvania Avenue; the President, too, speaks as if we still have the luxury of fighting our wars on other nations' soil. Indeed, with the failure to find weapons of mass destruction, and the (at best) fitful progress toward building a functioning democracy there, the central rationale for the increasingly quagmire-like war in Iraq is that it has become a central front in the war on terror.

The problem with our counterterrorism strategy is that we're basing it on the wrong metaphor. And, in so doing, we're forgetting history, true to form. If anything should be clear from Vietnam, it should be that the "domino" theory—"if we don't beat 'em in Saigon, we'll have to face 'em in San Francisco"—has its limits. Ho Chi Minh had no designs on the homeland.

Terrorism is really more like water than dominoes; like water, it seeks, finds, and takes the path of least resistance. For all the savagery and mayhem in Iraq, at least we have the mightiest war machine in the history of warfare defending our interests there. Our military installations and diplomatic facilities elsewhere in the world are relatively hard to penetrate and attack. By way of contrast, here at home, our defenses are down, and terrorists can easily seep and trickle into those cracks and crevices that our nation's leaders have yet to cover over and fill in.

The President got it exactly right, conceptually, when he said in a dramatic White House news conference in the run-up to the war in Iraq, "September 11th changed the strategic thinking, at least as far as I was concerned, for how to protect our country. . . . It used to be . . . that oceans could protect us. . . . September the 11th should say to the American people that we're now a battlefield"[7]; but the strategy being pursued remains based on the misperception that we still have the option of keeping danger "over there."

Going forward, our very existence may well depend upon whether our nation's leaders can be made to see that securing the homeland and defending the nation are the very same thing.

THE "VULNERABILITY GAP"

While the other factors I have cited here are partial causes, the main reason why America remains dangerously unprotected is that our leaders aren't quite sure what to do to increase our level of protection markedly. Everyone understands instinctively that we can't do everything—100 percent security is impossible to achieve, especially in a nation like ours, which rightly places a premium on civil rights and civil liberties—and everyone agrees that for all we've already done, we need to do even more.

But how much more? How much is enough? How little is too little? Exactly how secure are we? How much more secure do we need to be, or can we be?

These are the key questions, and yet no one inside or outside government seems to have the answer to them. Until we answer them, we will continue to essentially flail about, trying one thing and then another, with no real idea of whether any of it is doing appreciable good.

In Iraq, for example, it's easy to tell whether we're winning or losing—it's almost mathematical. We measure progress, or the lack of it, by whether the number of insurgent attacks is increasing or decreasing. In the global war on terror, we likewise measure progress by whether the number of terrorist attacks around the world is increasing or decreasing; however, if we were to use this criterion here at home, we would be led to conclude, erroneously, not just that we're winning the war on terror, but that we've already won it, since there hasn't been another terrorist attack in nearly five years. So, if the number of attacks isn't the criterion, what should the metric be?

The metric should be what I will call "the vulnerability gap," the difference between terrorists' intentions, resolve, and capabilities to attack, on the one hand, and our resolve and capabilities to prevent them from doing so, on the other. As I explain in detail in the chapters that follow, there is no question but that Al Qaeda and its disciples continue to want to strike America. Indeed, no less an authority on terrorists' intentions than Osama bin Laden himself has made it clear that he wants to attack us again, and he wants the next attack to be even deadlier and more spectacular.

This is not just a wish or hope. Terrorists are absolutely determined to carry out another attack. They are not just *willing* to give their lives to make it happen; they are *eager* to do so. According to their perverted conception of Islam, dying while killing "infidels" is an express ticket to Paradise.[8]

While the United States and our allies' toppling Al Qaeda's Taliban protectors and destroying their bases and training camps in Afghanistan, killing or capturing scores of their strategists and foot soldiers around the globe, disrupting their financial networks, and hardening our defenses marginally have certainly put a serious dint in terrorists' capabilities, the odds are still very much in their favor.

Millions of people cross our borders by air, land, and sea each year. Any one of those people could be a terrorist. Every day, thousands of shipping containers carrying countless tons of cargo arrive at our seaports. Any one of those containers could contain a weapon of mass destruction. Every day, our 300 million people depend upon our nation's "critical infrastructure," that is, the transportation industry, the energy sector, the banking system and financial markets, telecommunications and information technology networks, and the food industry, to provide essential goods and services. An attack on any of these systems could be so devastating in its economic impact as to adversely affect national security. Given this, the Department of Homeland Security inspectors, screeners, and air marshals who guard our borders; the Department of Homeland Security analysts who work with their colleagues in the intelligence community here at home and abroad to detect and analyze threats against the homeland; and the Department of Homeland Security law enforcement personnel who work with their counterparts in other departments in our federal, state, and local governments and with foreign governments to track down known terrorists and to keep track of suspected ones, all have to "get it right" every single moment of the day. One mistake could mean catastrophe. Would-be terrorists, on the other hand, have to succeed just once to kill thousands or even millions, and to devastate our economy and our way of life in the process.

Before the attack on our homeland, terrorism was recognized by our leaders as a danger, certainly, but it wasn't seen as the kind of danger it became all too clearly on the day terror struck—immediate, mortal, and existential. With the passage of time, the absence of another attack, and the establishment of a department that is supposed to "take care of it all" so the rest of us can focus on more pleasant and, seemingly, pressing things, the specter of terrorism on our own soil has returned to the shadows. While Al Qaeda is resolute, our leaders are anything but. While our leaders continue to concentrate largely on threats to America from abroad, the threat to America from our vulnerability within is still largely an afterthought, and addressing the threat is treated like an afterthought: fitfully, haphazardly, and lackadaisically.

Of course, the vulnerability gap can never be reduced to zero, but, as will be demonstrated by the weaknesses detailed in the chapters that follow, it remains far wider than it has to be. Knowing what we know about our enemies, it is urgent that we reduce the gap to as close to zero as possible before terror strikes the homeland again.

CHAPTER ONE

HOMELAND (IN)SECURITY

I'm a stickler for timeliness. To me, being late is almost a sin—not just any sin, but an unforgivable one. I'm the kind of person who showed up at the airport two hours before flight time years before terrorists forced everyone else to. So, there was no way I was going to be late for my first meeting with Tom Ridge.

The White House is at most a ten-minute walk from the State Department. In no time, I was waiting patiently, if a little anxiously, in the cozy, dimly lit, elegantly appointed West Wing reception area with at least a half-hour to spare. As I waited, I went over my mental script again. I had it all thought out, and my mind was made up. I wanted Ridge to like me, but I didn't want him to like me *too* much. I would do my best to do well in the interview, but I didn't want to do *too* well. I was perfectly happy at the State Department, and I would be perfectly happy to stay there.

Being as good as you can be is always a challenge. Being *almost* as good as you can be, but not an iota better, would be even harder. My mental calibrations were so intricate and distracting that Ridge's assistant had to repeat herself and speak louder when she finally came out of what appeared to be nowhere to tell me that the Governor was ready to see me.

Ushering me into his tiny office, Ridge greeted me graciously and motioned for me to sit down. I settled in for what was scheduled to be only a fifteen-minute "chat."

Tom Ridge is an extraordinarily likable man. It's easy to see why he had such a successful career in electoral politics: He is friendly, engaging, and sincere, and, he pulls off the rare feat of being an imposing presence, while at the same time being utterly unpretentious and easily approachable. He's a huge man, 6'6", and built like a football player, but his manner is so warm and welcoming that he creates a sense of intimacy with those he meets that has the immediate effect of bringing him down to eye level.

I found myself getting so comfortable with Ridge that I forgot that I was supposed to go only so far in selling myself and no further. I heard myself explaining why I would make not just a good Department of Homeland Security Inspector General, but the perfect one: I knew the job inside and out. I already had experience in visa matters, a key part of the border control aspect of homeland security. I was well versed in international affairs, and homeland security had a global dimension to it. I'd shown myself to be thorough, aggressive, and independent, and those were just the qualities the Homeland Security Department, more than any other agency in government, needed in an Inspector General. I could tell by Ridge's intense focus on me and his positive body language that I was racking up points on his mental scoreboard. The fifteen-minute chat stretched into an hour-long heart-to-heart session. By the end of it, we were remarking upon, and bonding over, the similarities between us. We both came from modest backgrounds. We had both gone to Harvard on scholarship. We had both lost our fathers to relatively early deaths. We were both trying to carve time out of our busy schedules to visit our aging mothers. As I walked out of the White House and into the dimming light of a chilly late fall Washington afternoon, it was clear to me that Tom Ridge and I had clicked. I was fairly certain that it would be only a matter of time before Presidential Personnel called back to offer me the job.

I would bask in the glow of that meeting for quite some time. It would take me a while to realize that I'd made a big mistake. Perhaps my time at Colin Powell's State Department had spoiled me: I'd thought that the Department of Homeland Security would be different from the run-of-the-mill agency where a "good enough for government work" mentality is pervasive. I assumed that the very best and brightest the country had to offer would be recruited to run and staff the agency charged with the task of preventing another terror attack on the homeland. I believed that the Secretary and his management team would move Heaven and Earth to close the gaps in America's defenses that my team and I would surely find the minute we set out to look for them. The very last thing I expected was to be made persona non grata for being impertinent enough to do my job.

If the story stopped here, this would be merely a history book, interesting perhaps to political junkies and students of government; but the story doesn't stop here. The gaps in America's defenses that my team and I uncovered during my time at the Department of Homeland Security largely remain, and, since then, still more gaps have been found.

Somewhere in the world today—perhaps right here in America, under our very noses, hiding in plain sight—terrorists are plotting another attack on the homeland. To succeed, they have to find out where we remain vulnerable, and then they need to figure out how to exploit those vulnerabilities to inflict the maximum possible degree of death, injury, and economic damage. So, the urgent question is, What is the state of homeland security today? In general terms, where are the gaps in security that terrorists can exploit right now to attack the homeland once again?

AMERICA'S OPEN DOORS

People in power in Washington, D.C., are bad at keeping secrets. The nation's capital is awash in a downpour of leaks. Many secrets are so poorly kept that they are secrets in name only. Probably the worst-kept secret is that our nation's borders are easy to slip through.

Until terror struck the homeland, this was mostly a political, social, and economic issue, and one of only secondary importance. After September 11, it became a national security issue, and one of first-order importance. Our approach to border control mirrors our approach to every other aspect of homeland security since the attacks: We've taken a half-step in the right direction, but we haven't done everything we can do. We haven't moved with the sense of warp-speed urgency that defending the nation requires; it's as if we think that terrorists are decent, honorable, reasonable, and empathetic. It's as if we think that they wouldn't dare attack until we get around to putting up as much in the way of defenses as we possibly can. In short, we're continuing to take what remains an essentially pre-9/11 approach, and moving at a pre-9/11 pace, in a radically different, post-9/11 world.

For example, in one key aspect of border security, DHS has made some progress. For the first time in our history, we're moving toward keeping track of who is entering our country—at least through legal channels. Thanks to the biometrics-based automated immigration system known as U.S. VISIT*, port

---

* "U.S. VISIT" is an acronym for United States Visitor and Immigrant Status Indicator Technology.

of entry inspectors can confirm the identity of some entrants, and a more extensive check against terrorist and criminal watch lists can be run.

However, millions of people come to the United States each year by land, and most of those who do so come by way of Mexico and Canada. Most of those countries' citizens aren't subjected to the scrutiny of U.S. VISIT. Moreover, the exit feature is still only in a nascent stage. Until that feature is fully operational, we can't be sure whether terrorists who have managed to legally enter the country undetected by the U.S. VISIT system remain here or whether they've managed to sneak back out.

What about the millions of illegal aliens who continue to come to our country with relative ease? Because the border is so vast, it is critical that the number of Border Patrol agents be increased as much as possible as quickly as possible. During the course of the 2006 budget process, both houses of Congress supported increasing the number of agents by between 1,000 and 2,000, but the President's budget proposed hiring only about 200, suggesting that the administration considered border control to be a low priority. In the end, Congress provided funds to hire 1,500 additional agents, a step in the right direction, but that was 500 fewer than the goal set in the intelligence reform law passed less than a year earlier. Congress' unwillingness to meet its own goal suggests that it, too, places a lower priority on border control than the security of the nation can afford.[1]

Even if the White House and Congress had agreed to even bigger increases in the number of Border Patrol agents, there can never be enough of them to cover the entire border. The wide deployment of effective technology such as sensors and unmanned aerial vehicles is vital to fill the gap. The department has begun to deploy this technology, but more needs to be done sooner rather than later. The technology has to work, and the government should not be overcharged for it. Little comfort in this regard can be taken from the expenditure of more than $200 million on a camera and sensor system so defective and riddled with problems that it proved to be worthless and had to be scrapped.

In the fall of 2005, Secretary Chertoff announced a border security initiative that promises to provide both more Border Patrol agents and more and better technology. But we've heard this all before, and our borders remain far easier to penetrate than they should be.

AIR ATTACK

As noted earlier, one of the first things I did as Inspector General of the Department of Homeland Security in the summer of 2003 was to send a team of undercover investigators to airports around the country to see whether there had been any improvement in the ability of airport screeners to detect concealed guns, knives, and explosives. My team found it far easier than it should have been to sneak these weapons past screeners. Had they been terrorists, my investigators would have succeeded all too often in bringing these instruments of death onto airplanes. One of the last things I did as my time as Inspector General counted down in the late fall of 2004 was to ask my staff to conduct a second round of undercover tests at the same airports to see whether screener performance had improved two years later. The tests were conducted, the results came in, and a disturbing conclusion was reached. In short, no improvement in screener performance was found.

In addition to screener performance, I remain concerned about what we found regarding the issue of criminal background checks for airport screeners. When my team of inspectors looked into the issue, we found convicted criminals within the screener workforce. The reality that criminals had been among the ranks of airport screeners raised for me the question of whether terrorists might have been, too, and TSA's laxity in vetting procedures at the time gave me little comfort as to the likelihood of that terrible possibility.

As for air marshals, how effective can they be if their identities can be discerned by the order in which they board flights, where they sit on flights, and which hotels they may check into while on the road?

On the issue of the security of airports themselves, the degree to which perimeters are vigorously patrolled varies from airport to airport. Further, the degree to which vendors, delivery personnel, and repair and maintenance workers are vetted before they are hired, and the degree to which they are permitted to access secure parts of the airport without adequate screening, is, in a word, unclear.

With regard to cargo on passenger planes, the Department of Homeland Security makes a point of boasting that all cargo is "screened" before it is loaded onto flights, but the term is misleading. "Screened" does not mean "inspected." What the department means is that all cargo manifests are scrutinized to see whether any red flags, which would warrant physically inspecting a particular container, are raised. In addition to such "targeted" inspections, there are occasional random inspections of this package or that. Most commercial flights contain some cargo, and the vast majority of cargo on passenger planes is not inspected, a fact that most passengers are unaware of. The explosive device that "shoe bomber" Richard Reid was trying to ignite on a flight from Paris to Miami could have killed every passenger on board. An explosive device hidden in the cargo hold could do the same thing.

With regard to international flights bound for the United States, there continue on a regular basis to be mid-flight diversions when the name of a passenger matches or appears to match the name of someone on the "no fly" list. That list contains the names of those throughout the world known to the United States government to be a threat to aviation. The mid-flight diversions will continue unless and until the Department of Homeland Security succeeds in working out an arrangement with international airlines and foreign governments whereby passenger manifests are sent to the U.S. government *before* flights take off. At present, airlines have up to fifteen minutes after planes take off to transmit passenger manifests to DHS. If a terrorist is intent simply on blowing up an airplane, as opposed to hijacking it and flying it into a target into the United States, fifteen minutes may be more than enough time to accomplish his goal.

Finally, the department has launched what is, in theory, a promising plan called the Immigration Security Initiative (ISI).* Reminiscent of a similar program to check oceangoing cargo for weapons of mass destruction known as the "Container Security Initiative" (CSI), the Customs and Border Protection bureau stations some of its port of entry inspectors at some foreign airports. Before flights bound for the United States depart, these inspectors question passengers whom they deem to be potential security risks, and they inspect passengers' passports and other such documents to ensure that they are genuine, valid, and otherwise sufficient for entry into the United States. Inspectors are stationed in less than a handful of airports around the world, however, and in those few countries where the program is operational, it is only as effective as a counterterrorism tool to the degree that our inspectors are actually permitted by foreign countries to do their work. Countries vary widely in the degree to which they permit other countries' security personnel to operate freely. Any limitations on the degree to which ISI inspectors can scrutinize passengers and their documentation limit the security protection provided by the program.

PORT SECURITY AND NUCLEAR ATTACK

Less than a quarter of the radiation detection devices needed to check all incoming cargo at America's seaports have been installed; in New York, *none* of the cargo that moves through the largest ship terminal or goods leaving the

---

* The program has since been renamed the "Immigration Advisory Program."

port by rail or barge is inspected for radiation, according to the security manager for the Port Authority of New York and New Jersey,[2] and, where radiation detection devices are installed, they are of limited value. They have proved to be unable to distinguish between innocuous, naturally occurring radiation in substances like ceramic tile, cat litter, and bananas, and dangerous weapons-grade uranium.[3]

Two key maritime security programs are riddled with problems. To focus for now on only one, the department's Container Security Initiative makes a lot of sense, in theory. The idea behind it is to "push the borders out" by stationing customs inspectors at foreign ports to see to it that high-risk cargo is inspected for weapons of mass destruction *before* it sails for the United States. But, according to a Government Accountability Office report, there are a variety of problems with the program in practice.[4]

For one thing, U.S. inspectors don't conduct the inspections themselves; they only review cargo manifests for suspicious items and other anomalies. If this "targeting" exercise leads them to believe that a particular shipment should be inspected, they must ask the host country's inspectors to do so.

For another thing, a significant percentage of U.S.-bound shipments from CSI ports were not targeted to determine whether they were high-risk enough to merit inspection, and, therefore, those shipments were not inspected. Furthermore, a significant percentage of the containers that were targeted and then referred to foreign governments for inspection were actually not inspected by those governments for one reason or another. Finally, as for those targeted containers that are inspected, there is limited assurance that the inspections are effective in detecting weapons of mass destruction because of variances in the capability of the detection equipment employed abroad.

To top it all off, monies awarded by the department to secure ports across the country have on occasion been misdirected to projects of dubious security value. For example, $180,000 was spent to install security lights in a "small, remote facility" that receives fewer than twenty ships annually.[5]

MASS TRANSIT ATTACK

Money isn't everything, to be sure, but how we choose to spend our limited homeland security funds says a lot about what our priorities are. Somewhere between $18–20 billion has been spent to secure aviation since terror struck in the United States five years ago. Only a small fraction of that— about $250 million—has been spent by the federal government to enhance the security of mass transit, despite the fact that 32 million people use mass transit systems each day, sixteen times the number of people who fly in airplanes.[6] Indeed, one week after the bombing in London that killed more than 50 people and wounded 700, the United States Senate failed three times to increase mass transit security funding. At the end of the budget process in that chamber, the Senate voted to actually *cut* mass transit funding by some $50 million.[7]

CRITICAL INFRASTRUCTURE AND "SOFT" TARGETS

Certain sectors—the food and water supply, the energy industry, telecommunications networks, the financial system, to name a few—are critical to our national security because a successful attack on them would cripple our economy and lower our standard of living, yet relatively little has been done in the last five years to secure them. Most critical infrastructure is owned and operated by the private sector, and the federal government has been reluctant to use its ultimate power to mandate security enhancements.

What little has been done to secure critical infrastructure is more than has been done to protect "soft" targets like shopping malls, sports stadiums, movie theaters, restaurants, and nightclubs. While the loss of life would likely be relatively small, the result of an attack on a soft target would be to terrorize the entire nation.

THE FAILURE OF INTELLIGENCE

A key challenge facing the Department of Homeland Security is ensuring that it has access to the intelligence it needs to protect the homeland. The department's Information Analysis unit is the poor stepchild of the intelligence community, with its nose pressed against the glass, looking in. The functions initially intended for it—synthesizing information from across all the various intelligence agencies concerning threats against the homeland and consolidating the various terrorist watch lists—have been taken over by the CIA and the FBI, respectively. According to the report of the Silberman-Robb commission established by the President to examine the nation's most recent colossal intelligence failures,[8] the department has trouble getting information from the FBI and the CIA-led National Counterterrorism Center. DHS itself is part of the problem when it comes to intelligence sharing: according to this report, it does not always share relevant information with its nominal partners at the federal, state, and local levels. So, the turf battles and stovepipes that can to some degree be held responsible for not detecting the last attack on the homeland continue to this day.

PREPARING FOR CATASTROPHIC ATTACK

Secretary Chertoff has made a point of stressing that we can't protect America from every conceivable threat, and we shouldn't even try to.[9] Some threats are likelier to materialize than others, and, within that subset of threats, some would have greater consequences in terms of death, injury, and economic damage than others. We should concentrate our necessarily limited time, attention, and financial resources on these threats, and focus our preparedness efforts accordingly.

The department is moving in this direction by using intelligence to devise likely terrorist scenarios that, were they to materialize, would have serious consequences. The department is working with its state and local partners in geographical areas likeliest to be targeted to provide them with the planning, training, and resources they would need in the event that any of these scenarios materializes.[10]

The department also conducts periodic exercises simulating multifaceted terrorist attacks to test the ability of federal, state, and local governments to respond quickly and adroitly enough to minimize death and destruction, but the flat-footed response to a predictable catastrophe like Hurricane Katrina—Secretary Chertoff's first big test as Homeland Security Chief—shows that our preparedness efforts are woefully inadequate to respond to a terrorist attack.

WASTEFUL SPENDING AND SLOPPY ACCOUNTING

In Washington, D.C., where some degree of wasteful spending is accepted as par for the course, the Department of Homeland Security has become notorious for it. Examples abound of the department's throwing money at contractors and then providing little or no oversight. There is the wholly defective $200 million-plus camera and sensor system cited earlier that was supposed to help our overstretched Border Patrol agents spot illegal aliens. It is probably fair to say that TSA has the worst contracting record of all the various DHS components. To cite but one example here, TSA contracted with a company to install and maintain explosive detection equipment at airports throughout the country, paying nearly $50 million for little or no work.[11]

Closing security gaps is not cheap, but these are tight budgetary times, and there is only so much money to go around. That makes it even more important that the Department of Homeland Security spend each dollar wisely. The department has proved to be such a poor steward of taxpayer money that the Congress is understandably reluctant to appropriate significantly more. Every dollar the Department of Homeland Security misspends or fails to keep track of makes us less safe by that amount and the absence of whatever security protections that amount could buy. Radiation portal monitors, for example, can cost as much as $25,000 apiece. The wasted $50 million could have bought 2,000 of them to help protect us from a catastrophic terrorist attack with a nuclear weapon. When it comes to wasteful spending at the Department of Homeland Security, the beat goes on, even though Secretary Chertoff has claimed to make procurement reform a priority. In the aftermath of Hurricane Katrina, scores of no-bid contracts were let and money misspent that could have been used to further secure the homeland.

In the chapters that follow, each of these security gaps will be explored in detail to explain exactly how a terrorist might exploit them to attack the homeland.

AMERICA'S
OPEN DOORS

I should have known. I'd been trying to get a face-to-face, one-on-one meeting with the Secretary for over a year. Ridge needed to hear directly from me that there were serious gaps in America's defenses that terrorists could slip through. My team and I had made that point time and again in report after report and congressional hearing after congressional hearing. It mustn't have sunk in. I was convinced that his management team must have been misleading him into thinking that the nation was safer than it really was. If I could just get to him, surely I could convince him that the sky really was falling.

I was delighted when I received a call from the Secretary's scheduler one day in late May 2004. "The Secretary would like to meet with you."

"That's great news," I replied. "As you know, I've been trying to get some time on his schedule for a long time now. Can you tell me what the agenda is? I want to make sure I'm prepared to discuss whatever he wants to talk about, and, of course, I'll have some things of my own to talk about."

"Well," the scheduler began, "let me check with him on that and get back to you."

I had two weeks to get ready for what would be a pivotal encounter. This could be the meeting that would turn the department around before it was too late.

Days passed with no word from the scheduler as to what exactly the Secretary wanted to discuss. I asked my assistant to call her and press her on the matter. Finally, the word came back that this was to be just a routine "get to know you better" session of the kind he'd been having lately with other senior officials in the department. "There's nothing in particular to prepare for, Clark," reported my assistant.

I was skeptical. Why, all of a sudden, was the Secretary willing to meet with me? Why was it so hard to find out what he wanted to talk about? Was I being set up? Was the session intended to rein me in and shut me up? I decided that there was no use agonizing over it—I'd just prepare myself for either contingency. Either it would be a chance for me to set the record straight about the real state of homeland security and why I was so insistent on calling attention to it, or it would be a knock-down, drag-out, no-holds-barred confrontation between an angry Secretary and "out of control" Inspector General.

The meeting was set for the late afternoon of June 9, and, as usual, I was half an hour early. I cooled my heels in the Secretary's spartan conference room, down the hall from his office suite. When the appointed hour arrived, the Secretary didn't appear. I waited and waited, wondering what was keeping him.

Suddenly, I heard a great commotion in the hallway. The outer door opened, and in walked the utility pole–tall, ramrod-straight Secretary, trailed by a phalanx of aides and bodyguards. He didn't look happy. "Sorry to keep you waiting, Clark. I was up testifying on the Hill, and they kept me longer than I expected. I'll be with you in a minute."

"Of course, sir. Take as much time as you need."

I was finally escorted into his small office. I took a seat on the couch opposite his chair, and waited for him to join me in that corner of the room. "Clark, hold on a minute more. I've asked Joe Whitley to join us. He'll be here in a minute."

"Sure," I said. But that's not good, I thought to myself. Joe was the department's General Counsel. It wasn't Joe that bothered me: He was amiable, capable, and diligent. In my opinion, he was among the handful of senior-level officials in the department who knew what they were doing and was easy to work with.

But why was Ridge bringing *anybody* to the meeting, especially the General Counsel? It probably meant, I feared, that my suspicions were well founded. This would be a gripe session. Ridge would try to read me the riot act and intimidate me into toning down my criticism.

Sure enough, as soon as Whitley arrived, Ridge lit into me. "Look, Clark. I was just on the Hill testifying on border security, and I got my head handed to me over this new report of yours on the visa waiver program. Why do you keep putting out these damning reports? Asa Hutchinson [the Under Secretary for Border and Transportation Security] tells me that there's no problem there, and you're making something out of nothing. And why don't you show these reports to us before you put them out? Why don't you give us an opportunity to point out the flaws in your arguments? Why don't you give us the opportunity to provide you with information contrary to your conclusions?"

"Mr. Secretary, I was afraid that the meeting was going to turn out this way. But if this is what you want to talk about, fine. I welcome the opportunity. Your people have really done you a disservice. You don't understand what's going on here.

"First of all, we do share drafts of our reports with your management team before we finalize and publish them. This is their opportunity to correct any mistakes we've made or to provide any contrary information. We sent a draft of this particular report to Asa months ago, and, you know what, he never gave us any comments. When he got word that we weren't going to wait any longer and we were going to release it without his comments, he called me to plead with me to hold off. You know what his argument was? The report discloses a serious security vulnerability, and publishing the report would give terrorists a road map as to how to attack us. The only problem with that argument is that I'd anticipated his making it and we did a Google search to see whether he himself had said anything about this particular gap on the public record. As it happens, we found that just a few weeks earlier, he was making precisely the point the report makes, and acknowledging that this represents a big hole in border security."

"Look, Clark. Are you *my* Inspector General? When I was Governor of Pennsylvania, I had an Inspector General, but he wasn't out there like you constantly criticizing and embarrassing us."

"Well, sir, you've put your finger on the problem we're having here. The fact is I'm not *your* Inspector General; I'm the American people's Inspector General. By law, I report to you and to the Congress, but I work for the American people. I don't know how things worked in Pennsylvania, but this isn't Pennsylvania. Here in Washington, the Inspector General is supposed to serve as a watchdog over his department. He's supposed to call things as he sees them. It gives me no pleasure to point out that the department is not carrying out its mission. I'm an American citizen, too. Every time we issue a critical report it means that we're more vulnerable to another act of terror than we need to be. I can't hide the facts because it might make you and the Administration look bad. I owe it to the country to tell it straight. Terrorists already know we're vulnerable; it's the American people who are in the dark."

Round and round it went like that for two full hours. The contrast between our first meeting and this one could not have been more stark. If there had been any doubt in my mind before, there was none now. This Secretary would be an adversary, not an ally. Instead of taking the terrorists on, he would take me on.

Two years have passed since I tried to bring these gaps to the Secretary of Homeland Security's attention. The same urgent questions continue to haunt me, because though the department is now under new management, to a large degree, the same old security gaps remain.

Will suicide bombers finally bring their bloodlust to America? Will there be an attack on the subway; a crippling virus in cyberspace; an explosion on a bridge, a bomb in a shopping mall, sports arena, or movie theater; or, worse yet, an apocalyptic attack with a nuclear weapon smuggled into one of our seaports? Despite the government's periodic attempts to reassure the public that it is doing everything within its power to secure the homeland, we are still vulnerable to terrorist attack and our enemies are seeking to find security gaps that they can exploit to bring us down.

Perhaps the biggest question mark hangs over what we don't know about the dangers that lie dormant in our own communities. Have terrorists already slipped into the United States? Have some native-born Americans been radicalized and converted to a nihilistic, hate-filled version of Islam such that they, too, pose a threat to the homeland? Have nuclear weapons in cargo containers already been smuggled into our country through our vulnerable ports? How easy is it to poison the food supply, cripple the financial markets and banking system, or shut down the nation's energy supply? How good is our intelligence about terrorists in our midst? How much do we know about terrorists' plans and capabilities?

As Inspector General, I would often lie awake at night, tossing and turning as I pondered these questions. While I struggled each day to get the department's leaders to take security gaps seriously enough to close them, I knew that the terrorists were working overtime to exploit them.

TERRORISTS ON AMERICAN SOIL—THE ENEMY WITHIN

Just how easy is it for terrorists to penetrate our country today? Once they get here, what and where are the security gaps they can exploit to perpetrate another deadly attack? Before turning to these important questions, it is worth pausing here to debunk once again the widely trumped notion that another attack can be averted simply by confining terrorists to wherever they happen to be overseas.

As the President put it in a June 28, 2005, address to the nation on the state of the war in Iraq, "Iraq is the latest battlefield in this war. Many terrorists who kill innocent men, women, and children on the streets of Baghdad are followers of the same murderous ideology that took the lives of our citizens in New York, Washington, and Pennsylvania. There is only one course of action against them—to defeat them abroad before they attack us at home."[1]

While we certainly should continue to take the fight to the enemy wherever he is, we need to face the awful reality that the enemy may already be in our very own backyard. Tracking down terrorists overseas and killing or capturing them before they manage to slip into the United States is, needless to say, preferable to fighting them on our own soil, but it is not as if terrorists are conveniently confined to some neatly contained, easily defined, and clearly labeled "BATTLEFIELD" overseas. The frightening truth is that there are already terrorists among us.

The war in Iraq has actually increased the pool of violently anti-American Islamic fundamentalists from whom Al Qaeda and likeminded groups can recruit jihadists to strike our homeland. As CIA Director Porter Goss pithily put it in February 2005 testimony before the Senate Select Committee on Intelligence, "The Iraq conflict, while not a cause of extremism, has become a cause for extremists."[2]

The frightening reality is that exactly who they are, where they are, and how many there are no one—not the FBI, not DHS, not the CIA—really knows, but our nation's top security officials all acknowledge that at least some of our nation's deadliest enemies are already here. It is clear that the global war on terror is a multi-front war, and America itself is one of the battlefields.

In the same hearing in which Goss made his arresting comments, FBI Director Bob Mueller identified the prospect of terrorist sleeper cells in the United States poised to launch another surprise attack against us as the number one threat to our national security today. "While we still believe the most serious threat to the homeland originates from Al Qaida members located overseas, the bombings in Madrid have heightened our concern regarding the possible role that indigenous Islamic extremists, already in the United States, may play in future terrorist plots. . . . We are also concerned about the possible role that peripheral groups with a significant presence in the U.S. may play if called upon by members of Al Qaida to assist them with planning or logistical support."[3] If the deadly bombing of a Madrid train station in the spring of 2004 heightened the FBI's concern about the potential presence of sleeper cells in the United States, surely the grisly bombing of subway stations and a commuter bus in London in the summer of 2005, which likewise bore all the hallmarks of Al Qaeda and its affiliates, can only have heightened such concern even more.

These are not merely theoretical concerns. For the first time ever, the President himself, in an October 6, 2005 address, disclosed that, "Overall, the U.S. and our partners have disrupted at least ten serious Al Qaeda terrorist plots since September the 11th, including three Al Qaeda plots to attack inside the United States. We've stopped at least five more Al Qaeda efforts to case targets in the United States, or infiltrate operatives into our country."[4]

For example, the Department of Homeland Security raised the threat level for financial institutions in New York, New Jersey, and Washington, D.C., in August 2004 based on the seizure of a computer from an Al Qaeda operative in Pakistan that contained hundreds of photographs of key buildings. The photos were so numerous and detailed that it was clear that extensive casing operations had been conducted to spot security gaps that could be exploited. Based on the information obtained, the authorities concluded that terrorists had intended to blow up the buildings by placing bombs in vehicles such as limousines, large vans, trucks, and oil tankers placed in underground parking lots or near heavily trafficked building entrances.[5]

Iyman Farris was arrested in 2003 for plotting to blow up the Brooklyn Bridge. He is now in federal prison, having pleaded guilty to providing material support to Al Qaeda.[6]

The so-called Lackawanna Six were a group based in upstate New York that allegedly trained in Afghanistan in the spring of 2001 to carry out terror attacks in the United States. The members of the group purportedly met with Osama bin Laden during the course of their training. Five of the six were born and reared in the sleepy, off-the-beaten-track town of Lackawanna. The six are serving sentences ranging from seven to ten years after pleading guilty in 2003 to providing support to a terrorist organization.[7]

In June 2005, a father and son in the town of Lodi, California, near Sacramento, Umer Hayat and Hamid Hayat, were charged with making false statements to the FBI by denying that the son had trained in Pakistan to kill Americans and that the father had helped to pay for his training. In an affidavit, the son later admitted attending an Al Qaeda training camp where photographs of prominent U.S. political figures, including President Bush, were used for target practice. Another father-son duo was caught up in this investigation, Mohammad Adil Khan and Mohammad Hassan Adil. The father headed a mosque in Lodi. According to the FBI, Khan planned to establish a *madrassa,* or fundamentalist Islamic school, to recruit people to wage *jihad* against the United States. Khan and his son agreed to be deported to their native Pakistan after being arrested in June 2005 for violating the terms of their visas.[8]

We all know the story of "dirty bomber" Jose Padilla, a Hispanic man who grew up in inner-city Chicago and converted to Islam in prison after being convicted of gang-related activities. He is alleged to have attended training camps in Afghanistan and Pakistan, and then to have returned to Chicago in order to carry out a radiological attack. The President declared him an "enemy combatant," and he was held for three years in a military brig as the constitutionality of his indefinite detention was being litigated. Padilla has since been turned over to the regular criminal justice system and charged with the less sensational crimes of providing support to terrorists and conspiring to murder people overseas.[9] Al Qaeda and affiliated groups are known to be particularly attracted to prisons as fertile ground for recruiting converts, especially African Americans.[10]

An African American convert to Islam with terrorist ties, Seattle-born Earnest James Ujaama, was sentenced to two years in prison in February 2004 for providing goods and services to the Taliban. Among other things, Ujaama was involved in a 1999 plot to establish a terrorist training camp in Bly, Oregon. One of the people with whom Ujaama is alleged to have conspired is purportedly Haroon Rashid Aswat, whom British authorities believe was connected to the deadly subway and bus bombings in London in the summer of 2005.[11]

Groups like Hamas and Hezbollah, which have a presence in the United States but have traditionally confined their activities to efforts to harm Israel, could be used by Al Qaeda and its offshoots to facilitate attacks on the homeland. There are also disaffected and alienated homegrown right-wing groups, personified by Oklahoma bomber Timothy McVeigh, who share Islamic terrorists' hatred of the American government and their animus toward Jews and Israel.[12]

To offer some sense of the scope of the danger facing America from terrorists already inside the country, the FBI knows of about a thousand Al Qaeda sympathizers in the United States today, and it has about 300 extremists under surveillance.[13]

Even more worrisome are terrorists and terrorist sympathizers whom we know nothing about. Of course, we don't know what we don't know, but we do know that there is reason to believe that the numbers cited above are low.

For example, in the aftermath of 9/11, the FBI and the CIA intensively screened the visa applications of all males between the ages of sixteen and forty-five from predominantly Arab and Muslim countries for any terrorist connections they might have. State Department consular officers, who process and issue visas at our embassies and consulates around the world, were told by their superiors to wait thirty days before issuing visas to such applicants, in order to give the FBI and CIA time to scrutinize their applications. If the consular officers received no word during this time period from the FBI or CIA connecting a given applicant to terrorism, the applicant was deemed eligible for a visa and one was duly issued to him.

Predictably, the FBI fell woefully behind in vetting these applications. By the time they began to catch up, 105 applicants to whom the State Department had already issued visas were found to have terrorism connections. Fortunately, 100 of the visas were revoked before the suspected terrorists who had obtained them attempted to use them to enter the United States. Of the remaining five, suspected terrorists did use them—three suspects were stopped at the border, but two made it into the country. According to an anonymous law enforcement source, those two suspected terrorists eventually left the United States without incident, thankfully. But this all too close brush with disaster raises the question of how often this kind of bureaucratic bungling continues to happen in the post-9/11 era, where the margin for error is zero.[14]

During my time as Inspector General of the Department of Homeland Security, my staff and I stumbled onto an equally, if not even more, disturbing discovery during a visit to our embassy and consulate in Saudi Arabia. While there to assess the effectiveness of DHS' Visa Security Officer (VSO) program[15] (more about this later), one of the consular officers we interviewed in Riyadh mentioned in passing that there were boxes and boxes in a storage room down the hall containing the applications of thousands of young Saudi men who had applied for and received visas around the time the fifteen Saudi hijackers did. In the months following the attacks, he explained, a team of FBI agents came to the embassy and asked the consular section to go through the boxes and pull the files of several hundred applicants, including those of the fifteen terrorists. The agents then reviewed those files to determine whether there might have been any connections (tribes, families, villages, occupation, addresses, and so on) between those applicants and the hijackers.

For reasons unexplained, the agents left without examining the thousands of other applications. Without going through them, there was no way to tell whether the other applications might have contained any relevant information, so the only reasonable guess as to why the FBI chose not to examine those too is that in their judgment doing so was too much trouble. While it is certainly possible that the remaining applications contained nothing important, it is equally possible that examining them might yet lead to tracking down other terrorists presently in the United States, lying in wait to launch follow-up attacks, or simply copycat cells hiding out until an opportune time to launch another attack. As I write these words today, these applications have yet to be examined, and the more time goes by, the less potentially useful any intelligence they might contain will be. It's safe to say, then, that a not insignificant number of suspected terrorists are known to be in the country today, and still more are, in all likelihood, here somewhere.

Laying aside the terrorists who are already here, how easy is it for even more terrorists to come to America today? The short answer is: harder than it's ever been. But, if we allow ourselves to think that it is hard enough, we are setting ourselves up for another rude awakening one day.

ENTERING THE UNITED STATES

If you are a terrorist who wants to come to America to launch an attack, there are two ways to come into the country to do so—legally and illegally. The attackers last time chose to enter through the proverbial "front door" of our somewhat regulated immigration system, by applying for a visa. I'll begin, then, by assessing the degree to which, since then, this legal route has been made harder. To explain fully the scope of the changes, it is important to step back in time and trace the steps leading up to the present day.

Diplomatic relations between the United States and twenty-seven countries[16] in the world are close, and there have been few instances of those countries' citizens committing fraud to get a visa or overstaying the terms of entry once they get here. As a result, foreign nationals from those countries may enter the United States without first applying for and receiving a visa from an American embassy or consulate in their own country or some third country. They need simply show up at an American airport, seaport, or land crossing and present their passports. American citizens are likewise not required to obtain visas to enter those countries. Needless to say, then, a terrorist will have an easier time entering the country with a passport from a "visa-waiver" country than he will with a passport from a non–visa-waiver country, as will be explained in detail later.

The citizens of most countries in the world, including those from the lion's share of predominantly Arab and Muslim countries, do need to apply for visas through our embassies and consulates abroad. If a foreigner succeeds in obtaining a visa, he may or may not be admitted to the United States once he shows up at a port of entry. A visa does not entitle a foreigner to enter the United States; Department of Homeland Security customs inspectors at ports of entry have the final say as to who may and who may not be admitted into the United States. But if a foreigner's visa and passport are in order, and nothing in the inspector's databases indicates that the foreigner is a terrorist or criminal, he is almost certain to be admitted into the United States. In short, a visa is essentially a pass key to get into the United States.

Before terror struck the United States, it was relatively easy to get a visa to enter this country. The State Department was largely focused on facilitating and expediting the visa issuance process. To the extent that the State Department scrutinized visa applicants back then, it tended to do so more with an eye toward weeding out those intending to become illegal immigrants than toward weeding out would-be terrorists.

As the years went by, the volume of visa requests increased, but the State Department's visa processing budget was not increased commensurately. The upshot was that more and more pressure was put on the State Department by friendly foreign governments, our own business community, academic institutions, and Congress to simplify and speed up the visa process in order to better promote trade, tourism, and scholarship. In response to this pressure, the State Department tended increasingly to exercise its discretion to waive the legal requirement that all visa applicants apply in person at an American embassy or consulate and be interviewed by a consular officer before being granted a visa. Even after the first Al Qaeda attack on the World Trade Center in 1993, the State Department's focus on processing visas faster, with fewer workers, and a minimum of hassle and fuss for foreign applicants, did not change. Even in 1998, the year that Al Qaeda bombed our embassies in Kenya and Tanzania, the investigative arm of Congress, the then-named General Accounting Office (GAO, which was renamed the

"Government Accountability Office" in 2005), issued a report critical of the delays and recommending ways to expedite visa issuance.[17]

According to our embassy in Saudi Arabia, less than 3 percent of Saudi applicants for a U.S. visa were interviewed prior to September 11.[18] Only three of the fifteen Saudi hijackers were interviewed. Applicants from Saudi Arabia were generally approved anyway with little scrutiny because most Saudi applicants were so affluent that they rarely overstayed the time period granted for entry. Only .5 percent of all Saudi visas were refused. Making matters worse, in hindsight, the U.S. Embassy in Saudi Arabia, four months before the attacks, initiated a program, similar to ones in other countries with friendly governments and low fraud and visa overstay rates, to speed up the visa application process even more. So as both to expedite the process and to reduce the number of visitors to the embassy who might either perpetrate an attack or be killed or injured in one (the major security preoccupation after the East Africa bombings), Saudi visa applicants were permitted to use the "Visa Express" program to bypass the embassy or consulate altogether and submit their applications to certain approved travel agencies within the Kingdom. Those travel agencies reviewed the applications for completeness and then passed them on to the embassy or consulate for approval or rejection.

Three of the fifteen Saudi terrorists used Visa Express to obtain their visas. Abdulaziz Al-omari was one of the hijackers on American Airlines Flight 11 that crashed into the north tower of the World Trade Center. Khalid al-Midhar and Salem Al-Hazmi were both aboard the American Airlines flight that crashed into the Pentagon.[19]

As if the controversy surrounding Visa Express was not bad enough, it soon came out that there were grounds for the State Department to have denied the hijackers' visa applications because of various defects and omissions. According to 9/11 Commission staff, "All . . . of these applications were incomplete in some way, with a data field left blank or not answered fully. . . . [T]hree of the 19 hijackers submitted applications that contained false statements that could have been proven to be false at the time they applied."[20]

To add insult to injury, a scheme to sell visas was uncovered in our embassy in the Persian Gulf state of Qatar. Seventy visas had been sold for $10,000 apiece by a Jordanian-born employee in the consular section to thirty-eight fellow Jordanians, twenty-eight Bangladeshis, and one Syrian. Three of the men to whom the visas were sold had roomed for a time with two of the Saudi hijackers.

As the controversy over Visa Express and associated issues swirled around Washington, I was still serving as the Inspector General of the State Department, and I was eager to weigh in on the issue by conducting my own examination of the State Department's handling of the visa issuance process, with or without a congressional request to do so. As it happened, at about this time I received a letter from Iowa Senator Chuck Grassley and Pennsylvania Congressman Dave Weldon requesting an examination of the by then infamous Visa Express program.

Between July and November 2002, I assembled a team of veteran consular experts from my office to examine the visa policies and practices of our embassies and consulates in the twenty-seven countries that are predominantly Muslim, or non-Muslim with a significant Muslim minority. To get a firsthand look at the issue myself, I traveled to Singapore, Malaysia, and Bangladesh—three predominantly Muslim countries—and France, the country in Europe with the largest Muslim minority.

The conclusion of our report was stark: "The post–September 11 era should have witnessed immediate and dramatic changes in CA's [the State Department's Consular Affairs bureau] direction of the visa process. This has not happened. A fundamental readjustment of Department leadership regarding visa issuance and denial has not taken place. The Department still does not fully appreciate the consular function as part of a coordinated national effort to manage border security. . . . If the visa process is to be made more secure, it must be considered a part of a larger process beginning with the visa process and continuing through the admission of aliens to the United States and tracking them while they remain in the country. . . . The Department at every level must approach this task and devote the necessary resources and effort to it."[21]

While recognizing that simply interviewing every applicant in and of itself is no guarantee that a would-be terrorist in the applicant pool will be identified, we nevertheless recommended that applicants be interviewed as a general rule rather than an exception, and that experienced State Department officers with the requisite language skills be used to supplement consular offices staffed by newer officers lacking the ability to speak the native tongue. Finally, we discouraged the use of programs around the world like Visa Express that allow third parties to process visa applications on behalf of U.S. diplomatic missions.

Most government reports gather dust on Washington bookshelves. This report resulted in action. The State Department began to significantly increase the percentage of visa applicants interviewed. Visa Express in Saudi Arabia, and similar programs elsewhere, were discontinued.

Still, in the fall of 2002, influential voices on Capitol Hill and in the media[22] were demanding that the State Department transfer the visa function wholesale to a new Department of Homeland Security. Had the Secretary of State been less influential, less politically adroit, and less skilled a bureaucratic infighter than Colin Powell, and had the presumptive Secretary of Homeland Security-to-be, then White House Homeland Security Adviser Tom Ridge, been more savvy and aggressive, it is virtually certain that visas today would be handled entirely by DHS; however, at Powell's insistence, a compromise was reached whereby the State Department would continue to process applications and issue visas, while Homeland Security would set overall visa policy and have the final say as to whether a visa could be issued and an alien admitted.

To ensure that counterterrorism, rather than "customer service," would become the primary focus of consular officers, the law creating the Department of Homeland Security established the "Visa Security Officer" program. Visa Security Officers, or VSOs, trained in fraud detection, interview techniques, and other tricks of the counterterrorism trade, would be dispatched to our embassies and consulates throughout the world to, as it were, look over the shoulders of consular officers to ensure that they reject visa applications from known or suspected terrorists. The presumption was that VSOs would serve in every U.S. diplomatic post abroad where visas are issued. Only if the Secretary of Homeland Security "determined that such an assignment at a particular post would *not* promote homeland security" would VSOs not be sent to that country.[23]

Because fifteen of the nineteen terrorists had come from Saudi Arabia, and because some of those Saudis had gotten their visas through the Visa Express program without any direct contact at all with an American government official, the one place where Congress explicitly mandated the stationing of VSOs was Saudi Arabia.

After becoming Inspector General of the Department of Homeland Security on its very first day, January 24, 2003, I made it a priority to examine the VSO program as soon as practicable. After giving it a while to get up and running, I traveled to Saudi Arabia with two of my best inspectors, Doug Ellice and Ken McKune, former State Department experts in consular affairs and counterterrorism, respectively, to see for myself how the Visa Security Officer program was working in practice. If having DHS look over the State Department's shoulder in a critically important country like Saudi Arabia would serve to keep Saudi terrorists out of the United States, at least some of the promise of DHS was being realized. If, on the other hand, DHS was adding no value to speak of, this would call into question whether the department was really the indispensable counterterrorism tool that its supporters claimed it to be, and that even its detractors wanted it to be.

Over the course of several days in the capital city of Riyadh, my team and I met with the ambassador and his deputy, officials in the consular section, those in the Diplomatic Security section who guard the embassy and its personnel, and the representatives of the other relevant government agencies other than the State Department, including, of course, the Department of Homeland Security's Visa Security Officers. It was sobering to be in the country from which so many of the hijackers had come, not to mention Osama bin Laden himself, and to be in the very building where visas for some of the terrorists had been approved. The anguish and strain of knowing the ghastly consequences of their colleagues' decision to admit the hijackers showed on the faces of the consular officers with whom we met, and a feeling of sadness and loss hung so heavily in the air that it was almost palpable.

After a few days in Riyadh, we moved on to the Red Sea city of Jeddah, Saudi Arabia's second largest city, where the United States maintains a consulate. I recall sitting in the Consul General's office for our initial meeting and thinking how unsettling it must be to work in a building that is *the* symbol of the much-hated United States government in a country increasingly under siege from radicalized and emboldened Islamic militants. Common sense and even a cursory knowledge of recent history suggested that it would be only a matter of time before an attack on the consulate itself.

My team and I would get a firsthand sense ourselves of the anxious mood of Saudi security forces in the city. As my colleagues strolled back along the seawall from dinner to our hotel one night, Saudi officers stopped them to hand out leaflets with photos of the twenty-six most wanted Al Qaeda terrorists in the Kingdom. This clear and present sense of danger, and this encounter with the faces of evil convinced us, as if we needed convincing, of how important it was for the security of the United States that our Department of Homeland Security be at work in our embassy and consulate in Saudi Arabia on the lookout for terrorists among those seeking entry into our country. (My sense of doom proved prescient when, months later, terrorists did storm the consulate, leaving five non-American employees dead.) What we found, to our shock and dismay, was that the VSO program was not working as intended, and, through no fault of their own, these officers were adding little, if any, homeland security value.

The first sign of how seriously DHS took the Visa Security program was how long it took the department to send VSOs to Saudi Arabia. Even though

Saudi Arabia was perceived to be a hotbed of terrorism, and even though the program was touted in the early days of the department as *the* antidote to the State Department's focus on customer service at the expense of counterterrorism, DHS failed to send Visa Security Officers to Saudi Arabia in a timely fashion. The applicable provision of the Homeland Security Act required VSOs to begin reviewing visa applications in Saudi Arabia "after enactment of this Act."[24] Though the law became effective on January 24, 2003, sixty days after the President's signature, VSOs did not actually arrive in the country until August 2003, some seven months later.

The Homeland Security Act did not authorize the Department of Homeland Security to create any additional employee slots to fill with Visa Security Officers, and no money was provided to transfer existing employees to Saudi Arabia. Furthermore, unlike the State Department and the Pentagon, which can, if need be, order employees to transfer to a new location, the Homeland Security Department is governed by Civil Service rules that generally do not allow for forced transfers. Accordingly, the department relied on volunteers to staff this critically important counterterrorism program. The volunteers served for only short, temporary periods of time, resulting in rapid turnover of personnel. As a practical matter, an officer would no sooner begin to learn the fundamentals of the job than he would be rotated out and replaced by another officer just as inexperienced as he was when he arrived.

Additionally, the temporary personnel who volunteered often lacked the skills necessary to be effective at identifying and foiling terrorists. For example, one officer had no law enforcement experience. Another had never worked outside the United States, and, as a result, he had no idea how an embassy works. Another had no knowledge of the visa process.

The VSOs' temporary status resulted in the classic bureaucratic Catch–22 that made them even less effective. Because of their temporary status, the State Department issued DHS personnel only "official" passports, not "diplomatic" ones. A person can get an official passport if he or she is abroad temporarily on official business for the United States government. If, however, a person is on official diplomatic business for the United States for an extended period of time, he or she is eligible for a diplomatic passport. The significance of this seemingly trivial distinction is that the Saudi government treats foreigners holding official passports like any foreign private citizen visiting the Kingdom. Foreign visitors cannot transact business at a bank, rent a car, or buy a cell phone, so VSOs were significantly limited in their ability to travel, communicate, and interact with the Saudi government.

To make matters even worse, the Saudi government has a rigidly compartmentalized approach to doing business with its foreign counterparts. The Saudi Foreign Ministry deals only with the State Department. The Defense Ministry deals only with our Pentagon. The Saudi Intelligence Service deals only with our CIA. While the Interior Ministry comes closest, there is no exact counterpart to DHS in the Saudi government. As a result, the VSOs do not have a natural partner or interlocutor in the Saudi government with which to work. DHS, then, must work through pre-existing U.S. agencies—principally, the State Department—to try to influence the Saudi government with regard to counterterrorism issues, when the whole point of the VSO program was that the State Department was to defer on such matters to a putatively more expert and focused Department of Homeland Security.

Only one of the ten VSOs sent to Saudi Arabia could speak Arabic. Needless to say, the officers' effectiveness was severely limited by their inability to speak and read the language of the visa applicants. The VSOs who were sent to Saudi Arabia to oversee the State Department and to ensure that no more visas would be issued to Saudi terrorists were, then, relying on State Department personnel to tell them what visa applicants were saying and what their documents said.

To my great surprise and disappointment, I found out that none of this bothered the Secretary of Homeland Security one bit. Tom Ridge made that crystal clear in an interview on National Public Radio less than two months before the 2004 presidential election.[25]

> NPR INTERVIEWER: In these final weeks before Election Day, Homeland Security officials have been warning of a possible terrorist attack. They've been watching airports, seaports and borders. Yesterday, Tom Ridge, the Secretary of Homeland Security, contended that the nation is getting safer. . . .
>
> Your department's inspector general found that when the U.S. government sent agents to Saudi Arabia to try to keep track of people who are applying for false visas, if that happens in Saudi Arabia, that they suffered from a lack of funding, from a lack of expertise, and, in fact, nine of the ten people sent to Saudi Arabia to look out for illegal entrance toward the United States couldn't even speak Arabic. How'd that happen?
>
> SECRETARY RIDGE: Well, it's interesting that the—we appreciate the work that the Inspector General does, but, frankly, you don't necessarily need to speak the language in order to check all the back-

ground information relevant to an application from someone in Saudi Arabia.

NPR INTERVIEWER: Do you think the program is working well?

SECRETARY RIDGE: Well, the program just began. Let's give the Department of Homeland Security and the Security Visa Program an opportunity to mature. The first place we wanted to go was Saudi Arabia. They had sufficient financial support, don't necessarily need the language training. Now make no mistake about it, there's a need for Arabic-speaking and foreign language–speaking analysts not just reviewing visas but frankly reviewing intelligence information that we glean in from around the world. So, the absence of foreign-speaking agents in the Security Visa Office is the least of our problems.

Tellingly, in a mere six-sentence response, the Secretary had made no fewer than six inaccurate assertions, ranging in importance from the minor to the major. The DHS agents in question were Visa Security Officers, not Security Visa Officers. The department's own formal written response to our report acknowledged that the program was unfunded. At the time of our review, the program had not "just begun"; it had been operational by that point for more than a year. VSOs were not sent to Saudi Arabia because that was the first country to which the department "wanted" to send them; they were sent there pursuant to an explicit congressional mandate because Saudi Arabia was perceived to be a center of anti-American militancy.

More important, Ridge's response indicated an utter lack of understanding on the part of the Secretary of Homeland Security as to what "intelligence" really is. Intelligence is *any* information that can be helpful in protecting the security of the nation, so to the extent that visa applications contain information about Saudi terrorists seeking to come to the United States to launch an attack, they contain "intelligence."

Finally, the Secretary's response indicated a misplaced sense of what the government's priorities should be as it seeks to wage a necessarily multifront war on terrorism. To be sure, Arabic-speaking counterterrorism professionals are in short supply in our country, and they are, admittedly, much in demand. The State Department, the Defense Department, the FBI, the CIA, and the other agencies that make up the intelligence community are all competing with DHS for the few who are available. But, that said, it is hard to see how *any* U.S. government mission—*including* finding bin Laden and breaking the back of the insurgency in Iraq—could be more important than preventing another terrorist from getting what amounts to a permission slip to enter the United States. Of course, not all foreign terrorists speak Arabic, but certainly many do, and, therefore, the Department of Homeland Security's agents in Arabic-speaking countries ought at a minimum to be able to communicate with them in their own language.

During the course of our review of the program, we also found that VSOs were spending the majority of their time inputting data into DHS computers that State Department consular officers had already entered into State computers. Even though DHS and State Department officers were located in offices just a few feet from each other, neither could access the others' databases, and both were sending essentially the same information back to the United States for a background check. As a consequence, precious time was being wasted by the State Department, the Department of Homeland Security, and other key members of the U.S. law enforcement and intelligence communities. While VSOs were wasting time doing what others had already done, they had less time to focus on what they alone were supposedly uniquely competent to do—reviewing the visa issuance process with an eye to discerning whether, and, if so, how, terrorists were exploiting it.

Furthermore, by the terms of the law, DHS was to develop general homeland security training for consular officers to supplement the training provided by the State Department. As of the time of our report, more than a year and a half after the creation of the department, DHS had not begun to provide such training, nor had it made plans to do so.

One of the key tools that Congress gave DHS to provide it with leverage over the State Department with regard to visas is the authority to develop performance standards against which to determine State Department consular officers' eligibility for pay increases and promotions. It is extraordinary, if not unprecedented, for one government agency to be given a say in how another government agency's employees are evaluated. An aggressive DHS secretary could have used this provision to force, essentially, the State Department to put counterterrorism concerns above everything else in administering the visa issuance process, but at the time of our examination, DHS had neither set performance standards, nor even identified personnel within the department to whom the task would be assigned.

The Homeland Security Act also required DHS to study the role that foreign nationals play in the visa issuance process, and to report its conclusions to Congress. True to form, the department missed the deadline, by eight months. Missing a deadline is only as important as the task to have been accomplished by the deadline, of course. By this standard, missing this deadline was very important, indeed.

Most Americans would be shocked and disturbed to learn that, to one degree or another, foreign nationals supplement the American workforce in our embassies and consulates abroad. Of course, some of these workers are service personnel like drivers, janitors, and groundskeepers, all of which is unremarkable. What *is* remarkable is the degree to which, in any given country, foreigners can outnumber American workers, and, more remarkable still, the fact that foreigners can and do play a large role in performing the most critical and sensitive tasks.

As we all know all too well, now that the homeland has been attacked, no task in an American diplomatic mission is more critical and sensitive than issuing visas. In America's diplomatic service, foreign nationals are not permitted to "adjudicate" visa applications, that is, decide whether to approve them; however, foreign nationals (or FSNs, as they are called, for Foreign Service Nationals) do process and review visa applications for completeness and legal sufficiency. They can and do help to determine whether an applicant is deemed eligible for a visa by helping to translate what applicants say in interviews for those consular officers who do not speak the local language. Drawing on their knowledge of local culture, customs, and conditions, foreign nationals can and do advise American officers as to whether a given applicant's story about why he wants to come to America is or isn't credible, and whether there is anything distinctive in an applicant's body language or demeanor that might signal trouble. In short, foreign nationals play a major role in the visa issuance process, and yet the American government has limited information about them and their bona fides.

For reasons of sovereignty and practicality, the American government cannot run a background check in another country on one of that country's citizens or "third-country nationals" (foreigners residing in a country), so our embassies and consulates rely on the word of the host government as to whether our foreign workforce in that country is free of terrorists and criminals. Some countries' background checks are more thorough than others', and some countries' "word" is better than others'. Be that as it may, experience has shown that most foreign nationals in our embassies' employ are not security risks; still, in today's world, knowing that even one terrorist can kill thousands, it was disturbing in the extreme to realize that we Americans are not in control of checking the backgrounds of those foreigners who help to decide who gets into our country.

A draft of the report on the role of foreign nationals in visa issuance was not finalized and circulated for comment with DHS until the very month it was to have been submitted to Congress. The reason DHS gave for the delay in the preparation of the report was revealing—the department was waiting for input from the State Department. No "meaningful" report could be written about the role of foreign nationals in the visa issuance process without the State Department's participation, DHS explained, because the lion's share of them are State Department employees. In the end, the report was more or less written by the State Department, DHS conceded to us. This being so, it was no surprise that the report concluded that foreign nationals are indispensable to the conduct of America's diplomatic business abroad, and that they pose no appreciable security risk to the United States.

Of course, this is exactly what anyone would expect the State Department to say. If the Congress wanted the State Department to ask itself whether it could make do without foreign workers, it could have asked the State Department to undertake such a study. By asking DHS—the government agency charged with looking at issues from a counterterrorism perspective—to do so, the Congress expected, presumably, that the report would be DHS' own work and that a Department of "Homeland Security" might at the very least question whether foreign nationals should play any role at all in sensitive areas such as visa issuance, especially after the disclosure that a Jordanian national in our embassy in Qatar had sold visas to associates of some of the September 11 hijackers.

In addition to requiring DHS to assign Visa Security Officers to our embassy and consulate in Saudi Arabia, the Homeland Security Act contemplated that, in short order, VSOs would be sent to most, if not all, American diplomatic missions abroad where visas are issued. DHS was to submit a report to Congress no later than one year after the signing of the Homeland Security bill into law on the reason for *not* assigning VSOs to those embassies and consulates to which they were not dispatched.

As of the date of our inquiry, DHS was unable to tell us who in the department would finalize the criteria for determining the additional countries to which VSOs would be sent, who would draft the report, and when it would be drafted and submitted.

Again, this was more than the failure to miss a deadline. In this instance, setting criteria by which to decide to which countries Visa Security Officers should be sent, dispatching VSOs throughout the world accordingly, and sending a report to Congress on these matters within a year was reasonable, necessary, and doable, but at that point, three years after the attacks and one year and a half after the creation of the Department of Homeland Security, the United States government had yet to assign homeland security-oriented specialists to any visa-issuing U.S. diplomatic mission other than the one in

Saudi Arabia, even though terrorists could obtain a visa by applying at any of the approximately 200 countries in the world with which the United States maintains diplomatic relations.

ENTERING ON A VISA TODAY

As disturbing as all of this is, what relevance does it have today? Has the Department of Homeland Security since closed those security gaps so that it's as hard as we can make it for terrorists to get a visa to come to America to carry out another attack? The short answer is that the gaps have been narrowed, but not nearly enough. It's still easier than it should be for terrorists to slip through the cracks.

Before the attacks, only about a fifth of visa applicants were interviewed. The State Department's policy was "to permit waiver of the interview when it [was] clear that the alien is eligible for the visa and an interview would be an unnecessary inconvenience."[26]

The presumption was so much in favor of granting visas that interviews were required generally only in those instances when an application was rejected for some reason on the initial review. An interview was not a prerequisite to getting one's visa application approved; it was a second opportunity to convince a consular officer to approve an application initially deemed to be questionable!

Fortunately for our security, most visa applicants are interviewed as a matter of course nowadays. More than 350 new positions have been created to give the State Department the manpower it needs to do so,[27] and to make them likelier to spot terrorists among the throngs of visa applicants, State Department consular officers undergo more extensive training in interview techniques and fraud detection. Today, the State Department's "consular lookout" database (also known by its acronym, CLASS), against which all visa applicants are checked, contains 21 million records of terrorists and other people who for some reason are ineligible for visas, nearly triple the number prior to the attacks.[28] About 70 percent of the database is based on information passed on to the State Department by the FBI, the CIA, and other law enforcement and intelligence agencies.[29] This is a notable advance, as some of the hijackers were known by other agencies to have ties to Al Qaeda. Had that information been shared with the State Department and entered into CLASS, those hijackers' visa applications would, presumably, have been denied by our consular officers overseas.

However, the system still has holes that terrorists know very well how to exploit. First of all, to this day, Department of Homeland Security Visa Security Officers are stationed only in Saudi Arabia and four other countries—Pakistan, Indonesia, the United Arab Emirates, and the Philippines—all of which were added to the program only in the fall of 2005. According to the department, the plan now is to expand the program at the rate of five countries per year, but as I pointed out in congressional testimony four years almost to the day after the terror attacks, "at that rate, it will take about 40 years for Visa Security Officers to be deployed worldwide, giving terrorists plenty of time to apply for a U.S. visa from countries lacking the putative protections of the program."[30]

Part of the reason why VSOs have thus far been dispatched to so few countries is the lethargy and incompetence of the lumbering DHS bureaucracy, certainly. Another part of the reason is that the State Department, through the so-called NSDD-38 process, still exercises what amounts to veto power over where Department of Homeland Security officers may be sent and how many may serve at any particular embassy or consulate. "NSDD" stands for National Security Decision Directive, a presidential order governing various and sundry national security matters. NSDD-38, promulgated in 1982, gives the American ambassador in each country, as the "Chief of Mission," the power to determine the overall size of the American government staff in that embassy, how those numbers are apportioned among State Department personnel and those from other U.S. government agencies, and what the mission of each agency represented within the embassy is.

Even in Saudi Arabia, where VSOs have been stationed for some time, terrorists' chances of being caught are not appreciably better than they were when my inspection team and I traveled to the Kingdom to examine the Visa Security Officer program. There are still only a handful of VSOs in Saudi Arabia—four, to be precise—and only two of them speak Arabic. They still serve for a relatively short period of time, one year, depriving the program of the experience and expertise that comes with longevity, and while there's anecdotal evidence that they've stopped some suspected terrorists from getting U.S. visas, there's no way to tell for sure because the Department of Homeland Security doesn't keep adequate records.[31]

Second, the role of foreign nationals in our embassies and consulates around the world has not changed since the attacks. We still know only such background information on them as foreign governments are willing to share with us. Our ability to validate that information is limited, at best. As they process and review visa applications for completeness and legal sufficiency before passing them on to American consular officers for final determination, foreign nationals still constitute the first line of defense against those of their countrymen and other foreigners seeking to obtain a visa who might pose a terrorist threat to the United States. This line of defense is only as strong as the weakest foreign national in the chain of responsibility. A single foreign national conspiring with terrorists, sympathetic to terrorists, or simply willing to take a bribe from terrorists could be the loophole through which the next Mohammed Atta slips.

Third, though there has been progress in sharing terrorist-related information between and among agencies, there are still holes in the system that could facilitate the issuance of a visa to a terrorist. The good news is that there is now a consolidated database of known and suspected terrorists, drawn from the separate watch lists maintained by various government agencies, including the State Department. The Terrorist Screening Database, or TSDB, is a huge advance. As noted above, the State Department's CLASS database contained no information linking any of the hijackers to terrorism, but other agencies' databases did. Had the TSDB been in place at the time, chances are high that the visa applications of those hijackers previously linked to terrorism would have been denied.

Government investigators have found, however, that the TSDB is not foolproof. The Justice Department's Inspector General concluded, "Although we found that the TSC [the FBI-led multi-agency organization responsible for developing and maintaining the database] has successfully created and deployed a consolidated watch list database, we also determined that the TSC could not ensure that the information in that database was complete and accurate. We found instances where the consolidated database did not contain names that should have been included on the watch list. In addition, we found inaccurate information related to persons included in the database."[32] Accordingly, there is still no guarantee that every known and every suspected terrorist will be identified as such when State Department consular officers query the now consolidated terrorist watch list, and that every entry about identified terrorists is accurate and complete.

The final gap to be mentioned lies in the limits of the U.S. VISIT system. As noted above, the Department of Homeland Security has, for the first time in American history, installed the early stages of an automated entry-exit immigration system to keep track of who enters our country legally. When some foreign travelers arrive at a port of entry where U.S. VISIT is operational, a digital photograph is taken of them and their two index fingers are scanned. For travelers entering on a visa, inspectors at the port of entry can match the photos and finger scans they take with those stored in databases and other information stored therein to confirm that the person in front of them is the same person who applied for a visa abroad. The entry feature of U.S. VISIT is now operational at the 115 airports with international traffic, 15 seaports, and all 154 land border crossings.

One security gap is that U.S. VISIT is applied at the fifty busiest land crossings (and, presumably, at the less busy crossings as well) only if inspectors are suspicious enough of a traveler to pull him aside for more thorough scrutiny in a "secondary" inspection. If a terrorist fails to arouse the suspicions of the border inspector, that terrorist would not be subjected to U.S. VISIT.

Yet another security gap is that the exit feature of U.S. VISIT is still in the pilot stage, operational at only twelve airports and two seaports. There is no way to determine definitively whether someone who exits the country from any other airport, seaport, or land border crossing has done so or whether he is still somewhere in this country to be tracked down by law enforcement personnel before (ideally) or after an attack. Partly because the exit feature is in its infancy, it is easy for foreigners to remain in the United States past the deadline set by the terms of their visa. "Visa overstays" are supposed to be apprehended by the Immigration and Customs Enforcement bureau's Compliance Enforcement Unit and returned to their home countries, but according to a September 2005 report[33] by my former colleagues in the DHS Office of Inspector General, only a small fraction of people who overstay the terms of their visas are apprehended. Less than 1 percent of the leads generated by U.S. VISIT and other tracking systems for foreign visitors resulted in apprehensions in the year 2004. Out of more than 300,000 leads generated by these tracking systems, the CEU referred 4,000 cases for investigation. Of the cases investigated, about 700 aliens who had overstayed their visas were found and apprehended, but among the thousands of aliens who, for one reason or another, could not be located, there could well be terrorists lying in wait to perpetrate another deadly attack.

Finally, at those ports of entry where U.S. VISIT is operational, and even in the few places where it has both an entry and exit feature, we are still failing to detect known terrorists and criminals. This is because a key FBI database is incompatible with key Homeland Security and State Department databases. The FBI uses a ten-fingerprint system to identify criminals. DHS uses two finger scans to identify illegal aliens and to process visitors through U.S. VISIT. The State Department uses a two-finger system to process visas. The upshot is that "99 percent of foreign visitors to the United States do not have their fingerprints checked against an FBI database that contains 47 million prints, including non-American citizens suspected of terrorism."[34]

To his credit, in a speech outlining his plans for reorganizing the department and rethinking its programs and operations, Secretary Chertoff recognized the huge vulnerability presented by this lack of interoperability, and he pledged to do something about it. "In the category of strengthening security, after extensive consultation with the Department of State and the Department of Justice, DHS has decided to strengthen our U.S. VISIT program. In the future, first time visitors to the U.S. will be enrolled in the program by submitting ten fingerprints. Subsequent entries will continue to require only a two-print scan for verification. This enhanced use of U.S. VISIT will dramatically improve our ability to detect and thwart terrorists trying to enter the United States, with no significant increase in inconvenience."[35]

If, indeed, going to a ten-fingerprint system will dramatically improve our ability to detect and thwart terrorists, with no significant increase in inconvenience, why not do it *immediately* rather than in the indefinite "future"? How far into the future will it be before this is done? How many terrorists will slip in through this loophole in the meantime?

So, in sum and substance, while it is harder now than it was when America was attacked for a known or suspected terrorist to obtain a visa to enter the United States, it is still far from impossible.

ENTERING FROM A "VISA WAIVER" COUNTRY TODAY

A terrorist intent on entering the United States through the legal immigration system can make things even easier on himself by entering on the passport of a country whose citizens, at least under certain circumstances, do not need visas to enter the United States.

The contrast between the scrutiny applied to travelers who need visas to enter the United States and those who enter from "visa waiver countries" is marked. As my team of inspectors put it when we examined the Visa Waiver program during my time as DHS Inspector General, "The visa is more than a mere stamp in a passport. It is the end result of a rigorous screening process the bearer must undergo before travel. By the end of the process, U.S. authorities have collected and stored considerable information about the traveler and the traveler's planned journey. When the visa is waived for broad classes of travelers, those travelers avoid this extensive examination and the United States does not collect comparable information regarding them."[36]

All visa applicants must complete a forty-question form. Male applicants between the ages of sixteen and forty-five must complete a supplemental form. Applicants' name, date of birth, place of birth, employment history, travel purpose and itinerary, visa history, and the immigration status of close family members are recorded. Starting in 2003, consular officials take prints of two of the applicants' fingers. This information is stored in the Consular Consolidated Database (CCD), and much of it can be accessed electronically by port of entry inspectors to enable them to verify travelers' identities. The inspector checks that information against an additional thirteen-question form, the Form I-94, Nonimmigrant Arrival/Departure Form, which the traveler completes and presents to the inspector upon arrival at the port of entry.

The visa waiver traveler, on the other hand, completes only the Form I-94, and, accordingly, gives only his name, present citizenship, country of residence, passport number, and address in the United States where he will be staying. The more biographical information the authorities obtain, the greater their chances of verifying a traveler's identity and tracking him down, if that proves to be necessary. Accordingly, it is significant that visa waiver travelers are not required to disclose their place of birth, any previous citizenship, or their visa history.

Whereas consular officers schedule their interviews of visa applicants at such lengths and at such intervals as to give themselves time to question them adequately, port of entry inspectors have just minutes to make an evaluation of a traveler's bona fides, lest the lines of waiting passengers back up unduly. Inspectors feel pressure to clear international flights within forty-five minutes, leaving them little time to scrutinize passengers, and while consular interviewers are likelier than not to speak the local language, few port of entry inspectors speak foreign languages other than Spanish.[37]

Terrorists understand well the advantages of entering the United States with a passport from a visa waiver country.[38] Recruiters are on the lookout for the citizens of visa waiver countries. It is not for nothing that the "twentieth hijacker," Zacarias Moussaoui, is French. It is no coincidence that the so-called "shoe bomber," Richard Reid, is British.

Terrorists also know that it is relatively easy to obtain citizenship in certain visa waiver countries. Third-country nationals (that is, people who are citizens of countries other than those in which they reside) can acquire Belgian, Swedish, or Danish citizenship after living in one of those countries for only three years.

It is even easier to obtain visa waiver entry into the United States by acquiring "derivative nationality" in certain countries. Without ever setting foot in Italy or Ireland, for example, one can claim citizenship in those countries, and thereby acquire a passport, if one or more of his parents or grandparents were Italian or Irish nationals.

For those terrorists not inclined or able to acquire citizenship in a visa waiver country legally, they can, with varying degrees of ease, simply steal blank passports from government issuing offices and substitute their own photographs and biographical data for those of the real applicants, or they can steal already issued passports from unsuspecting holders. A number of countries have been known over the years to have a lost and stolen passport problem, notably, Britain, France, Italy, Spain, Belgium, Portugal, Denmark, Slovenia, and Japan. Though the Department of Homeland Security is supposed to review each visa waiver country every two years to assess the extent of lost and stolen passports and the extent to which its nationals overstay the terms of their entry into the United States, when my office examined this issue in the spring of 2004 the department had yet to do so.[39]

The extent of the problem of lost and stolen passports from visa waiver countries is unknown because of the laxity of reporting, but to give some sense of the scope, twenty-eight foreign governments reported 56,943 of their passports stolen from January 2002 to June 2004, according to State Department records.[40] Complicating the reporting of lost and stolen passports is the fact that most countries' passports have two numbers—an "inventory control number" or "book number," when the passport is initially manufactured, and another number, the "passport number," assigned when the passport is personalized for the particular person to whom it is issued. If a bundle of blank passport books is stolen from a foreign government before they are issued to individuals, there is only one number that government can give us—the book number. Our immigration records, however, are all based on the passport number later printed into the book with the bearer's biographic information and photograph. When terrorists or criminals use stolen passports to forge a passport for an individual, they assign a fictitious passport number when they print the biographic data and affix a photo. Since our immigration inspector will check that number, and not the book number, against our database, a terrorist will likely be admitted, even if the book number in his forged passport is in our database of stolen passports.

Incredibly, we found that, rather than arresting people who present lost or stolen passports and retaining the passports so that they can't be used in the future to attempt another entry into the United States, in most cases inspectors return the passports to the traveler to facilitate his removal to the country from which he came. Port of entry inspectors told us that they wanted to retain the passports, both for their own future training purposes and to prevent re-use, but they were forced to return them because otherwise the traveler would not be re-admitted to the country from which he had arrived. There are "travel letters" that will sometimes be accepted by foreign governments when people carrying their passports are refused entry into other countries and those countries deem the passports to be lost or stolen, but sometimes foreign governments refuse to accept travel letters. In those instances, inspectors told us that it was better to return the documents than to admit an obviously suspicious person into the country.

That said, when my team of inspectors attempted to determine the extent to which lost and stolen passports are successfully used to enter the United States, we found that "aliens applying for admission to the United States using stolen passports have little reason to fear being caught and are usually admitted."[41] In arriving at this conclusion, our investigators focused on the nearly 4,000 blank passports from visa waiver countries reported to the U.S. government from 1998 to 2003 as stolen.

We found 176 attempts to use some of the 3,987 passports reported stolen to enter the United States. Some entries were made before "lookout" notices were posted in customs inspectors' computer systems indicating that the passports in question were stolen, and some were made after the lookout notices were posted. Aliens presenting stolen passports before lookout notices were posted for them were successful in being admitted to the United States 81 percent of the time. Shockingly, the success rate of aliens presenting stolen passports after lookout notices were posted was almost as high—73 percent. Of the 57 aliens in the latter category, 33 were admitted into the country after 9/11, when, presumably, our government should have been on high alert. Even more incredibly, some of the aliens used stolen passports to enter the United States multiple times after a lookout notice was posted. Because there was no exit system at the time to determine when people legally admitted to the United States left, there was no way for us to tell whether any aliens entering the country with stolen passports remain among us. For all we know, some of those admitted with stolen passports are terrorists, and at least some of them might still be in America waiting for the optimal time to launch another attack.

This problem continued after the Department of Homeland Security was created in 2003. For example, Spanish passports stolen from the Spanish consulate in Rio de Janeiro, Brazil, in September 2003 were posted as such in the customs database the following month. But nine aliens used these stolen passports to enter the United States between December 2003 and August 2004.[42]

There is no way to be sure that admitting aliens with stolen passports won't happen again. The Department of Homeland Security's Customs and Border Protection unit told us that "there is no procedure to screen the numbers of newly reported stolen passports against admission records to determine whether the stolen passports were used to enter the United States." Doing so presently requires multiple database searches, which is deemed to be too "labor intensive." CBP has "considered" modifying its software to permit simultaneous searches, but it has yet to do so.[43]

Furthermore, when the department does learn that stolen passports have been used successfully to enter the United States, it does not as a matter of course refer this information to its immigration law enforcement arm, the Immigration and Customs Enforcement bureau (ICE), so that ICE agents can try to find and arrest the miscreants.

We learned that some stolen passports were connected to 9/11, and yet ICE had not made a priority of investigating those incidents to determine whether any of those admitted might still be in the country. For example, forty-six blank passports were stolen in June 1999 from a certain European country. For reasons we could not determine, lookout notices for them weren't posted until March 2000. Of the six aliens who used some of these passports between October 1999 and May 2000 to try to get into the United States, five were successful. One of the five succeeded *after* a lookout notice was posted. One passport within the block of forty-six stolen was among the belongings of one of the Al Qaeda terrorists who killed the leader of the anti-Taliban Northern Alliance group in Afghanistan, Ahmad Shah Massoud, the day before 9/11 as a prelude to those attacks. Could the five aliens who used passports in the same block to enter the United States have been connected to the hijackers and any co-conspirators yet unidentified? We don't know the answer to that question because, despite our urging, ICE has yet to look into it.

In another incident, on June 6, 2001, three months before the attacks, 708 blank passports were stolen in a visa waiver country from a city that served as a center of financial and logistical support for the hijackers. The U.S. government was not advised of the theft until nearly three years later, in April 2004. Twenty-one of these passports were used between December 2001 and March 2004 by aliens attempting to enter the United States. All but one of the passports was successfully used to do so. Because of the nascent state of the U.S. VISIT exit feature, we could not determine for sure whether any of the aliens had left the country or whether they might still be here today. Again, we recommended that ICE investigate this incident and attempt to ascertain the whereabouts of these aliens, but there's no evidence that ICE has done so, raising once more the possibility that terrorists directly connected to the last attack might be here somewhere planning the next one.

A further weakness in the Visa Waiver Program that terrorists could already have exploited is that the department initially excluded visa waiver countries from the scrutiny of U.S. VISIT. As explained earlier, U.S. VISIT makes the port of entry inspection process more thorough because the digital photograph and fingerprints taken at the visa-issuing embassy or consulate are compared against those taken at the port of entry to confirm that the visa applicant and the traveler standing before the customs inspector are one and the same person. Further, as a result of taking biometrics at the port of entry, more extensive terrorist and criminal database checks can be run than with those based solely on names.

We issued our report on the flaws in the visa waiver process that terrorists could exploit in August 2004, but we shared the results of our work with department managers months earlier. Still, it was not until December 2004 that U.S. VISIT was extended to visa waiver travelers. There is no way of knowing whether any terrorists took advantage of the delay to slip into the United States under the proverbial radar screen, and, if so, how many did so, when they did so, who they are, and where they are now, but the possibility alone should keep us awake at night.

While including visa waiver countries in U.S. VISIT was certainly a step in the right direction, albeit a potentially dangerously belated one, that system enrolls only a small fraction—2.7 percent—of the millions of people who come to the United States legally each year through land border crossings. Of course, the lion's share of people who come to the United States by land do so from our neighbors to the south and north, but, notably, most of these Mexicans and Canadians are exempt from U.S. VISIT.[44]

Mexicans who crossed the border with Border Crossing Cards (BCCs) constituted approximately 43.8 percent of foreigners crossing our land borders in fiscal year 2002. To put that percentage in perspective, nearly seven million Mexican nationals use the BCC to make 104 million border crossings annually. A BCC may be used to stay in the United States for up to thirty days and to travel up to twenty-five miles into the interior of the United States. Only if a Mexican wishes to stay in the United States for longer or to travel further within the country must he apply for a visa.

To get a BCC, a Mexican must apply for it at an American consulate and a background check is conducted. But, when the Mexican presents the BCC at a land border crossing, the Department of Homeland Security customs inspector at the primary inspection point is unlikely to scan it into a card reader to verify the holder's identity and to make an electronic record of entry because the card readers are placed only at secondary inspection points in most ports of entry. Only if the inspector's visual inspection of the BCC or the holder leads him to suspect that something is out of order is the holder referred to secondary and his card scanned. There being no exit system in place to record whether BCC holders are leaving the country when they are supposed to, there is no way to know whether they are overstaying the terms of their entry. So as to avoid the scrutiny of the visa issuance process and U.S. VISIT, a Mexican with a BCC (his own or someone else's) need merely enter with it and then go about his business wherever he chooses and for however long he chooses. If that business is terror, the authorities are unlikely to discover that in time to prevent it.

As for Canada, most Canadians may enter the United States without a visa or passport.[45] They may stay in this country for up to six months, and there are few restrictions on where they can travel. A Canadian driver's license is all a Canadian needs to gain entry into the United States, and yet there is no way for U.S. border inspectors to verify his identity.

When my inspectors looked into the shortcomings of U.S. VISIT at land ports of entry, they pointed out that eight Canadian citizens suspected of terrorist activities were intercepted at either American airports or American pre-clearance facilities at Canadian airports between January 2004 and August of that year. It was possible to intercept them because DHS customs inspectors at airports and seaports receive the list of incoming passengers in advance of their arrival. The inspectors then have time to run the names against multiple databases to determine any terrorist or criminal connections. If any such connections are found, the passenger is referred to secondary inspection, where more intensive scrutiny is applied to determine conclusively whether the person at issue is in fact a terrorist or criminal.

By way of contrast, land port of entry inspectors receive no advance passenger data to check against watch lists, and the volume of passengers arriving at land border crossings is so overwhelming that there is limited time to query databases on arrival. Instead, during the primary inspection process, the inspector merely runs a database query on the license plates for those travelers arriving by car. The query determines only the bona fides of the vehicle; it determines nothing about the occupant(s) of the vehicle, who may or may not be the vehicle owner. There is even less scrutiny of people who cross the border on foot. It is, then, unlikely that the eight Canadians with terrorist ties intercepted in 2004 at an airport would have been intercepted if they had entered by land, as more than 50 million other Canadians did one calendar year earlier.

Because most Mexican and Canadian travelers are exempt from U.S. VISIT, and American citizens and legal permanent residents are, too, U.S. VISIT affects only about 42 percent of all those who officially enter the United States each year by air or sea. In short, then, U.S. VISIT is still far from the comprehensive border check-in check-out system it needs to be.[46]

AMERICAN PASSPORTS

Of course, the best way for a terrorist to enter the United States legally with a minimum of fuss is to obtain an American passport somehow. This is not as difficult as you might think. The scale of passport fraud in the United States each year is huge.

According to a GAO report,[47] the State Department issued approximately 8.8 million passports in fiscal year 2004. The department suspects that "tens of thousands" of applications each year are fraudulent, referring them to fraud prevention offices for review. In fiscal year 2004, the State Department's Bureau of Diplomatic Security, which takes the lead on investigating passport fraud, arrested 500 people for this crime, of whom about 300 were convicted. GAO found that identity theft "is the primary tactic used by individuals fraudulently applying for U.S. passports. Imposters' use of legitimate birth and other identification documents accounted for 69 percent of passport fraud detected in fiscal year 2004, while false claims of lost, stolen, or damaged passports and other methods accounted for the remaining 31 percent."[48] Terrorists outside the United States can use these fraudulent means to obtain American passports at various passport-issuing offices overseas. Those offices handled about 300,000 passport applications in fiscal year 2004.

The most disturbing finding in the GAO report is that the State Department does not have access to the Terrorist Screening Database, the consolidated terrorist watch list discussed earlier that is maintained by the FBI-led Terrorist Screening Center (TSC). Nor does the FBI routinely make available to the State Department the names of people wanted by federal, state, and/or local law enforcement authorities for known or suspected criminal activity, comprehensive information that only the FBI has.

Establishing that this was no mere theoretical problem, the Government Accountability Office tested the names of sixty-seven individual federal and state fugitives; fewer than half were in the State Department database. Some of the sixty-seven were wanted for serious crimes such as murder and rape. Indeed, one of them was on the FBI's Ten Most Wanted List, and he managed to get a passport some seventeen months *after* he was first placed on the list.

Of course, the news of this vulnerability caused a political firestorm when the report was released.[49] On the very day of the hearing called by the Senate Homeland Security and Governmental Affairs Committee to highlight the report, the State Department, as if by a miracle, announced progress toward the agreement with the TSC that had long eluded them to obtain access to the consolidated terrorist watch list.[50] What we don't know is how many terrorists managed to get American passports and use them to enter the United States with relatively little scrutiny in the interval.

DIVERSITY VISAS

Yet another vulnerability that terrorists can exploit to enter the United States is the Diversity Visa Program. Established by Congress in 1995 to encourage immigration from countries whose nationals are underrepresented in America's immigrant population, the diversity visa program is essentially a lottery system based on education level or work experience. A computer randomly selects applicants who, to be deemed eligible for a visa, must prove that they have completed the equivalent of a U.S. high school education, or at least two years experience in a field that requires at least two years of training or experience within the five-year time period immediately preceding their application. If, as a threshold matter, one of those requirements is satisfied, an applicant can still be denied a visa on the same grounds that all other visa applicants can be denied, including factors like having terrorist ties and/or a criminal record. If an applicant clears these hurdles, he is entitled to reside in the United States permanently and to do as he pleases, in contrast to other visa applicants who are entitled merely to stay in the country for a set period of time and for a set purpose. Having a diversity visa is almost as good as having an American passport.

The good news is that the Diversity Visa Program has been tightened considerably in the last five years along with the visa process generally. According to the State Department's Inspector General, Howard Krongard, "Consular officers interview all diversity visa winners and check police and medical records once applicants begin the actual visa application process. CA [the Consular Affairs bureau in the State Department] now requires all immigrant and non-immigrant visa applicants to be fingerprinted. This allows consular officers to run visa applicants' fingerprints through United States databases of criminals and terrorists in about fifteen minutes. It also means that if an applicant applies for a non-immigrant visa using one name and later applies for a diversity visa under a different name, the fingerprint system will identify him as a fraudulent applicant."[51]

Despite these security enhancements, the Inspector General went on to testify before Congress, "[The Office of Inspector General] continues to believe that the diversity visa program contains significant risks to national security from hostile intelligence officers, criminals, and terrorists attempting to use the program for entry into the United States as permanent residents."[52] The reason for this concern is that, while the nationals of countries that are deemed by the United States government to be "state sponsors of terrorism"— Syria, Iran, Libya, Sudan, North Korea, and Cuba—are barred by law from being issued visas to visit the United States absent a determination by the Secretary of State that a particular alien is not a threat to national security, there is no such restriction barring the nationals of these states from gaining *permanent* residence in the United States through the diversity visa program.

Syria continues to foment trouble in Iraq and Lebanon, and, at least indirectly, in Israel as well. Iran likewise is a key instigator and facilitator of unrest in these countries. Relations between the United States and Libya are improving, but Libya's long record of supporting terrorism should raise concern.

ENTERING THE COUNTRY ILLEGALLY

As easy as it still is for terrorists to slip into our country through the "front door" of legal immigration channels, it is easier still for them to slip in through the "back door" by coming in among the throngs of illegal immigrants who sneak into America each year. No one knows for sure how many illegal aliens there are in America today, and "no one" includes top officials in the Department of Homeland Security's Border Patrol unit. In a hearing before a Senate subcommittee, Chief Tom Walters, the acting assistant commissioner of the Office of Training and Development in the department's Customs and Border Protection bureau, did not dispute the Chairman's estimate that at least half a million people come across our borders undetected each year. The Chief candidly admitted, "I don't have a substitute figure for that. I think everyone's entitled to their own view on it. Statistics indicate that it's a fairly large number, but we just don't really know, and I don't personally have any better information than what you've seen, sir."[53]

America's top security officials have acknowledged that terrorists can exploit our virtually open borders to perpetrate another attack. In testimony before the Senate Intelligence Committee, then Deputy Secretary of Homeland Security Jim Loy noted various improvements in border security but went on to conclude, "we assess that the threat of illegal and even covert entry is still present and likely will be for the foreseeable future . . . entrenched human smuggling networks and corruption in areas beyond our borders can be exploited by terrorist organizations. Recent information from ongoing investigations, detentions, and emerging threat streams strongly suggests that al-Qaida has considered using the Southwest border to infiltrate the United States. Several al-Qaida leaders believe operatives can pay their way into the country through Mexico and also believe illegal entry is more advantageous than legal entry for operational security reasons. . . . In addition to the problems posed by the Southwestern border, the long United States–Canada border, often rugged and remote, includes a variety of terrain and waterways, some suitable for illicit border crossings. A host of unofficial border crossings can be utilized when employing the services of alien smugglers, especially those winding through mountain ranges and across the vast western prairie."[54]

In testimony before a House subcommittee,[55] FBI Director Robert Mueller did not dispute a congressman's claim that the Department of Homeland Security had determined that nearly 10,000 "special interest" aliens from countries with connections to Al Qaeda entered the United States between October 2002 and June 2004. Additionally, Mueller confirmed that at least some of those aliens had used false identities to evade detection by, among other things, changing Arab surnames to Spanish ones and posing as Hispanics.[56] The congressman zeroed in on the particular appeal to terrorists of the identity card that many Mexicans use to enter the United States legally, the "matricula consular."

> CULBERSON: One of the principal sources of concern, sir, that I wanted to ask you about are the—in June 2003, your director at the office of intelligence, Steve McGraw, testified to the Judiciary Subcommittee on Immigration and Border Security and claims that the FBI had a particular concern about the use of the matricula consular card. He testified at the committee that the Department of Justice and the FBI have concluded the matricula consular is not a reliable form of identification due to the nonexistence of any means of verifying the true identity of the card holder. Is that still the opinion of the FBI, sir?

MUELLER: Yes.

CULBERSON: He also said that the matricula consular is a perfect breeder for establishing a false identity. Is that still the opinion of the FBI?

MUELLER: Yes.

CULBERSON: He also testified that the ability of foreign nationals to use a matricula consulars [*sic*] to create a well-documented, but fictitious identity in the United States, provides an opportunity for terrorists to move freely within the United States without triggering name-based watch lists that are disseminated to local law enforcement officers. Is that still the opinion of the FBI?

MUELLER: Yes, that could happen.[57]

Congressman Culberson went on to discuss with the Director the tri-border area in South America where Brazil, Argentina, and Paraguay converge. The area has been known to house Arabs with links to terrorism.

CULBERSON: I've got reports . . . very reliable reports that there are special interest aliens traveling into Brazil, changing their identities and then crossing into Mexico. And, because these are visa waiver countries, these individuals are then crossing using false identities into the United States from these countries that have visa waivers. Are you aware of this, sir?

MUELLER: Yes.[58]

Time magazine has reported that the head of Al Qaeda in Iraq has considered ways to slip into America from Mexico to conduct terror attacks on the "soft" targets such as movie theaters, restaurants, and schools. "Two weeks after intelligence officials confirmed that Osama bin Laden had sent a message to Jordanian-born terrorist Abu Mousab al-Zarqawi's lieutenants about what the man behind many of the terrorist attacks in Iraq could have in mind. Intelligence officials tell TIME that interrogation of a member of al-Zarqawi's organization, who was taken into U.S. custody last year and has been described as a top aide, indicates that al-Zarqawi has given ample consideration to assaults on the American homeland. . . . The bulletin also notes the Iraq-based master terrorist's apparent belief that 'if an individual has enough money, he can bribe his way into the U.S.,' specifically by obtaining a 'visa to Honduras' and then traveling across Mexico and the southern U.S. border."[59]

Of course, it is unrealistic to think that the chance of illegal immigration can be reduced to zero; the 7,000 miles of shared border with Mexico and Canada make that impossible. But the more Border Patrol agents we have, the better trained they are, and the more the sophisticated detection equipment and technology we deploy, the greater our chances of limiting it significantly.

In recognition of the need for additional Border Patrol agents, the law passed in response to the 9/11 Commission's recommendation to overhaul the intelligence community authorized the administration to hire up to an additional 10,000 over a five-year period. The congressional appropriators who actually decide how much money government agencies get to spend were of like mind. The House allocated money to hire 2,000 agents in the succeeding 2006 budget year, and the Senate allocated enough to hire 1,050. The Administration apparently believes, however, that there are higher priorities than increasing the number of Border Patrol agents, since it requested only enough money to hire an additional 210. In the end, Congress appropriated money to hire an additional 1,500 agents, but that was 500 short of the goal set in the 2004 intelligence reform law.[60]

In addition to increasing the number of Border Patrol Agents, any serious strategy for combating the problem of illegal immigration must include the increased use of technology. But the department's "American Shield Initiative" (ASI), designed to do just that, has yet to get off the ground.

The $2.5 billion multiyear project is designed to use a mix of satellites, ground sensors, unmanned aerial vehicles, high-resolution and infrared video cameras, and yet-to-be-developed technologies to serve as a back-up detection monitoring system for the miles of border that there are too few agents to cover. ASI project managers are on record as hoping for annual appropriations in the range of $200–300 million, but the President's 2006 budget called for spending only an additional $20 million on top of the pre-existing approximately $30 billion in base funding.[61]

Until ASI is fully funded and fully operational, the nation must continue to depend upon the current Integrated Surveillance Intelligence System(s) (ISIS). That $239 million program pays for more than 11,000 infrared, seismic, and magnetic ground sensors, a remote video surveillance system with 269 high resolution cameras, and a system known as the "Intelligent Computer-Aided Detection" system that alerts Border Patrol Agents to the activation of ground sensors[62]—but the General Service Administration's Inspector General has found the program to be so defective and dysfunctional as to put "national security at risk."[63] According to news reports, criminal or administrative charges could result from the probe.[64] The contractor, International Microwave Corporation, is said to have overcharged the government by nearly $13 million, and the General Services Administration, which let and administered the contract, exercised little if any oversight. Among the problems noted was the lack of cameras in places where they were supposed to be. For example, the government was billed for fifty-nine cameras near Buffalo, New York, but only four were installed. Unassembled gear was discovered lying in the desert in Naco, Arizona. The sixty-four cameras installed in Washington State (where it's often rainy or cold) either broke down completely or failed to operate in rain and cold.

In presentations to potential contractors for ASI, the Department of Homeland Security itself acknowledged the limitations of ISIS. The equipment is defective, hard to maintain, and obsolescent. Only 2 percent of the border is covered by electronic surveillance. Ground sensors cannot distinguish between human beings and animals. That Border Patrol agents have too few hand-held radiation detection sensors also adds to the problem.[65]

In short, then, five years after the attacks, lacking the manpower, equipment, and technology we need to stanch the flow of illegal aliens, our borders remain a sieve. As a consequence, terrorist penetration remains easier than it should be.

When illegal aliens are caught, they are all too often released. Part of the reason for this is the chronic lack of money to detain them.

The applicable component of the Department of Homeland Security— the Immigration and Customs Enforcement bureau—has only 20,000 beds in its own facilities and those under contract. This is not enough to house the aliens in custody each day, much less the approximately one million illegal aliens arrested each year.[66] And, just as Congress funded fewer Border Patrol Agents in the 2006 budget than the 2004 intelligence reform law called for, it likewise funded fewer beds to accommodate illegal alien detainees than were called for in that law. The intelligence reform law called for 40,000 new beds at the rate of 8,000 over five years; the 2006 budget provided money for a few more than 2,000 beds.[67]

This problem has only worsened as time has gone by because the Immigration and Customs Enforcement bureau is so inept at financial management that it can't keep track of the money it does have.[68] The ICE budget must pay not only to house detained aliens, but to track down approximately 80,000 fugitive criminal aliens, as well as the more than 320,000 aliens who were ordered to leave the country but disappeared without a trace before their departure could be confirmed.[69]

All of this leads to a "catch-and-release" policy. Each day in America hundreds of Mexicans are arrested on immigration grounds or for other criminal law violations only to be released a few hours later on account of the lack of detention space. While the aliens are given a written notice demanding that they appear in court for an immigration hearing, more than 85 percent of them fail to show up.[70]

But at least the United States government has the option of returning Mexican aliens to Mexico because of the willingness of that government to take its aliens back. Of particular concern are "OTMs," or, aliens from nations other than Mexico. The former DHS Under Secretary for Border and Transportation Security summed up the problem in congressional testimony in February 2004 before a Senate Judiciary subcommittee on immigration: "At present, DHS has no specific policy regarding OTMs apprehended at the southern border. While OTMs as well as Mexicans are permitted to withdraw their applications for admission and can be returned voluntarily to their country of nationality, as a practical matter this option is not readily available to them, as it is for Mexicans, whose government will accept them back into Mexican territory. Thus, when apprehended, OTMs are routinely placed in removal proceedings under Immigration and Nationality Act 240. It is not practical to detain all non-criminal OTMs during immigration proceedings, and thus most are released."[71]

Senator Diane Feinstein, a California Democrat, has correctly linked the catch and release policy as it is applied to aliens other than Mexicans as a serious vulnerability that terrorists can exploit. "[W]ith respect to the Southwest border, in 2003 there were 30,147 other-than-Mexican intrusions. In the next year, 2004 . . . there were 44,617. That's a 48 percent increase, which indicates that other-than-Mexicans are seeing the Southwest border as a point of vulnerability, going to Mexico and stealing into our country through that border. . . . So you can look back and say that the likelihood is, in 2004, some 44,000 people, other-than-Mexicans, came across the border and just disappeared. . . . In the so-called countries of concern—Syria, Iran, and Iraq—the numbers are up of penetrations through our Southwest border. Clearly, we're deficient in a mechanism to deal with these. Thus, it seems to me, if I were a terrorist and I wanted to come to the United States, this is the way I would do it."[72] The problem of OTMs, and the potential terrorists among them, is only growing. As of July 2005, the number of apprehensions of OTM has far exceeded the total for all of last year.[73]

Secretary Chertoff's "goal" is to end the catch-and-release policy, and he says that "it should be possible to achieve significant and measurable progress to this end in less than a year." It bears noting that this is awfully "flexible" language. A "goal" is not a pledge; and "significant" is subjective. Until the goal is reached, a serious security gap will remain. Chertoff concedes that "today, a non-Mexican illegal immigrant caught trying to enter the United States across the southwest border has an 80 percent chance of being released immediately because we lack the holding facilities."[74]

The dangerous state of border security and the lackadaisical approach that the Department of Homeland Security's senior leaders would take to it was made frighteningly apparent to me just three months into my tenure as Inspector General.

It was about 6 P.M. on Friday, April 4, 2003. I was packing up my briefcase to head home when the phone rang. It was Lisa Redman, my Assistant Inspector General for Investigations. "Clark, we've got a problem. I just heard from the department that someone played a very bad April Fool's joke this past Tuesday. There's this lawyer whose job is to advise the DHS facilities that house illegal aliens on the immigration status of each detainee. Basically, the lawyer checks immigration records to see whether each detainee is an illegal alien. If a particular detainee is determined to be an illegal alien, the facility is supposed to keep him in custody and then he goes through deportation and removal proceedings. If the person is determined to be an American citizen, he's released. Well, this genius lawyer sent an e-mail to a detention facility officer claiming that a particular alien was an American citizen. So, the officer released him. The problem is that at the bottom of the email approving release, the lawyer had written 'April Fool's,' but, apparently, the detention officer didn't read all the way to the bottom before letting the guy back out on the streets. To make bad matters worse, the guy they let out is not only an illegal alien; he's a convicted kidnapper. If they don't catch him, he might kidnap or, even kill, somebody else!"

I couldn't believe it. A Department of Homeland Security employee, an officer of the law no less, had pulled a practical joke that resulted in releasing someone gravely dangerous. I immediately put down the phone and picked it up again to call Asa Hutchinson. It took a while for me to get him on the line, but he eventually took the phone.

"Asa, I just heard from my top investigator about this April Fool's thing. This is *serious!* I'm launching an immediate investigation, a *criminal* investigation, and if this turns out to be true, I'm referring this to the Justice Department to be prosecuted to the full extent of the law."

"Clark, hold on. You're overreacting. What crime could have been committed here?"

"How about reckless endangerment, for starters? I mean, how much more serious could this be? This guy is a convicted kidnapper. Your people better be trying to find him. What if he kidnaps someone else, or kills somebody? This lawyer should rot in jail."

It went on like this for quite some time, but I couldn't convince Hutchinson, or, later, the head of ICE, Mike Garcia, to take this as seriously as I was. It astounded me even more than this reaction was coming from men who were both former federal prosecutors. Indeed, Garcia today is the United States Attorney for the Southern District of New York.

Fortunately, the kidnapper turned himself in two days after his release, and he'd committed no crime in the interim. But, as promised, we conducted a thorough investigation and confirmed that the facts were as we had been told. (During the course of the investigation, it came out that the detainee himself had actually questioned his release, insisting that he was an illegal alien who deserved to be in detention!) For reasons I'll never understand, the Justice Department declined to prosecute the lawyer in question, and for all I know she's still working in the same job at the Department of Homeland Security today. I had no choice but to refer the case to Hutchinson and Garcia for administrative discipline, the same border security officials who had thought the incident was no big deal in the first place. By this point, I'd made enough of a public fuss about the incident that they all but had to impose some punishment. The lawyer in question was placed on leave without pay for one month, and on "administrative" leave *with* pay for six months.

So, at the Department of Homeland Security, releasing a criminally dangerous illegal alien can get you a paid vacation. I could only conclude that, to the department's senior managers, border security was quite literally a joke. In brief, there are a number of terrorists already in America, doubtless waiting for just the right moment to strike us again. And, for those terrorists outside America who wish to do us harm here, there are still a wide variety of loopholes they can slip through to get in.

CHAPTER THREE

AIR ATTACK

Once inside the United States, there are numerous targets for terrorists to choose from to launch an attack. As we all know too well, the last time the homeland was attacked, terrorists chose to use our aviation system against us by hijacking airplanes and turning them into deadly missiles aimed at iconic buildings representing American political, economic, and military power. As noted earlier, it's harder to attack our aviation system now than it was then, but it's far from impossible. For all the notable advances, the degree to which aviation remains vulnerable to terrorist attack even to this day is alarming and distressing. In this chapter I explain these vulnerabilities in detail, while taking you behind the scenes as I do so.

CAN TERRORISTS STILL SNEAK WEAPONS ONTO AIRPLANES?

Before bringing us up to date as to the state of aviation security today, it is worthwhile to put our present situation in some context. How far have we come since the 9/11 attacks? What is the baseline against which progress, or the lack of it, can be measured? To answer these questions, I have to start at the beginning of my time at DHS.

One of my first orders of business upon becoming Inspector General of the Department of Homeland Security in 2003 was to try to determine whether there had been any improvement in the ability of airport screeners to detect concealed deadly weapons hidden on passengers' bodies or in their carry-on luggage since the Department of Transportation's Inspector General, Ken Mead, looked into the issue in 2001.

Shortly after the attacks, the President asked Mead's office to undertake a series of undercover investigations at airports around the country to test the effectiveness of the then privatized screener workforce. Mead's teams fanned out across the country to airports large and small between November 2001 and July 2002. Their results were alarming, pun intended. While the results varied from airport to airport, weapon to weapon, and mode of concealment to mode of concealment, they were consistently bad. Considering what nineteen hijackers were able to do with box cutters, one could imagine what terrorists could do with guns, knives, and bombs.

The first step in our investigation was to assemble an undercover team. To minimize the chance of their being recognized and their mission's being compromised as a result, we needed diversity in every particular. The team would include men and women, younger people and older people, shorter ones and taller ones, and a range of racial and ethnic backgrounds. Just as the Department of Homeland Security was an amalgam of different agencies and parts of agencies related in one way or another to homeland security matters, so my Office of Inspector General consisted of bits and pieces of other federal Offices of Inspector that had previously overseen aspects of homeland security. Some of Ken Mead's staff had been transferred to me to help me oversee the Transportation Security Administration (TSA) and the Coast Guard. For reasons of continuity and expertise, I included on the undercover team some of the Mead staff I had "inherited" and who had participated in his undercover airport tests two years earlier.

Each member of the team was to be issued a top-secret security clearance. This would enable them to examine the highly classified results of Mead's tests that would provide the baseline against which progress or slippage would be measured. Each would be given a badge indicating that he or she was an employee of the Department of Homeland Security's Office of Inspector General, and, as such, was duly authorized by federal law to carry and conceal weapons and to try to sneak them past unsuspecting airport screeners.

The competition to be on the team was intense, and nearly everybody in the office wanted in, even though the demands placed on the chosen ones would be considerable. The investigators would endure months of dangerous and stressful work in the field trying to exploit gaps in aviation security, all the while confronting the realization that each "success" would simply demonstrate the peril that they, their loved ones, and the rest of the American people lived in each and every day. But given the number, smarts, and dedication of the investigators vying to take on the assignment, we had no trouble assembling a crack undercover team. We promptly sent them off for weeks of intensive training in handling and concealing weapons, evading detection by TSA screeners and security personnel, and the ins and outs of the screening process.

The next step was to decide which airports to test. In the interest of time, we decided to test only some of the airports that Mead's team had tested, but we were determined to go to as wide a range of airports, in terms of both passenger loads and location around the country, as possible. Depending on the size of the airport, we would vary the amount of time we spent from a matter of hours to, in the case of larger ones, several days.

Of the 450 or so airports in the country, screeners in only five of them—San Francisco, Kansas City, Rochester, Jackson Hole, and Tupelo—work for private contractors. The rest of the screeners in the 45,000[1] overall workforce are employed by the federal government, specifically, the Transportation Security Administration. The first major initiative the government undertook after the attacks was to federalize airport screening and to create TSA to oversee it. The ease with which the hijackers were able to penetrate airport security confirmed that airlines had neglected the task, contracting with the lowest bidder and paying little attention to whom they hired and whether those hired knew or cared about what they were doing.[2] The law creating TSA contained a pilot provision, however, intended to test whether a more sensitized private sector could do the job better than the federal government. It was under this provision that the five airports noted above were permitted to operate.

The nation's commercial airports are categorized by the number of people who board a plane in each airport annually. The busiest airports are called "Category X" airports, such as San Francisco International; the least busy are called "Category IV" airports, such as the one in Tupelo, Mississippi. Those in the middle are called "Category I" (Kansas City, for example) and "Category II" (Rochester International, for example), and Category III (Jackson Hole, Wyoming, for example) airports, respectively. Of course, the bigger airports tend to have more resources—more security personnel, more sophisticated equipment and technology for passenger and luggage screening, and better trained, supervised, and sensitized screeners to do the screening.

But, interestingly, Mead's results had shown that no conclusion could be drawn from an airport's size as to the ability of the screener force to detect weapons hidden on passengers or in luggage—and 9/11 had shown that terrorists weren't partial to any particular size of airport. We would have to test every kind of airport—large, small, public, private, and everything in between. Each kind of airport and each individual airport had its own particular weaknesses and vulnerabilities, and given the asymmetrical nature of terrorist warfare, any vulnerability, anywhere, might well be exploited.

To keep themselves fresh and to keep screeners off guard, the members of the undercover team would, over time, try to conceal different weapons in different ways. In order to ensure that our results could be fairly compared to those of the Department of Transportation's Office of Inspector General (DOT OIG), each investigator was required to spend hours with Mead's team, learning their methodology and protocols so that, to the extent possible, we could duplicate them.

The team also spent hours with TSA personnel. Following DOT OIG's nine months of testing from late 2001 to mid-2002, TSA established its own internal evaluation office—the Office of Internal Affairs and Program Review (OIAPR)—to assess how well screeners were performing and to test the system for its ability to withstand terrorist penetration. Our team studied TSA's test protocols and borrowed guns and knives (real ones) and explosives (fake ones) from OIAPR to use in our own penetration tests.

Congress also had gotten into the act. The Government Accountability Office, Congress' investigative arm, established its own team of undercover airport "penetration" testers, and our team spent hours with the GAO team learning as many of the tricks of the trade from them as possible. The GAO team shared with ours how they chose the airports to visit; the length of their visits; whether and, if so, when, airport managers should be advised of the presence of government investigators; the kinds of weapons concealed; and specific concealment tactics.

Our final tactical decision was whether to let key personnel at the airports know in advance that we were coming. My management team and I were conflicted on this point. On the one hand, we wanted to protect the traveling public and our own investigators from understandable overreaction on the part of airport security guards if and when screeners discovered a hidden weapon. Under the circumstances, a guard might well draw his weapon on someone attempting to sneak a gun, knife, or bomb onto an airplane. In the confusion and pressure of the moment, a guard's instinct might well be to shoot first and ask questions later.

Alternatively, a guard, in an abundance of caution, might well order the evacuation and re-screening of the terminal, or that of the entire airport and its occupants. In that event, thousands of travelers at that airport and airports around the country would be inconvenienced for hours, all on account of a test.

On the other hand, the more people we told of our coming, and the longer in advance of our arrival, the greater the risk that word would leak out as to our presence and mission.

Ultimately, we decided to strike a balance between security and the efficacy of our tests by informing just the top airport security official, and then doing so only minutes before our team arrived on site. That, we thought, would give our team and the traveling public the maximum degree of protection possible under the circumstances, while at the same time minimizing, to the degree possible, the risk of compromise. Still, once our tests got under way, members of the team would occasionally get the feeling that they'd been spotted and recognized, even though they'd done everything we thought reasonable to minimize that possibility.

With everything in place, the team set out in July 2003 for four months of undercover tests at airports large and small throughout the country. Amid the clutter of a carry-on bag, or tucked on their bodies in sensitive areas underneath layers of clothing, my investigators tried as hard as they could to breach the last line of defense before would-be terrorists board airplanes. Back in my office high atop downtown Washington, as summer turned to fall, all I could do was wait.

After a few weeks, preliminary results were in. While the exact results varied by airport, length of test, type of weapon concealed, and mode of concealment, on average, airport screeners were no better able, two years after the attacks, to detect concealed deadly weapons than they were on that fateful day. As the week went by and more results came in from still more airports, to my growing astonishment and alarm, our preliminary conclusions were only being confirmed and reinforced.

Perhaps most shocking of all was the finding that, at least at certain airports, the longer we tested, the worse the screeners performed. Common sense would suggest that the longer we tested, the likelier it was that word would get out that we were testing, and, knowing that they were being watched and evaluated, the more vigilant and alert the screeners would be.

That we could test and test, and probe and probe, and probably even eventually be recognized, and the screeners would still fail our tests as often as they did was disturbing in the extreme.

When the teams came back from the field for a break, I probed them for details. We gathered in our twelfth-floor conference room in the early fall of 2003, a brightly lit room on whose walls hung poster-size photos of scenes from the aftermath of the attacks—among them the now iconic shot of the President at Ground Zero with one hand resting on the shoulder of a grizzled firefighter and other holding a bullhorn for shouting words of encouragement to the exhausted crowd of recovery workers. All manner of guns, knives, and bomb components were arrayed before me on the conference table.

My chief investigator, Dick Berman, kicked off the discussion and then asked each of the six or so team members present to say a word or two about how he or she concealed his or her weapon, how often screeners failed to detect the weapon, and so on. It was one thing to hear what the testers had done; it was quite another to see it for myself. I wanted to see exactly how the weapons had been concealed, and each tester took turns showing me in considerable detail what he or she had done, and how.

The session was going past an hour now, and I was still pressing with more questions. What happened, exactly, when screeners missed a concealed weapon? Did any screener or security guard overreact? Did any team member feel endangered at any point? What was the reaction of screeners who missed a weapon—nonchalance or even defiance, or sorrow and regret? Fortunately for my investigators, there were no dangerous incidents. No weapons were drawn on them. Our notifying the airport security chief beforehand must have helped. There were no needless airport evacuations, either. As soon as a screener missed a weapon, the investigators would immediately flash a badge, identify themselves as duly authorized federal investigators, call for a supervisor, and immediately explain to the supervisor and screener how the weapon had been concealed and why it had been missed. The team said that, poignantly, every single screener who had missed a weapon felt awful. Some even broke down in tears, sobbing uncontrollably and shaking their heads at the prospect of a terrorist's slipping by them in the same way our investigators had. Some wondered aloud whether Al Qaeda operatives, lying in wait for another wave of attacks, might already have sneaked weapons past them.

By late November, the teams had finished their work. They'd conducted hundreds of tests at airports all throughout the country—airports large and small, airports where the screener workforce was federalized as well as airports run by private contractors. They'd concealed real guns and knives, and several types of fake explosive devices in every conceivable way—on their person, in checked bags, and in carry-ons. They'd tested at different checkpoints, in different parts of the airports, at all different times of the day. The average results were an exact match with those of the Transportation Department's Inspector General two years earlier.

No one expected that screeners would be able to detect weapons 100 percent of the time. In an imperfect world of fallible human beings and sometimes unreliable equipment, there could be no reasonable expectation of perfect security, but it was far easier than it should have been to get these weapons past a screener workforce that was larger, more focused, and better trained than any before it in American history. To make bad matters even worse, our results were not isolated. At or about the same time we were conducting our tests, TSA's Office of Internal Affairs and Program Review was conducting hundreds of its own tests at the same airports as ours, using the same kinds of weapons and the same testing protocols and methodology as we. On average, TSA's results matched ours exactly.

We had the results, but we didn't yet have an explanation for them. Why, exactly, were screeners failing so much of the time to detect these deadly weapons? As Inspector General of the department, I had an obligation not only to spot weaknesses and call attention to vulnerabilities, but also to make recommendations that could address those weaknesses and vulnerabilities. The team had done the easy part—going to the various airports around the country and finding out that, somehow, contrary to TSA's chest-beating public pronouncements, things were in fact going terribly wrong.

Now, back in Washington, we had to do the hard part—figuring out why things were going so wrong and what could be done about it. All of us felt a profound sense of urgency. While we pondered the situation, the ease with which terrorists could duplicate our work and penetrate the screening system loomed over us like a dark cloud. We had to diagnose the problem and prescribe remedies as quickly as we could, lest another attack come and render our efforts in vain. At the same time, we would have to brief department management and the key congressional committees on our results. They had to know as soon as possible what we were finding. I had hoped that our briefings would result in a collaborative effort among the department, the

Congress, and the OIG to do everything possible to implement whatever recommendations my investigators could come up with before it was too late.

The reaction of our own two audiences couldn't have been more different, however. Congress, appropriately, was aghast and demanded answers. The department's senior managers, simply shrugged their shoulders.

I sent a draft of our report to the two department officials with the principal authority over TSA, Jim Loy, the former Coast Guard commandant who was by then the head of the unit, and, his nominal boss, Asa Hutchinson, the Under Secretary for Border and Transportation Security. I fully expected my phone to ring off the hook as soon as the report landed on their desks, with Hutchinson and Loy on the line desperately seeking an answer to the question of what could be done to turn this dangerous situation around. But days turned into weeks, and my phone lay silent in its cradle.

As for Ridge, by this time, I'd been frozen out of the regular staff meetings he'd made a point of inviting me to early on. The corridor talk was that I was causing problems and giving the Secretary and his team a bad name. One adviser to Ridge is said to have said of me, "The Inspector General is kind of like a necessary evil, except that he's not necessary." That put-down perfectly captured the sentiment that was becoming pervasive throughout the department. My staff and I had a good laugh about it. I even considered buying T-shirts for them labeled, "INSPECTOR GENERAL—NECESSARY EVIL," with a big line through "necessary." But I knew that this attitude was no laughing matter. Here we were trying to alert the Secretary and his management team as to where the nation remained vulnerable and how he and his team could close security gaps before terrorists exploited them, but our reports and recommendations weren't seen as the solution to the problem, but as the problem itself.

Though I heard nothing from the Secretary's office, word of our penetration test results was getting out. The investigators were briefing lower level officials at TSA. Surely, Ridge was getting wind of them, I figured.

By law, the Inspector General has a dual reporting responsibility, not just to the Secretary but to Congress as well, specifically, to the applicable oversight committees. Despairing of meeting with Ridge, Hutchinson, or Loy, we began to schedule congressional briefings. Even though the long holiday season was fast approaching, we had no trouble attracting key House members, senators (though, interestingly enough, not Susan Collins or Joe Lieberman, the leaders of the key Senate homeland security committee), and staff to a series of briefings. Each time we shared our results, the reaction on Capitol Hill was the same—disbelief, alarm, dismay, and anger that the department wasn't doing more about the situation.

In mid-November 2003, John Mica, the Republican congressman from Florida who chairs the House Aviation subcommittee, welcomed a few members of the undercover team and me to the imposing room where his committee holds its hearings. His dark eyes widened and his brow furrowed as we laid out our results and different members of the team showed how they had evaded detection. "This is outrageous," he thundered. "It seems to me that this is largely a technology issue. There's technology out there, I know, that can significantly increase screeners' ability to detect these deadly weapons. Why they haven't deployed it escapes me." Harold Rogers, the fiery Kentucky Republican who chairs the House committee that appropriates money to DHS was, if anything, even more upset and aghast when we met with him a few days later. "This has got to stop," he said. "Somebody has to be held accountable for this. This simply can't go on. If there's no action, heads are gonna roll!"

The reaction on the other side of the Capitol was much the same, though, in typical Senate fashion, more decorous and subdued. Trent Lott, the courtly Mississippian and former Majority Leader who chairs the Senate Transportation Committee, convened a closed-door members briefing so that my team and I could present our classified results. The gravity of the occasion was such that at least a half dozen Senators from both parties showed up and spent over an hour listening to our presentation and asking questions. The Republicans and Democrats assembled were equally outraged and incredulous that the results were so bad after all the much time, attention, and money had been poured since the attacks into making aviation more secure. "Mr. Inspector General," Chairman Lott declared in his Southern baritone, "these are very disturbing results, and we've got to get to the bottom of this. The American people deserve better than this."

I answered with the only reply I could muster under the circumstances, "Mr. Chairman, I quite agree."

If Ridge and his senior management team weren't listening, key players in Congress certainly were, and that counted for a lot. If the department wouldn't act on its own to improve the performance of the screener workforce, I knew that Congress could force them to.

The only power center with even more influence than Congress was the White House. Next to the Oval Office, probably the most powerful office in the Executive Branch is the little-known "OMB," for Office of Management and Budget. At the direction of the President, OMB develops the

Administration's budget, deciding how much money the Administration will ask the Congress to appropriate to each department and agency. Somewhat like Offices of Inspector General do, OMB evaluates federal programs and operations for effectiveness, efficiency, and economy. Those programs and operations that, over time, show poor results can be radically restructured, downsized, or done away with altogether.

I was delighted, then, when a few days after our last congressional briefing, we received a call from OMB. They'd heard about our report and our briefings, and asked for a copy of the secret version containing all the details. I eagerly agreed to send over the full classified report outlining exactly which airports we visited, when, and for how long; what the results were for each type of test at each airport; and exactly how and where our weapons were hidden. Surely OMB would be as shocked and distressed as Congress, and surely they would pressure the department to make aviation security the top priority that TSA was only professing to make it. As it turned out, I would never hear another word from OMB.

Briefings for all who requested them behind us, the team pored over the results for clues as to what lay behind them. Within a few weeks, the team had identified four areas of weakness that accounted for the consistently poor results: training, equipment and technology, policy and procedures, and management and supervision.

While screeners were obliged to take forty hours of classroom instruction and sixty hours of on-the-job training after being hired, there was at the time no requirement that they undergo additional training on a periodic basis to keep their skills sharp. It was no wonder, then, that the screeners were doing so poorly, since they weren't required to be regularly assessed. Our first recommendation was that there be a mandatory minimum amount of documented, standardized training during duty hours in their work location for screeners each calendar quarter. We recommended that the tests be designed to assess the degree to which screeners could detect weapons in real-world situations, and that their performance be a factor in screeners' annual evaluations. We maintained that repeated poor performance should be grounds for termination.

Aside from the lack of recurrent training, another major cause of failure was the lack of adequate equipment and technology. One of the reasons why screeners missed concealed weapons in baggage so often was that hidden items can be harder or easier to spot depending on how the bag is positioned on an x-ray belt. Sometimes, simply putting a bag lying on its side upright can reveal an item that would otherwise be concealed, or vice versa. Accordingly, we recommended that TSA deploy dual or multiview X-ray machines at airports throughout the country. These machines project high-resolution, three-dimensional images of baggage onto the viewing screen that can be rotated to enable the screener to examine the bag from every possible angle. Under these circumstances, the ability to detect hidden items or those merely obscured by clutter and dark recesses is greatly increased.

Another device that we recommended was the backscatter X-ray. A common problem was that one of our undercover investigators would walk through a metal detector with a gun or knife concealed underneath his or her clothing or near a sensitive part of the body. The alarm would sound. The screener would get out his or her wand and try to find the source of the alarm. Trying to avoid too intrusive a search, the screener would eventually let the investigator pass even though the alarm was continuing to sound. A backscatter X-ray avoids the awkwardness of a physical pat-down by providing a way for the screener to see through the clothing, directly to the body on which the weapon is being hidden. To allay privacy concerns, technology exists to convert the image of the body to a cartoon-like stick figure, revealing only the outline of the body and the presence of any hidden metal object. To further allay security concerns, the image can be viewed by someone other than a screener in a location some distance from the checkpoint.[3]

As an additional security enhancement, we recommended the deployment of "TIP" (Threat Image Projection) machines at all checkpoints at all airports throughout the United States. As the name implies, TIP is a software program that can superimpose on the X-ray screen images of fictional threat items in real bags, or fictional bags with fictional threat items in them. The occasional flashing of such images on X-ray screens can keep screeners' skills sharp and their eyes peeled for real weapons in real bags.

We found that some airports had no machines at all with TIP installed, some airports had such machines at only some checkpoints, and some had machines that were not enabled to permit the installation or operation of TIP. We further recommended that the TIP library of images be as extensive and innovative as possible, and that it be updated and changed regularly so that screeners wouldn't memorize the images and become desensitized to the importance of being ever vigilant for novel threats.

Probing for other explanations for poor screener performance, the team noticed that a big part of the problem was management and supervisory

laxity and inattention. Screener supervisors and airport managers were letting instances of poor performance go uncorrected. Bad habits were becoming ingrained and regularized. We recommended, accordingly, that supervisors and managers themselves be regularly trained on how well and how
rigorously they detected and corrected screener lapses, and that their supervisory skills in this regard be made a part of their own evaluations.

Finally, we recommended certain changes in the policies, procedures,
and protocols that TSA uses to screen people and baggage for weapons.
These recommendations must remain secret for reasons of national security.

The 2003 holiday season was upon us, but there was no time for merriment,
or even rest. Team members busied themselves through November and December, devising recommendations and drafting a classified version of the
report for key department officials and key congressional members and
staff.[4] The report contained the complete details as to which airports we visited and exactly how the team managed to sneak as many weapons as they
did past the screener workforce; a less detailed version was prepared for the
media and the general public.*

Once our public version of the report was released in early 2004, the reaction was predictable. It unleashed a firestorm. Even though we had kept
the details secret so as not to give a road map to Al Qaeda, there was enough
information in the public version of the report for the American people to
understand the bottom line—though more money and attention had been
devoted to aviation security than to anything else, and even though the
whole federal government had been reorganized and a whole new department created to focus on securing the homeland, screeners were no better at
keeping deadly weapons out of the hands of terrorists and off of airplanes
than they were on the day of the attacks.

At this point, however, in December 2003, Congress was all but ordering
the department's senior managers to take our report seriously and to implement our recommendations. Congressman John Mica demanded that Asa
Hutchinson and Jim Loy get a briefing from our office.

Within days, members of the undercover team and I found ourselves
seated at a long conference table in a non-descript, bunker-style building at

---

* This account is based, of course, on the unclassified version of the report.

the department's gulag-like headquarters in Washington with Hutchinson, a former Arkansas congressman, DEA chief, and federal prosecutor. In his typical fashion, Asa received us and our briefing graciously, but he asked few, if any, questions, appearing to be totally unfazed by the whole thing. As we rose to leave after an hour or so, I could only wonder why the man in charge of border and transportation security seemed so blasé about how easy it had been to sneak guns, knives, and bombs past airport screeners.

Shortly thereafter, we met with Jim Loy in his more expansive and elegant quarters in a modern high-rise virtually across the street from the Pentagon and Washington's Reagan National Airport. It was clear from the choreography of the meeting that Loy was a military man through and through. In typical military fashion, he brought an entourage of what seemed like thousands with him to the briefing. The conference table probably seated thirty, and there were at least that many assistants, advisors, attendants, and assorted courtiers and hangers-on arrayed around it. We began the briefing and gave Loy a copy of the presentation so that he could follow along.

After a few minutes, he interrupted me. "You keep talking about 'failure rates' at this or that airport, Clark. Why are you using the negative term, 'failure rate?' Why not use the positive term, 'pass rate,' to describe your results?"

I could hardly believe what I was hearing. Here I was reporting to the head of TSA that, after hundreds of tests at airports of all kinds throughout all parts of the country, screeners—federalized and private—were still doing an abysmal job of detecting concealed weapons that could be smuggled onto airplanes to be used in another 9/11-style terrorist attack—and he was more worried about how we described our results than he was about the results themselves!

"Because, Jim, the key thing is not that at, say, Airport X, screeners were able to keep weapons off planes six times out of ten; it's that they weren't able to do so four times out of ten. We should all know by now that even one mistake can be one mistake too many. If we're getting it wrong four times out of ten, we can take little comfort in the six times out of ten that we're getting it right."

Loy stared at me blankly and continued to press the point that we were needlessly making TSA look bad by emphasizing how often screeners missed concealed weapons instead of how often they caught them. Instead of trying to find ways to make bad results better, Loy was trying to find a way to make bad results *sound* better. His relentlessly positive perspective on inherently negative things must have endeared Loy to his superiors. He was soon to get a big promotion. The White House subsequently nominated him to be

Deputy Secretary of the department, and the Collins-Lieberman committee that was still stalling my nomination promptly and enthusiastically approved his.

I would soon learn that Loy's reaction was not anomalous. It was representative of the thinking of Secretary Ridge himself, and that thinking would pervade the department. Time and again, my inspectors, auditors, and investigators would find a weakness in homeland security that terrorists could exploit, and instead of embracing our findings and making haste to implement recommendations for corrective action, the department's managers would by turns either ignore the problem, belittle it, or claim, erroneously, that it had long since been solved and we were simply rehashing old news and trying to make sensational headlines.

No wonder the homeland is still so insecure, I came to think. I was beginning to realize that its leaders thought that all it took to secure the homeland was the creation of a Department of Homeland Security.

Given Loy's reaction to our briefing, Asa Hutchinson's lack of a reaction to it, and the fact the Secretary didn't even bother to ask for one, I doubted TSA's promise in its formal, written response to our report to implement our recommendations. I decided to give it a year or so and then order another round of undercover tests at the same airports to see whether there was any improvement in screeners' ability to prevent terrorists from making it onto airplanes with deadly weapons. As an American, I hoped that the department would live up to its promise and be true to its word. But as the Inspector General of the department, I'd come to doubt almost everything the department's leaders said.

Nearly two years later, on the afternoon of April 15, 2005, I happened to be walking down the streets of Manhattan, the city where more people died than any other on the day terror struck the homeland. By then, I'd been out of the Department of Homeland Security for a few months. Though on the outside looking in, I was still following developments within the department closely. Nothing interested me more than finding out whether the second round of undercover airport tests that had begun under my aborted watch would find any improvement in the ability of screeners to spot concealed weapons before it was too late.

As I glanced down at the street below me, I noticed that the red light was blinking on the BlackBerry in my hand. I had a new message.

My eyes widened and my countenance fell as I read the breaking news from the AP wire. The headline read, "Airport screeners perform poorly, reports will reveal." I read on. "Two upcoming reports will show the quality of screening at airports is no better now than before the September 11 attacks, according to a House member who has been briefed on the contents. The Government Accountability Office—the investigative arm of Congress—and the Homeland Security Department's Inspector General are expected to soon release their findings on the performance of Transportation Security Administration screeners. 'A lot of people will be shocked by the billions of dollars we've spent and the results they're going to see, which confirm previous examinations . . . Rep. John Mica, R-Fla., told The Associated Press on Friday."[5]

Basically, my old colleagues had concluded that there had been little, if any, improvement in screener performance.[6] It is still far easier than it should be to sneak guns, knives, and bombs past screeners. In fact, the Office of Inspector General determined that TSA screeners have reached the limits of their ability on their own to detect deadly weapons. The only hope of increasing performance now lies in the greater use of technologies that we had recommended two years earlier. Despite our having recommended it years ago, promising equipment like the backscatter X-ray machines is still to this day only in the testing phase. The bottom line is that if government investigators today can consistently evade detection—despite all the billions spent and all the focus and attention on aviation security—terrorists can, too.

BACKGROUND CHECKS ON AVIATION WORKERS IN SENSITIVE POSITIONS

Among the more shocking and disturbing findings that my team and I made during my time as the Department of Homeland Security's Inspector General was that the Transportation Security Administration had hired airport screeners *before* completing criminal background checks on them. Moreover, we found that some screeners were allowed to stay on the job for months even after TSA headquarters had obtained fingerprint results indicating that those screeners had committed crimes. The crimes at issue ranged in seriousness from false identification to burglary and rape. TSA found out that one screener had been convicted of voluntary manslaughter, but it did not notify the airport where the convict worked until some four months later.[7]

We also chided TSA for not determining before screeners' backgrounds were investigated what level of risk to national security they posed given their particular jobs if it turned out that they had questionable histories. By not determining applicants' risk level beforehand, TSA had no way to know whether the degree of background investigation conducted was adequate. So, while TSA probably "over-investigated" some screeners, it likely "under-investigated" others, leading us to question whether TSA knew everything it should about applicants who were ultimately hired. TSA agreed to determine risk levels before background checks are conducted and to complete the background investigations before hiring screeners, but questions continue to be raised about whether some of those who work in the most sensitive areas in our airports pose a threat to the security of the nation.

Even though airports have repeatedly asked it to do so, the Department of Homeland Security does not check the immigration status of the workers airports hire. The airports, through the American Association of Airport Executives, have asked DHS to give them access to the relevant databases so that they can check potential hires' immigration status themselves, but for unspecified "legal" reasons, the department has refused to provide access. A spokesman for the Immigration and Customs Enforcement bureau has admitted that the failure to check immigration status before workers in sensitive areas are hired is "certainly a homeland security vulnerability."[8]

To the extent that the department has a policy on this issue, it appears to be based on enforcement rather than prevention. In other words, the Department of Homeland Security waits until illegal immigrants are hired by airports and allowed to work in sensitive areas before determining that they are illegal immigrants. Since the terrorist attacks, through a program called "Operation Tarmac," ICE agents have arrested more than a thousand illegal immigrants at nearly 200 airports across the country, and nearly 800 criminal indictments have been handed down. Nearly 6,000 illegal workers have been identified.[9] To cite some examples, 14 illegal aliens were working as janitors at Boston's Logan International Airport, the airport from which two planes used in the last terrorist attack departed[10]; 24 were working as mechanics and technicians at the airport in Greensboro, North, Carolina.[11] The president of the Coalition of Airline Pilots Associations put it well when he said, in summing up the security concern, "These workers had easy access to the most security-sensitive areas of both the airport and its aircraft. We need the same level of security below the plane as we have in the plane."[12]

And, while TSA issued an order in July 2004 requiring airports to screen restaurant employees and those who work in gift shops and other retail concerns before they enter secure areas, no such order has been issued for caterers and janitorial and maintenance workers.[13]

It is disturbing, to say the least, that TSA has had such problems with the TWIC (Transportation Workers Identification Card) program. To prevent fraud and to verify the identity of workers in airports, seaports, mass transit stations, railways and the trucking industry, the card is embedded with biometric information, namely facial scans, iris scans, and fingerprints. Such a card would ensure that only workers with clean backgrounds can access secure transportation facilities. But, the program has been plagued repeatedly by missed deadlines, production delays, and cost overruns.[14]

AIR MARSHALS

After the terror attacks, the number of air marshals on U.S. airlines covering high-risk domestic and international flights was significantly increased. (The exact number is classified for security reasons.) But does a program intended to reduce the risk of terror attacks itself contain an element of risk? When we looked into the air marshal program during my time as Inspector General, we found problems similar to those we found with airport screeners.[15] Specifically, we found that TSA's standards for determining what information in an applicant's background is derogatory enough to disqualify him from the program were too lenient.

TSA provided us with the files of 161 marshals whose backgrounds contained questionable information but who, nevertheless, were determined to be suitable for duty. Some of the files contained indications of various forms of financial impropriety; others contained indications that the marshal had had a history of being disciplined for one infraction or another by previous employers. What concerned us most, however, was evidence in some files of serious criminal behavior. Sixty-two out of a sample of 161 applicants whose files had raised questions had been arrested for or accused of various crimes. Fifty-eight percent of those crimes related to assault or domestic violence within the preceding ten year period; drunk driving accounted for 27 percent; and sexual harassment for 11 percent. Fifty percent of the applicants had been arrested more than once for similar offenses within the preceding ten years.

We brought these files to TSA's attention, but TSA insisted that only 2 of the 161 cases should have raised enough concerns to merit further inquiry. One of those cases concerned an applicant who had been denied a gun permit by New York State. The adjudicator who had initially cleared the applicant did not bother to find out why the permit was denied. When we pointed out that air marshals must carry guns for their jobs, and that they must have the training, temperament, and record to permit them to do so responsibly, TSA agreed to review that file a second time. Upon a second review, TSA reaffirmed the initial decision to approve the applicant for hire.

After the attacks, to beef up the ranks of air marshals, TSA hired a number of people who had worked for the Bureau of Prisons (BOP). The unit in the BOP charged with investigating internal misconduct determined that 104 of those people had been involved in 155 separate cases of misconduct prior to their transfer to the air marshal program. The infractions included misuse of government property and credit cards, breach of security, and falling asleep on duty. Sixty-eight percent of these cases were not discovered during the initial background investigation conducted on the employees by the federal government's Office of Personnel Management. When we brought these 104 cases to TSA's attention, TSA's Credentialing Program Office (CPO) agreed to take a second look at them. Upon further review, the CPO sustained the initial clearance for 103 of the cases. CPO's grounds for doing so were that the OPM background investigation upon which the initial clearance was based did not uncover the derogatory information that the Bureau of Prisons had. (The 104th case was sustained, too, once it was determined that the air marshal in question had been cleared of the allegations against him.)

We also determined that, under its disciplinary standards, TSA could and *should* have meted out stringent punishments to air marshals found to have engaged in serious misconduct, especially since law enforcement officers are to be held to higher standards than other employees. We found nearly 800 cases—753, to be precise—of serious misconduct over a nine-month period. The misconduct included stolen or lost weapons, sleeping on the job, and testing positive for illegal drugs or alcohol. Though TSA policies permitted officials to fire air marshals for certain serious first-time offenses, many miscreants were simply placed on paid leave for an extended period. One air marshal was required by law to surrender his weapon on account of criminal misconduct, thereby rendering him unable to perform his duties. TSA took no action against this marshal, even though it could (and *should*) have suspended him without pay indefinitely.

TSA, per usual, agreed to implement our recommendations to weed out criminals and simple bad actors from the air marshal program before they're hired, and to discipline to the maximum degree possible those found to have engaged in criminal and serious noncriminal misconduct once on the job. Nevertheless, the fact that illegal aliens can continue to work in the most sensitive areas of our airports, even though terrorists might well be

among them, calls into question whether TSA to this day takes its vetting responsibilities seriously enough.

There are other potential security vulnerabilities in the air marshal program. For quite some time, marshals had rightly complained that their effectiveness was limited by how easy it was for terrorists to spot them. Early in
his tenure, Secretary Chertoff met with air marshal representatives and
agreed, commendably, to changes in the air marshal dress code to make
them less conspicuous. Marshals had been required to wear a jacket and tie,
when even many business travelers dress casually nowadays.

Marshals also complain about other policies that continue in place that
can have the effect of revealing their identity. Air marshals, or "FAMs," as
they are called, for Federal Air Marshals, are required to stay at certain
budget hotels. To get the discounted rate at those hotels, they must identify
themselves as FAMs, and hotels maintain a list of the marshals who routinely stay at their establishments. This remains TSA's policy, even though
the law overhauling the intelligence community requires FAM management
to "continue operational initiatives to protect the anonymity of federal air
marshals."[16]

UNSCREENED AIR CARGO

As my undercover teams' tests showed, it is still easier than it should be to
sneak deadly weapons past screeners by concealing them on passengers'
bodies or in their carry-on bags, but at least passengers and their carry-on
bags *are* screened. Checked luggage also is screened (or least, it is supposed
to be, and it usually is—more about this later), but according to the GAO,[17]
about 22 percent of all cargo shipped by air is transported by passenger aircraft, not airplanes dedicated to ferrying cargo—a fact unbeknownst, I
would wager, to most travelers. So, chances are, at some point in their air
travels, most Americans have flown on a plane carrying some cargo. The
horrifying thing is that most of that cargo is *not* inspected at all.

While the Department of Homeland Security makes a point of boasting
that all cargo aboard passenger airlines is screened, the claim is misleading.
"Screened" does not mean "inspected." "Screened" simply means that shipping documents are scrutinized to see whether there is anything about a
container's declared contents, route, shipper, or receiver that raises a red flag
indicating that it might contain a weapon of mass destruction or some other
deadly item. If something anomalous is spotted on the shipping "manifest,"
the particular container at issue is opened and physically inspected to ensure

that it contains nothing dangerous. In addition, there are supposed to be occasional random inspections, to further decrease the chances that terrorists can slip a threat item into the cargo hold undetected, but most cargo is not targeted for inspection or randomly inspected; most cargo is not inspected at all before it is loaded onto a passenger airliner.

To make bad matters still worse, the inspections that are done, if any, aren't done by the Department of Homeland Security or, for that matter, any other government agency. Believe it or not, domestic airlines and foreign carriers flying into the United States are supposed to inspect the cargo themselves, even though the whole point of federalizing the passenger and baggage screening system after the last attacks was that the airlines had proved to be so focused on profit and efficiency that they were incapable of adequately policing themselves.

No one knows how many inspections the airlines are doing now, and "no one" includes the so-called Transportation *Security* Administration. In a letter to Democratic Congressman Ed Markey of Massachusetts, the department's spokesman wrote that, "Air carriers do not report cargo screening data to TSA." So, the department has no idea how much of air cargo is screened, nor does it know where and when any screening is done. All of this came to light when another Congressman who heads the House committee that decides how much money the Department of Homeland Security gets each year decided to cut its budget to punish the department for failing to meet a congressional mandate to triple the amount of cargo that is inspected. There was no way to tell whether tripling the amount of cargo would do much good because TSA had no idea how much cargo was being inspected in the first place! Zero times three still equals zero.[18]

TSA is supposed to visit carriers periodically to make sure that they're inspecting some percentage of cargo, but in the absence of any independent verification, there's no way to know whether TSA is really doing this, or how often and how effective any such spot checks are. Only "known shippers," that is, shippers who have completed the necessary forms, pledged to put a rigorous security system in place, and developed a history of shipping items without incident are allowed to place cargo aboard passenger planes, but the degree to which TSA verifies shippers' representations as to their bona fides is unclear. TSA has admitted that it has not investigated most known shippers, and we know that some known shippers' security programs are suspect. In September 2003, for example, an employee of a company participating in the Known Shipper program shipped *himself* from New York to Texas. An additional concern is that shippers participating in the program are not required to inspect packages weighing less than sixteen ounces, even though the bomb that brought down Pan Am Flight 103 and killed 270 people over Lockerbie, Scotland in 1988 weighed less than sixteen ounces.[19]

To be fair, the Pan Am flight was brought down by a bomb hidden in passenger luggage that was not inspected before it was loaded onto the plane, but we know of at least one incident in which uninspected cargo loaded onto a passenger flight proved to be dangerous and potentially deadly. A bomb subsequently linked to the notorious Unabomber and concealed in the cargo hold of a passenger plane exploded in 1979, forcing the plane to make an emergency landing at Washington, D.C.'s Dulles International Airport.[20]

The airline industry maintains that it is either technologically impossible to inspect all air cargo or, alternatively, that while possible, it would be unduly costly and create an intolerable bottleneck in the economic supply chain that increasingly depends upon "just-in-time" deliveries. A representative of the Coalition of Airline Pilots Associations contends that "securing all cargo that is carried aboard commercial airlines is a very achievable goal," though, and a bipartisan team of Congress members who are pushing a bill to require 100 percent air cargo inspections by 2008 point to a number of companies that are already installing technology at various airports around the country and the world that can do the job. They also point out that air cargo is inspected as a matter of course in Britain, Israel, and the Netherlands.[21]

Between the claims of the Department of Homeland Security and airlines on the one hand, and those of members of Congress and admittedly self-serving contractors on the other, I would put my money on the latter. After all, before the attacks, the government and airlines likewise contended that it was too costly and disruptive to screen passengers' checked baggage. After the attacks, it was determined that the security of the homeland required it. Will it take a terrorist attack by means of a bomb hidden in the hold of a passenger plane to convince the Department of Homeland Security to inspect air cargo, too?

IMMIGRATION SECURITY INITIATIVE/ IMMIGRATION ADVISORY PROGRAM

The Customs and Border Protection (CBP) bureau in the Department of Homeland Security introduced a program in 2004 called the Immigration

Security Initiative (ISI). The program has since been renamed the Immigration Advisory Program (IAP). Similar in concept to a program designed to secure cargo shipped to the United States by sea known as the "Container Security Initiative" (more about this later), IAP stations American customs agents at foreign airports to screen passengers for possible terrorist connections *before* they board airplanes bound for the United States.

Specifically, IAP agents review the airline passenger manifest to identify potentially "high-risk" passengers. Working with the airlines and the relevant foreign government authorities, the agents question these passengers and examine their identity and travel documents to determine whether they are valid and genuine. If the questioning and/or document examination process lead an agent to conclude that a particular passenger might be a terrorist, the agent has the legal authority to deny that passenger entry into the United States.

While an IAP agent does not have legal authority in a foreign country, he can assert de facto control over the boarding process. This is so because CBP has exclusive authority under U.S. law to determine admissibility into the United States, so an IAP agent's determination that a particular person should not be permitted to board an airline bound for the United States should be respected by the applicable foreign airline and government. Furthermore, airlines must pay a hefty fine if they are found to carry an alien deemed to be inadmissible to the United States.

Other nations—Great Britain, Canada, Australia, the Netherlands, Israel, and Thailand—have programs similar to IAP, and, indeed, a similar program was tried even here in the United States before the creation of the Department of Homeland Security, by the old Immigration and Naturalization Service.

According to the Commissioner of CBP, "Operation Global Shield," a five-month-long program run in 2003, resulted in nearly 3,000 interceptions of inadmissible aliens who were headed to the United States. It is unclear whether any known, suspected, or potential terrorists were among the 2,791 intercepted, but it is certainly possible that there were. The INS claimed that with Operation Global Shield the American government saved more than $45 million in processing and detention costs, the airlines avoided more than $9 million in fines and costs, and the entire program cost only $2.4 million. In the words of then Commissioner Robert Bonner, "ISI will pay for itself and then some. . . . We need it to add to our layered, extended border defense against the terrorist threat. We need it to better protect passenger aircraft and the civil aviation. And, it will give the U.S. government . . . an option *other* than canceling flights. We need another, less blunt, tool in our toolbox to identify potential terrorists, and [to] make determinations on whether these particular individuals should be allowed to fly. ISI will give us that tool."[22]

It is hard to argue with any of that. If we can stop terrorists *before* they board flights bound for the United States, so much the better; by the time terrorists arrive at their destination, it may well be too late. If IAP is such an effective counterterrorism tool, though, if it has proved its worth in the past, if other countries have similar programs, if it pays for itself, and if, as a practical matter, foreign governments and airlines have no choice but to allow it to operate abroad, why has it been implemented in only two countries—The Netherlands and Poland—so far? Why isn't it operational in at least the top seven airports that account for 40 percent of all passengers flying to the United States, as originally envisaged by the Customs and Border Protection Commissioner? Indeed, why isn't it operating at *every* airport in the world from which people can fly to the United States? To the extent that we could add another "tool in our toolbox to identify potential terrorists," and we have not yet fully done so, we are not taking steps that we could take to make America safer.

MID-FLIGHT DIVERSIONS

Every so often international flights heading for a destination in the United States are either forced to return to their point of origin or diverted in mid-flight to the nearest American airport where a thorough security check can be conducted. This happens whenever the name of someone on the "no-fly" list (a list of people, terrorists or otherwise, who are known to pose a risk to aviation), or some other list of people who might pose a security threat, matches (or appears to match) the name of someone on the list of passengers aboard the flight.

At present, the Department of Homeland Security gives airlines a version of the U.S. government's no-fly list and then relies on airlines to check each passenger's name against that list before he or she boards a flight. The U.S. government maintains a more extensive no-fly list, as well as other lists of known or suspected terrorists, criminals, and immigrant law violators, which it does not share with airlines or foreign governments for understandable security reasons. In brief, the wider this information is disseminated, the greater the chances of a leak that could tip off terrorists, endanger sources, identify our methods of collecting intelligence, undermine counterterrorism investigations, or otherwise compromise the security of the homeland.

Once airlines check passengers against their truncated version of the no-fly list and the aircraft takes off, the airlines have fifteen minutes to electronically transmit passenger names and certain other personal information about them—birth date, gender, citizenship, country of residence, address, itinerary, form of payment—to the Customs Service's National Targeting Center. At the Center, Customs personnel check this information against the U.S. government's extensive lists of those who might pose a security risk. Depending on the number of passengers and the amount of relevant information, it can take as long as two hours to complete this check. The "turn-backs," or diversions, result when someone aboard the plane appears to be someone on one of the U.S. government's watch lists.

The fact that the passenger manifest is not checked by our government against its extensive watch lists until *after* a plane has already departed for the United States is, of course, a security gap of potentially immense proportions. If, like "shoe bomber" Richard Reid, for example, a terrorist simply wants to blow up an airliner, fifteen minutes can be more than enough time to do so. Needless to say, it is imperative for security reasons that passenger names be checked against U.S. government watch lists *before* flights depart, and that the checks take place as long before the flights depart as possible. Recognizing this imperative, Congress directed DHS to use its rulemaking power to enact a new regulation requiring international airlines to share passenger name records before takeoff, but the department has yet to do so because of pressure from the airlines and resistance from foreign governments. A *proposal* to require the airlines to submit passenger manifests to the U.S. government one hour before departure remains just that.

The airline industry's position is essentially that commerce and convenience must trump security. In the remarkably candid words of the president of the Air Travelers Association, "So here's the choice: either you have to occasionally inconvenience 250 passengers or you otherwise inconvenience hundreds of thousands of passengers every day."[23]

The Air Transport Association and the Association of European Airlines wrote in a strongly worded letter to Homeland Security Secretary Chertoff, "While we understand the government's goal, . . . such a rule [requiring airlines to submit passenger data sixty minutes before flight departures] will result in severe adverse consequences for the airline industry, and, indeed, to the world economy. . . . Airlines operate network systems, both on their own and in conjunction with other airlines. These networks are designed to connect as much traffic as possible to multiple destinations, in as brief a period as practicable. This benefits everyone by compressing transportation time and increasing the efficiency of the world economy. The APIS [Advanced Passenger Information System]–60 rule would disrupt both objectives by requiring either wholesale rescheduling of flights on much less efficient schedules or simply eliminating connecting traffic."[24]

The rest of this letter has been little noted, but that's much the most important part of it: "In addition, we continue to urge the development of a real-time passenger pre-clearance system that would allow DHS to vet each passenger at the time of check-in for a flight, before a 'person of question' proceeds to the sterile area of the airport to board a flight. As you know, there have been very positive results with real-time, interactive, passenger-clearance systems elsewhere in the world. An interactive system, such as that operated by the Australian government, would be far superior to APIS–60."[25]

If American and European carriers are supportive of a mechanism for transmitting passenger information to the United States government at the time of passenger check-in, which in the post-9/11 era generally takes place up to *two* hours before departure time; if they've been urging the development of such a mechanism for such time; if such a mechanism is already operating effectively in other parts of the world; and, if the Secretary of Homeland Security knows all of this, why hasn't the department moved forward with it? Why does a department spokesman take the position that, "It's an extraordinarily complex issue. We're not going to rush this"?[26]

Of course, it should be technologically possible in the Information Age to transmit passenger information to the United States government automatically at the time when a traveler makes his reservation and/or pays for his flight, which is generally some time before check-in. If key domestic and foreign airlines are supportive of a system that would get this information to the United States no later than check-in, our government could have this vital information long before it gets it now, and long before an hour from departure. Until the Department of Homeland Security moves forward on this issue, the possibility will remain that terrorists who could have been stopped beforehand will manage to board airplanes bound for the United States. By the time DHS finds out about it, it may well be too late.

UNSCREENED BAGGAGE

Is every single checked bag screened for explosives before it is loaded onto airplanes? The disturbing answer to that is no. Some airports lack the necessary equipment or a sufficient number of screeners, so as it is authorized to do under the Aviation and Transportation Security Act (the law that created the Transportation Security Administration), TSA permits airports, when it is deemed necessary, to use "alternative screening procedures."

At the request of a Senator, during my time as DHS Inspector General we visited an airport (which must remain unnamed for security reasons) to test the effectiveness of an alternative procedure that this particular airport used. We concluded: "Although the alternative procedure is authorized, we have concerns about its use. Given the sensitivity of the equipment, it is likely that the procedure would identify explosive traces. However, TSA provided inadequate guidance to standardize screeners' use of the procedure, and we encountered variations in use that could diminish its effectiveness."[27]

In response to a request from Congressman Jim Turner, the then senior Democrat on the House committee with chief jurisdiction over the Department of Homeland Security, we launched an investigation into local media reports that TSA management at both major Houston airports was encouraging screeners to ignore alarms indicating dangerous items in checked baggage. We concluded: "With one exception, which occurred after our initial visit to the airport, we found no conclusive evidence that TSA airport managers and supervisors purposely directed or encouraged screeners to ignore alarms, standard operating procedures, or alternative operating procedures for screening checked baggage allowed under TSA guidelines. However, screeners whom we interviewed at both airports said that inconsistent direction from their managers and supervisors was a problem. Inconsistent direction from managers and supervisors creates confusion, suspicion, and stress."[28]

While we could not go into detail, the bottom line is clear. Because there is insufficient equipment and too few screeners in at least some airports, corners are occasionally cut. The question is whether we can afford to cut corners when the security of the homeland is stake.

SCREENER TRAINING

When we conducted our undercover tests at airports throughout the country in 2003 and determined that it was easier than it should have been for terrorists to sneak deadly weapons past screeners and onto airplanes, one of the key reasons for this, as noted above, was that screeners weren't adequately trained. Indeed, the training program in the department's very first year was *literally* a joke.

By the time June 11, 2003 rolled around, I had been Acting Inspector General of the Department of Homeland Security for six months. It was already becoming clear to me that the nation's security was *not* in good hands. At first, I didn't believe it. I certainly didn't want to believe it. But, as time went by, more and more evidence was piling up to lead me to this conclusion. As I sat at my desk one day going through my burgeoning stack of incoming mail, a letter caught my eye that would only to the add to the pile of damning evidence.

It was a copy of a May 9, 2003 letter from TSA Administrator Loy to New York Senator Chuck Schumer relating the results of an internal TSA investigation into media reports that screeners at LaGuardia airport who were being trained by contractors to operate explosive detection machines were given the answers to test questions in advance to ensure that they would pass the tests. This allegation had come to Schumer's attention through accounts in the New York press, and he'd quite rightly insisted that TSA management look into it. If the allegation were true, there'd be no way to tell whether screeners really could operate the equipment, and a bomb might get through that a properly trained screener would have been able to detect.

As I read Loy's letter, I couldn't believe my eyes. He confirmed that twenty-two of the twenty-five questions on the final exam were identical to questions on the daily quizzes, but he then went on to say that the testing and training had been done to TSA's specifications, and that the instructors had done nothing wrong! I didn't know which was worse—that screeners weren't being trained to detect explosives, or that TSA saw nothing wrong with that.

I immediately determined that we would look into this issue ourselves, and I wrote to Schumer to tell him so. A couple of months later, we completed our investigation and I summed up the results in another letter to the Senator.[29] "Upon learning of the [TSA] review and [its] letter of May 9, 2003, I wrote to you to advise that my staff would review work performed by TSA and advise you of the results of our review as soon as it was completed. I took this action because it seemed incongruous to me that TSA would confirm this pattern of testing but limit its consideration of the allegations to a carefully circumscribed conclusion that no misconduct occurred," I began.

Not only did we confirm that most of the questions on the final exam were identical to questions given screeners on practice quizzes beforehand, but we found that some of the questions gave away the answers and others were "simply inane." For example, one question was, "What is the role of a detonator in an explosion?" The correct answer, of course, was "Creates a small explosion that *detonates* the main explosive charge." Another question was just as leading and just as inane:

> "How do threats get aboard an aircraft?
>   a. In carry-on bags.
>   b. In checked-in bags.
>   c. In another person's bag.
>   d. All of the above."

Most important, we found that "not a single question called upon a student to demonstrate a sufficient mastery of the class content to achieve the purpose of the training, i.e., to examine a real or simulated EDS [explosives detection system] screen to identify correctly objects in baggage that constitute threats or are prohibited."[30]

This was why having an aggressive and independent Inspector General was so important at the Department of Homeland Security, I thought to myself. If left to evaluate and investigate itself, it was becoming clear to me that the department would invariably conclude that all was well. In fact, however, the homeland was still dangerously vulnerable to terrorist attack. If anything, the illusion of safety that the department was creating was actually making us *less* safe and *more* vulnerable. By pretending that the country was safer than it really was, the leaders of the Department of Homeland Security were fooling the American people, certainly.

The question was whether they were also fooling themselves. Did they really believe what they were claiming, I wondered? If so, this was irresponsible in the extreme because facts to the contrary were right there in the black and white of our reports for them to see for themselves.

But, the alternative was even worse. If they didn't believe what they were claiming, and they knew perfectly well that they were failing to close security gaps that could be easily closed, I could only tremble for the country.

We followed up on this report by conducting a comprehensive review of TSA training about a year later.[31] While there were improvements, problems remained. The following year GAO looked into the issue[32] and there were still problems. Among other things, limited high speed Internet/Intranet connectivity at some airports made it difficult for screeners in those facilities to access training materials and to meet the three hours per week training (averaged over a quarter and within regular duty hours) requirement that TSA implemented in response to one of our early recommendations.[33]

The GAO report confirmed allegations made by screeners two months earlier at the nation's busiest airport, Hartsfield-Jackson, in Atlanta. Screeners there complained that they were given only twenty-five minutes of training a week, not the required three hours. Furthermore, they alleged that they were required to falsify paperwork by claiming that they had received the requisite amount of training.[34]

Everyone can agree that airline safety is no laughing matter. A properly trained screener workforce is a critically important component of airline safety. If screener training is a joke, every person who boards an airplane is in some danger as a result.

REGISTERED TRAVELER

TSA launched a pilot program in 2004 called "Registered Traveler." In exchange for agreeing to undergo a background check and to have their irises or fingers scanned to verify identity, travelers are routed to shorter security lines at participating airports and, at least generally, they can bypass the secondary screening process. The program is intended to balance the twin imperatives of security and efficiency. The traveler gets the benefit of expedited processing; the government gets the benefit of concentrating its more intensive screening efforts on travelers about whom less is known.

There were five participating airports—Minneapolis-St. Paul, Los Angeles, Houston's George Bush International, Boston Logan, and Reagan National in Washington, D.C. In Orlando only, a private company has operated the program. At that airport, travelers paid a fee of about $80 to participate in the program; participants in the program at other airports did not pay.

According to the company's founder, Steven Brill, CEO of Verified Identity Pass, some 10,000 travelers signed up for the program, and their average wait time was 4 seconds versus about 4 minutes for passengers in regular screening lines. The average maximum wait time for the "registered traveler" in Orlando was said to be 3 minutes versus 32 minutes.

TSA declared the pilot program a success and announced plans to expand it nationwide. The government would conduct the background checks, but private companies would be engaged to promote the program, enroll travelers, and issue the identification cards. TSA Administrator Kip Hawley said that thought was being given to expanding the benefits under the program to include letting travelers keep their shoes and jackets on when they go through the screening checkpoint.[35]

Like the Immigration Advisory Program discussed above, and the Container Security Initiative to be discussed below, the Registered Traveler program makes perfect sense in theory. If TSA can be confident that participants are not terrorists because they have passed a background check and submitted biometrics to confirm their identity, limited screening personnel are freed up to concentrate limited resources on those travelers who might be terrorists. So, the more participants in Registered Traveler the better.

But the security of the program depends entirely on how rigorous the background check is, and whether periodic updates are conducted. To date, there's been no independent examination of how rigorous the background check process is, and the laxity of TSA's processes for checking the backgrounds of screeners and air marshals calls into question the rigor of its background checks for Registered Travelers. Absent rigorous initial checks and regular updates, a terrorist might well exploit the program to get an "easy pass" to launch a deadly attack.

SECURE FLIGHT

Currently, as noted above, airlines check passenger names against a watch list that the government provides them. As nearly every American can attest from direct or indirect experience, the list is riddled with errors. Law-abiding citizens—including prominent ones who help to make law, like Senator Ted Kennedy, whose names are identical or similar to those on watch lists—are mistaken all the time for terrorists or suspected terrorists and subjected to humiliating scrutiny as a result.

The theory behind the Secure Flight program is that the government, rather than the airlines, should be checking names against watch lists. After all, the watch lists are the government's; the government has more extensive lists than the one given to airlines; and the government has more of an incentive to make security its principal concern since it doesn't have to worry about the proverbial bottom line. Furthermore, through Secure Flight, the department will have access to the copious information about travelers in private databases, enabling DHS to more confidently confirm that a traveler is who he says he is and not a security threat to the nation. But Secure Flight has been slow to take off because of various missteps related to privacy.

To safeguard our civil liberties, the Privacy Act requires the government to inform the public that it's collecting information on them; the type of information collected; the reason for collecting it; whether, and, if so, how and why such information is being stored; and how individuals can access and, as necessary, update and otherwise change the information. GAO has found that TSA violated this law by failing to tell the public that it was accessing information about them in private databases in order to test Secure Flight, and that it was storing this information.[36]

It's hard to believe that TSA has so bollixed an effort like this that could actually enable the government to have its cake and eat it too. Properly administered, Secure Flight could both enhance security and legitimate travelers' convenience.

If TSA were simply to be up front with passengers, to clearly explain to them that it would collect information on them in private databases so as to better confirm their bona fides, and that it would need to retain this information for some period of time, at a minimum it would be in compliance with the law. Furthermore, it is not unreasonable to think that many passengers would understand and support such a quid pro quo. Finally, those passengers opposed to the program could be given the chance to opt out of it, with the understanding that they would face a greater chance of being mistaken for terrorists than those who opt in. As it stands now, ironically, the vast majority of the travelers, who have no ties to terrorism whatsoever, are subjected to more scrutiny and hassle than is necessary, while, as a consequence, the tiny minority of travelers who actually are terrorists have a greater chance of slipping through the cracks.

FEDERAL AIRPORTS VS. PRIVATE ONES

As noted above, the screening process was federalized after the terror attacks, out of the recognition that the private contractors who had previously hired and supervised screeners were too focused on profit to pay enough attention to security. So as to test whether a newly sensitized private sector might be able to do a better job than the government, five airports were permitted to contract with private vendors—San Francisco, Kansas City, Rochester, Jackson Hole, and Tupelo. This pilot program is known as the "PP5" program.

The law creating the TSA, among other things, allowed airports to apply to opt out of the federal system in November 2004, though TSA would have the authority to deny such an application. If the application were approved, TSA would determine the private contractor, and TSA would retain oversight authority over the screening process.

To date, only two small airports—Sioux Falls, South Dakota, and Elko, Nevada—have applied to opt out. Both applications have been accepted.

Sioux Falls will be the first airport to return to private control. Elko, too, will be allowed to opt out of the federal system, but it is unclear whether a private contractor will take over screening or whether the Elko airport authority itself will take over from the federal government. Elko hopes to compete against private contractors for the contract, confident that it can make a profit if it wins the competition.

Unfortunately, because of TSA's ineptitude, we have no way of knowing whether, in the post-9/11 world, the federal government or private contractors can do a better job of screening. When I looked into the issue during my time as Inspector General, I caused a firestorm at a congressional hearing (which was to review the pilot program under which the five private airports were operating). I called the TSA Administrator on his misleading suggestion that the federalized airports and the private ones were performing equally well.[37]

To be sure, we found that both kinds of airports were performing at about the same level, but each was performing "equally poorly" in the critical area of spotting concealed weapons before they can make it onto airplanes. When we conducted our "penetration" tests, we found no difference in the ability of federal and private airports to catch these deadly weapons. Our conclusion was understandable, since TSA controlled every single key variable at both kinds of airports. The pilot program was, then, a "pilot program" only in name. (A report on the issue prepared for TSA by private contractors at or about the same time came to essentially the same conclusion.)

Going back to a privately run system seems to me to be a step in the wrong direction. One of the two airports returning to a private system has admitted that it is doing so in the hope of making a profit, and it is the profit motive that led airports, disastrously, to slight security issues before the terror attacks.

Furthermore, at least anecdotally, there are suggestions that private contractors at airports today cut corners where security is concerned to maximize their profits, just as they did prior to the terror attacks. A former supervisor for the private contractor that runs the screener program at one of those airports, San Francisco International, filed a wrongful termination suit against the contractor, alleging that the company cheated when federal investigators showed up to test security. Specifically, a supervisor for the contractor Covenant International alleged that the first time covert Office of Inspector General investigators showed up at a checkpoint, the screeners would invariably fail to detect the guns, knives, and mock explosives that the investigators had concealed under their clothing or in their carry-on bags.

Once screeners at one checkpoint failed a test, they were told to notify the contractor and to describe the investigator who'd sneaked the weapon through, the kind of weapon concealed, and the manner in which it was concealed. Then, the investigators were followed on closed-circuit cameras to the next checkpoint, and screeners at that checkpoint would be tipped off to expect them. As a result of this scheme, Covenant was able to pass the covert tests 90 percent of the time, the suit alleged. The contractor's motivation for cheating was to keep the $72 million screener contract and to increase its chances of getting additional contracts. To make bad matters still worse, at least according to the supervisor, who claims that he was fired for complaining about the cheating, when federal investigators were not at the airport, dangerous items routinely got past screeners. Those items included bricks, golf clubs, a baseball bat, electric drills, a "small" blowtorch, and box cutters (which the September 11 hijackers used).[38]

To be sure, these are merely allegations in a lawsuit at this point; those allegations have yet to be proved, and they have been denied by Covenant. Without confirming or denying that my investigators ever tested this particular airport, they would occasionally get the feeling that they had been recognized at airports around the country, and there would often be improvements in screener performance the longer we stayed at particular airports. If these allegations are proved in a court of law to be true, it will be a powerful argument against going back to the "bad old days" when security took a back seat to profit and speed.

GENERAL AVIATION

Another sign of creeping complacency when it comes to aviation security is the decision to reopen Washington, D.C.'s Reagan National Airport to general aviation. "General aviation" refers to private business and personal aircraft and charter flights, as distinct from commercial aviation.

Immediately after the attacks, a general prohibition on aviation was instituted nationwide. The only exceptions were for certain military, law enforcement, and emergency flights. The general ban was lifted on September 13, 2001, but, because of its strategic location in the nation's capital, close to the White House, the Capitol, the Pentagon and other symbols of American power, restrictions on the use of Reagan National Airport (known in airline parlance as "DCA") remained. Gradually, most of those restrictions were also lifted, but the ban on general aviation at DCA stayed in place. Business interests, both locally and nationwide, and members of Congress in the

Washington, D.C. area and elsewhere had complained bitterly about the restriction, stressing the economic costs and the inconveniences it caused for
those business executives and politicians who routinely used this rarefied
mode of transportation. The government finally yielded to the pressure in
October 2005.

To be fair, the conditions under which general aviation at DCA has been
resumed are stringent. TSA must conduct a "name-based threat assessment"
on each passenger and crewmember. There must be an armed security officer aboard, and TSA must have conducted a threat assessment on him. The
aircraft's most recent point of departure must be a TSA-approved "gateway
airport,"[39] meaning that at that airport, TSA must have inspected the aircraft, and screened the passengers, their carry-on bags, and any cargo in the
hold. The operator must observe all Federal Aviation Administration rules,
including the prohibition on traveling within a certain distance of the White
House and other such sensitive sites. TSA must be reimbursed for these various security costs by the aircraft operator.

If each of these security measures is taken, and if the threat assessments
and inspections are thorough, there would appear to be little reason to fear
re-opening DCA to general aviation, but it sends the signal that the nation
has turned a corner, and that we no longer remain under serious threat. Of
course, nothing could be further from the truth.

Furthermore, the timing is odd. Since the terror attacks, there have been
literally thousands of violations of the restricted airspace in Washington,
D.C. According to GAO, between September 12, 2001 and December 31,
2004, there were 3,400 violations, 88 percent of which were made by general
aviation pilots.[40] In May 2005, an errant private plane wandered into within
three miles of the White House, prompting an evacuation of the Executive
Mansion and the Capitol. For a few minutes at least, it appeared as though
the nation was under attack again. In congressional testimony on the subject
of restricted airspace around the capital, GAO made a point of noting that
" . . . intelligence agencies believe that terrorists remain highly interested in
U.S. aviation in both commercial and general aviation, to attack airports, or
to use aircrafts to attack targets, including critical infrastructure."[41]

To those who question whether a private aircraft could do much harm,
GAO pointed out that one could contain "fairly dangerous material" or
"horribly hazards [*sic*] material," and that the Secret Service considers any
threat to the White House to be serious ipso facto.[42]

Members of Congress have complained to DHS about the lax controls
over smaller airports. The Connecticut congressional delegation complained

about a twenty-year-old's having taken a plane stolen from the small airport in the town of Danbury for a joy ride. In the same month (June 2005), an Alabama teenager managed to steal a plane and cruise over neighboring towns for nearly half an hour. Senator Hillary Clinton summed up the concern in her letter to DHS about the Connecticut episode. The plane in question crossed state lines and landed in New York. "This incident seems to indicate a significant, looming danger. . . . It suggests the possibility that general aviation aircraft can be easily stolen, without detection, flown over populated communities, all without action or alerts by the federal government."[43] Indeed.

So, the question is whether restrictions should be relaxed in the absence of any relaxation in the terrorist threat. Until the prospect of another terrorist attack recedes into the realm of the improbable, it seems to me that general aviation restrictions around the nation's capital should remain. In fact, security should be tightened at general aviation facilities throughout the country.

30-MINUTE RULE

Likewise, the department has lifted the rule requiring passengers on commercial aircraft flying into Reagan National Airport to be seated for the last thirty minutes of the flight and those flying out for the first thirty minutes of the flight. In and of itself, it is hard to see how this will compromise homeland security. And, certainly things will be far more comfortable for those (like me) who travel from and back to Washington all the time. But, given the security gaps, and given terrorists' intentions, determination, and capabilities, shouldn't we be tightening security rather than loosening it?

LIFTING THE BAN ON CERTAIN SHARP OBJECTS

Likewise, in December 2005, the department lifted its post-9/11 ban on certain sharp objects aboard passenger planes, namely scissors four inches in length and less and tools like screwdrivers seven inches and less. Is it likely that terrorists nowadays would attempt to use scissors or screwdrivers to carry out a terror attack aboard an airplane? No. If they were to do so, is it likely that the loss of life or injury would be catastrophic? No, especially now that cockpit doors are hardened, the number of air marshals has significantly increased, some pilots are armed, and both flight attendants and passengers are presumably more vigilant and assertive. But again, unless and until the threat to aviation recedes to pre-9/11 levels, I question whether post-9/11 security measures should be relaxed. After all, if someone had asked me before 9/11 whether box cutters could realistically be used to hijack an aircraft, kill nearly three thousand people, destroy the Twin Towers, damage the Pentagon, and cause billions of dollars of economic damage, I would likely have said, "absolutely not."

The department's rationale for the relaxation is that it forces harried screeners to focus more on an even greater threat—explosives. It seems to me that this should not be an either/or proposition. Screeners should be able to look for potentially deadly sharp objects *and* explosives. If there are too few screeners to do both, then there should be more screeners.

On the same day the TSA announced the lifting of the ban on certain sharp objects, the agency announced three additional steps that move in the right direction—an intention to vary screening procedures so as to introduce an element of randomness to make it harder for terrorists to game the system; an intention to subject people to the more intensive secondary screening process at random; and an intention to pat down people's arms and legs as wells as their torsos.

But coming against other measures that relax security, and given the various gaps in aviation that remain, these steps in the right direction are too few to make up for the ground lost by all the steps in the wrong direction.

ARMED PILOTS

One of the programs instituted after the last attacks to increase aviation security was the "Federal Flight Deck Officers" program. It allows trained commercial aviation pilots who volunteer to do so to carry guns in the cockpit, the better to protect passengers and other crew members in the event of a terrorist attack.

But only a fraction of the pilots who want to participate in the program have signed up to do so because of various restrictions that TSA has imposed that appear to be counterproductive. Only about 4,000 out of the 95,000 commercial pilots in the country have been trained and deputized. About 50,000 pilots are said to have wanted to participate in the program but have chosen not to do so because of these restrictions.[44] For example, pilots are not permitted to holster their weapons when they're not in the cockpit; they must keep the guns in boxes. Pilots say that, as a consequence, they must periodically transfer the guns to and from the boxes, and that every time they do so the risk of an accident increases.

Furthermore, pilots say that if they were given a badge of some kind similar to that carried by law enforcement officers, they would have greater credibility convincing screeners at checkpoints and passengers, in the event of an incident, that they are authorized to carry a weapon. The plastic cards TSA does provide are not generally recognized as law enforcement-like credentials. Adding to these issues is the fact that pilots are not permitted to carry guns on international flights, and training is given in only one location—an obscure town in New Mexico.

Certainly, TSA should be cautious about permitting guns on aircraft. On the other hand, as repeated undercover government investigations have shown, it's easy enough for terrorists to sneak guns aboard. Shouldn't pilots who've been checked out and trained be allowed to even the score? It seems to me that the answer to that is yes, and, the more and the sooner, the better.

DO WE HAVE ENOUGH SCREENERS?

In response to the terror attacks, some 60,000 airport screeners were hired by the Transportation Security Administration. Since that time, so as to contain costs, Congress has capped the total number of screeners at 45,000. There appears to be no rhyme or reason for having chosen this number. Certainly, there has to be some limit on the number of screeners; we can't afford a one-to-one ratio between screeners and passengers, but it would be preferable, surely, for the TSA, which is supposed to have the requisite expertise, to set the number on the basis of security needs, than for Congress to do so on the basis of cost. As things stand now, TSA must cover the nation's airports as best it can within the confines of this arbitrary overall cap, but some of TSA's allocation decisions have been questionable at best.

For example, it makes no sense to cut screeners from the busiest airport in the nation. But, that's exactly what TSA proposed to do in April 2005 at Atlanta's Hartsfield-Jackson International Airport, until word got out and a media storm ensued. In the end, screeners were cut, but only 21 instead of the proposed 350 to 400. Documents obtained in July 2005 showed that JFK International Airport in New York, certainly one of the nation's busiest, was to lose 162 screeners.[45]

TSA should be given the resources and legal authority to hire the total nationwide number of screeners that maximum feasible security demands. Within that number, it should allocate screeners according to threat and risk. It is axiomatic that the busier an airport is the more screeners it needs; the less busy it is, the fewer. Until the screener numbers are recalibrated according to this commonsense calculus, the nation will remain at needless risk.

CHAPTER FOUR

PORT SECURITY AND NUCLEAR ATTACK

During the course of the hard-fought 2004 presidential campaign, President Bush and his Democratic challenger, Senator John Kerry, disagreed on almost everything. The one notable area of agreement was highlighted in this exchange during the first presidential debate.

> MODERATOR: If you are elected president, what will you take to that office thinking is the single most serious threat to the national security of the United States?
>
> KERRY: Nuclear proliferation. Nuclear proliferation. There's some 600-plus tons of unsecured material still in the former Soviet Union and Russia. . . . Now there are terrorists trying to get their hands on that stuff today. . . .
>
> BUSH: . . . well . . . I agree with my opponent that the biggest threat facing this country is weapons of mass destruction in the hands of a terrorist network."[1]

It is no wonder that bitter rivals vying over the world's most powerful office would agree on this one thing—the ultimate "nightmare scenario" is the introduction by terrorists of nuclear weapons on American soil. While such a weapon could be smuggled by air or land, it is widely agreed that the easiest way for terrorists to do so would be by sea. As the Commissioner of the Department of Homeland Security's Customs and Border Protection put it, "the sum of all fears is a 'nuke in a box.'"[2] This is no mere theoretical concern. There were some 650 confirmed cases of illicit trafficking in radiological and nuclear material across the globe between 1993 and 2004, according to the International Atomic Energy Agency.[3]

Every year approximately nine million cargo containers arrive at America's 361[4] seaports from all over the world—about 26,000 a day. It is no secret that only about 6 percent of those containers are inspected.[5] Any one of those containers could contain a weapon of mass destruction.

According to estimates cited by a key senator, "a 10 to 20 kiloton nuclear weapon detonated in a major seaport would kill between 50,000 to one million people and would result in direct property damage of $50 billion to $500 billion, losses due to trade disruption of $100 billion to $200 billion, and indirect costs of $300 billion to $1.2 trillion."[6] The maritime sector, which encompasses 26,000 miles of navigable waterways and some 95,000 miles of coastline, contributes some $750 billion to the gross domestic product of the nation, and it handles 95 percent of total annual international trade.[7]

There can be no higher national priority, then, than doing everything possible to prevent this nightmare scenario from becoming a terrible reality some day. To sum up the message of this chapter in a nutshell, our nation has a long way to go—a *very* long way to go—before we can say with assurance that the chances of this scenario's unfolding are as close to zero as we can make them.

During my time as the Inspector General of the Department of Homeland Security I had a number of occasions to examine this issue. One such occasion arose when I received a request from two Democratic members of Congress, John Dingell of Michigan and Jim Turner of Texas, to follow up on two extremely disturbing ABC News reports, the first broadcast on September 11, 2002, and the second on September 11, 2003.

One year to the day after the terror attacks, ABC News reported that one of its undercover investigative teams had conducted an experiment to test the vulnerability of the nation to terrorist attack by means of a nuclear weapon smuggled into one of our seaports. The team had shipped a steel pipe containing a fifteen-pound cylinder of depleted uranium shielded with lead from the port at Istanbul, Turkey to one in the United States. The Customs and Border Protection (CBP) unit at the Department of Homeland Security duly targeted the applicable container for inspection, but Customs officers failed to detect the uranium when they inspected it.

The cylinder was placed in a suitcase and then taken by train from Austria to Turkey. The team knew that such a route would likely arouse the attention of Customs inspectors, since the region of Central and Eastern Europe encompasses former Soviet nations where considerable radioactive material remains to this day, even though the Cold War ended more than a decade ago. The huge quantity of material available, the laxity of the controls over it, and the cultural and economic susceptibility of the few security guards there are to bribery make it relatively easy for terrorists to get their hands on it.

Once the suitcase arrived in Istanbul it was placed inside a chest that was then placed inside a crate. The crate was then placed inside a large metal shipping container alongside large vases and Turkish horse carts, and then finally placed on a ship bound for the United States. Appropriately, Customs targeted this particular crate for inspection upon its arrival, and Customs inspectors duly inspected it when it showed up at port, but they failed to detect the uranium.

One year later, on the second anniversary of the attacks, ABC News reported that it had succeeded a second time in smuggling the very same shipment of uranium into the United States. In the second incident, the cylinder was again placed in a suitcase and then placed in a teak trunk. The trunk was then loaded at the port in Jakarta, Indonesia (Indonesia is the world's largest predominantly Muslim nation) into a container filled with other furniture and shipped to the United States through Malaysia (another predominantly Muslim nation). Again, the crate was targeted for inspection and duly inspected, but Customs missed the uranium once again.

Depleted uranium is harmless; but weapons-grade uranium is deadly. Enough weapons-grade uranium can cause a catastrophe.

During the course of our investigation into how Customs missed these potentially deadly shipments, we were told by government scientific experts that the "signatures," or the emanations indicating the presence of radiation, are the same for shielded depleted uranium and shielded weapons-grade uranium. The significance of this is that since Customs missed this cylinder of depleted uranium, it likely would have missed an otherwise identical one containing weapons-grade uranium.

After looking into the issue, we determined that there were flaws in the radiation detection equipment that Customs used, and also that certain policies and procedures were inadequate. We made detailed recommendations to correct these flaws and deficiencies, which must remain secret for reasons of national security. CBP agreed with our recommendations and promised to implement them.[8] Would that the story stopped there.

I had my doubts that Customs would take our recommendations seriously enough to implement them because we had such a hard time convincing Customs' leadership that there was a problem. Customs kept stressing to us that they had correctly targeted the container each time for inspection and that they had inspected it. We kept stressing that those were only two steps in a three-step process. What good was it to target a suspicious container and to inspect it, if, in the end, the potentially deadly nuclear material was not discovered? This "accentuate the positive; eliminate the negative" attitude on CBP's part was typical of the reaction that we would get whenever we examined a Department of Homeland Security program or operation, but this reaction to our assessment of port security was particularly troubling to me because of the enormity of the stakes involved.

Sure enough, my fear that Customs would not take our findings and recommendations seriously was borne out and confirmed by subsequent examinations. Numerous news reports, expert studies, and congressional testimony since my time at DHS make clear that we remain vulnerable to a catastrophic attack by virtue of continued inadequacies in cargo security.[9]

CONTAINER SECURITY INITIATIVE (CSI)

The Customs and Border Protection unit bases its cargo security strategy largely on two programs, the Container Security Initiative (CSI) and the Customs-Trade Partnership Against Terrorism (C-TPAT). These programs make eminent sense in theory; it's how they work in practice that's the problem.

Like the Immigration Advisory Program (IAP) discussed in chapter three, the theory behind CSI is that the farther away we can keep terrorists and the weapons they would use to attack us, the better. Like IAP, the Container Security Initiative "pushes the borders out" by stationing U.S. Customs inspectors at foreign seaports to target and oversee the inspection of potentially dangerous cargo *before* it sails for the United States.

CSI began in January 2002, and, as of October 2005, it was operational at forty foreign ports. Twenty of these ports collectively sent 66 percent of all the containers that arrive in the United States; the remaining ports are in countries that are either of strategic importance to the United States or ones deemed vulnerable or attractive to terrorists as a shipment point.[10] In total, the ports account for approximately 70 percent of the maritime cargo sent to the United States each year.[11]

To determine the effectiveness of any DHS program as a counterterrorism tool, it is important to begin by understanding the terms that the department uses. As noted above, when explaining TSA's failure to inspect the lion's share of cargo on commercial flights, the Department of Homeland Security tends to use language with an "Alice-in-Wonderland" quality to it. Words don't mean what they normally do. For example, to say that the department "targets" every container does not mean that it "inspects" every one of them. "Targeting" means assessing containers to determine the level of risk that each poses to the security of the homeland. The *goal* of CSI is to target every shipment bound for the United States, and then to inspect those that are determined by the targeting process to be "high-risk" before those shipments set sail.

Of course, the inspection process can be only as effective as the targeting process upon which it is based. The targeting process, called the "Automated Targeting System," or ATS, is not that effective, regrettably. According to assessments by my former colleagues in the Office of Inspector General, the Government Accountability Office (GAO), and the shipping industry itself, the information upon which ATS is based is insufficient to determine with any degree of assurance a given container's level of risk.[12]

ATS is based on the manifests of cargo containers' contents that are electronically submitted to CBP twenty-four hours before shipments arrive at port, but the descriptions in the manifests are often too general—"used machinery" or "general department store merchandise"—to be of much use in making a determination as to whether the contents might be suspicious. Even the president of the World Shipping Council has said that "An ocean carrier's bill of lading by itself is not sufficient for effective cargo carrier security screening."[13] Furthermore, manifests can be amended for up to sixty days *after* shipments arrive in the United States, further reducing their reliability at the time they are initially received. It is not surprising, then, that my former colleagues concluded that "improvements were needed in the data to which ATS targeting rules are applied, and the use of examination results to refine the ATS targeting rules."[14]

An industry advisory group has called for importers to provide more detailed cargo manifests, information on the origin of shipments, and the names of the buyers and sellers.[15]

Legislation to this effect has been introduced as well.[16] Proving the point, even the department has implicitly acknowledged the weaknesses in the current targeting system by launching, in phases, "the Advanced Trade Data Initiative," or ADTI. The stated goals of ADTI are to: (1) identify shipments' true ports of origin and any and all stops along their way to the United States; (2) determine all the parties—from manufacturer to retailer—who were in any way involved in the shipment process; (3) confirm the accuracy of the manifest's description of container contents; and (4) improve Custom's risk management and targeting strategy.[17] As of now, however, the proverbial bottom line remains that the CBP targeting system constitutes a weak foundation, indeed, for a program touted as a key layer of defense against a potential nuclear catastrophe.

An unreliable targeting system is only one of the things wrong with CSI, though. Another is that American Customs officers lack the legal authority under foreign laws to do inspections themselves; they are dependent upon foreign inspectors to inspect the shipments determined by us Americans to be high-risk. The DHS officers' functions are limited to targeting based on ATS and any other available intelligence; referring any "high-risk" containers to the host government's customs agents for inspection; and observing and documenting the results of any inspections that are done by those agents.

Actually, there's some question as to whether our Customs agents always get to observe foreign inspections. In some cases, they have to take foreign governments' word that thorough inspections have been conducted. According to one Democratic senator, Frank Lautenberg of New Jersey, "We don't oversee some of these foreign inspections. In some cases, DHS personnel in the CSI program are stationed an hour away from where the actual loading takes place."[18]

Moreover, CBP is unable to station enough American customs agents to target every single container. Foreign governments are sovereign on their territory, so only they get to decide how many Americans may serve at their ports. "Practical" constraints like insufficient workspace can also limit the number of Americans deployed. Furthermore, like the case with Visa Security Officers in Saudi Arabia, the U.S. State Department (in the person of our ambassador there) must agree to the deployment of CBP inspectors in any given foreign country. Finally, at least in the early days of the CSI program, CBP inspectors were deployed only on a temporary basis. The rapid turnover limited the ability of American inspectors to build rapport with foreign inspectors and to acquire the skills and experience they need to perform optimally.

The consequence of these limitations is that 35 percent of cargo headed for the United States from a CSI port is *not* targeted for inspection before it sets sail. Chillingly, GAO concluded from this that there is no assurance that all high-risk shipments are identified as such.[19] That's a big problem because it's only if a high-risk shipment is so identified that it is inspected.

With regard to those containers that CBP targets and determines should be inspected, foreign inspectors don't always agree to inspect them. Between the inception of the program in January 2002 and September 11, 2004, foreign inspectors refused requests to inspect 4,013 containers, or 28 percent of the total referred to them within this period for inspection.[20] The reasons for refusal varied. On occasion, referrals were refused because the host government claimed to have superior knowledge as to whether the container at issue really posed a high-risk threat. On other occasions, "practical" considerations prevented host governments from inspecting containers. For example, sometimes inspections couldn't be carried out because the cargo at issue had already been loaded onto a ship and the ship was about to set sail!

Are there consequences if CSI port officials consistently refuse to inspect containers that our inspectors ask them to? Apparently not. The port in LeHavre, France, for example, refused our inspection requests 29.61 percent of the time, or nearly one times in three. Our Commissioner of Customs said that he was "troubled" by this, but rather than suspending France from the program, he said that he was merely "evaluating and working with the French customs authorities . . . to increase the percentage of requests that are honored because that's the whole point of CSI."[21]

The good news here is that if CBP targets a shipment as high-risk and the foreign inspectors refuse for whatever reason to inspect it, CBP is supposed to see to it that the American port of destination inspects it before it leaves that port. Likewise, CBP can require a domestic inspection if a foreign inspection is not done to CBP's satisfaction. The bad news is that some shipments referred by CBP for domestic inspection aren't inspected when they arrive at an American seaport, either. Because no records were kept for the first two and half years of the program, there's no way to tell how often this happened during that period. So, while it's certainly possible that no weapon of mass destruction was sneaked into the country at the time because of this security gap, it's equally possible that one was. The only way we may ever know for sure is the "hard way," when a mushroom cloud appears in the sky.

Between July and September 2004, 7 percent of shipments referred for domestic inspection were let into the country without being inspected. Of this percentage, 2 percent were not inspected because additional intelligence was obtained indicating that the shipment at issue was not high-risk after all. Knowing that intelligence is necessarily imperfect, one can only hope that this additional intelligence was sound. Of the remaining 5 percent, there's no way to tell whether there was a good reason, a bad reason, or no reason at all for giving it a pass because of "data input errors."[22]

Not only is it disturbing that some containers targeted by Customs as high-risk are not inspected either at the foreign port of departure or the

American port of arrival; it's just as disturbing that Customs' leadership is in a state of denial about this. The following telling exchange occurred in a hearing before the Senate Homeland Security and Governmental Affairs Committee.

> CHAIRMAN SUSAN COLLINS: Are you saying that when you have a case where there is a high-risk container that's been targeted for inspection but was not inspected by the host government it is now inspected upon arrival?
>
> BONNER (the Commissioner of Customs): Yes, I am saying that. I'm making an assumption that it was targeted because it had a risk targeting score for the terrorism threat of 190 or above, and I will say that in each and every case—I mean, I can't sit here and say that somebody didn't fail in their job in some way, but I can tell you if you look at, for example, just taking last month, April, the total number of containers that scored above 190 was about 32,000, and 99.9% of those containers were inspected on arrival. So, I do have a pretty high degree of confidence that if it's been loaded and we deemed it as a high risk, that we would get it on arrival."[23]

Commissioner Bonner's flat, declarative claim that every single shipment targeted as "high-risk" and not inspected at the foreign port of departure is inspected once it arrives here in the United States becomes in his very next sentence merely an "assumption." Even then, the assumption isn't that 100 percent of these shipments are inspected; it's only that 99.9 percent of them are. What about the remaining (admittedly miniscule) percentage? Again, it just takes one shipment containing a weapon of mass destruction to kill hundreds of thousands, if not millions of people, and to shut down national and international commerce as well. By the end of the exchange, the Customs Commissioner's assurance is whittled down to a "*pretty high degree of confidence.*" In the age of terror, a pretty high degree of confidence that weapons of mass destruction aren't getting into our country isn't high enough.

Later in the hearing, the GAO was asked about the Commissioner's assurances by the Senator chairing the hearing.

> SENATOR COLEMAN: Mr. Stana, I want to just clarify a couple of things that the Commissioner stated. He indicated very clearly that all high-risk containers overseas, if they're not inspected overseas, are inspected when they get here. Was GAO able to verify that?

RICHARD M. STANA (GAO witness): No. In fact, of the 65 percent of the containers that were classified as high-risk and were reviewed by the staff overseas, our detailed work at the ports suggested even within that 65 percent there's no guarantee that all those were high-risk or not high-risk. That's the first point.

The second point is when the CSI port people called the U.S. port people and verified [to] them that they couldn't get it inspected for whatever reason, we found no records that could assure us that in all cases the inspection was done stateside. So, we don't have the high level of assurance that Commissioner Bonner has."[24]

As for those high-risk shipments that are inspected by foreign inspectors, there's no assurance that all the inspections are effective in detecting weapons of mass destruction. There are two kinds of inspections, "non-intrusive" ones and "intrusive" ones. Of course, non-intrusive means are used first because of the length of time it takes to unload a container, open it up, and physically inspect it. In the twenty-first-century global trading environment, time literally is money, so every second counts. In a non-intrusive inspection, X-ray or gamma-ray scanning equipment such as a VACIS (Vehicle and Cargo Inspection System) machine is used to scan a container for any anomalies. If the cargo manifest indicates that the container's contents are one thing and the density of the items inside suggests otherwise, such a container should be physically inspected to resolve the ambiguity.* Radiation detection devices are also used. If any radiation is detected, Customs officers need to pinpoint the source of it and then determine whether the radioactive material is the kind that is dangerous.

To complicate matters further, different kinds of potentially deadly radioactive material vary in the degree of ease with which they can be detected. The kind of radiation used in a "dirty bomb" is easy to detect because it is highly radioactive. Highly enriched uranium, on the other hand, is hard to detect because it gives off relatively little radiation, ironically enough. It's harder still to detect if it is shielded, as the non-weapons-grade uranium ABC News managed to smuggle was.[25]

---

* Regrettably, the X-ray images of those containers that are scanned by non-intrusive means are not retained. This is a missed opportunity, for example, to spot patterns and trends that might indicate terrorist plotting and casing methodology, or to conduct forensic analysis after an attack occurs.

Through the "Megaports Initiative," the U.S. Department of Energy provides major international seaports with radiation detection equipment. There are three types of radiation detection devices—radiation isotope identifier devices (RIIDs), radiation portal monitors (RPMs), and personal radiation detectors (PRDs). These devices are not interchangeable; each has its own capabilities. PRDs are helpful only to protect individual inspectors from radiation exposure; they can detect radiation and warn of its presence, but they can't find it. RPMs can detect and pinpoint radiation, but they can't distinguish between the harmless kind that occurs naturally in, say, bananas, and the dangerous kind found in nuclear bombs; only RIIDs can do that.[26]

And yet, in sworn testimony before Congress, the Customs Commissioner has called radiation portal monitors "the best available technology there is,"[27] conveying the impression that a CSI port with an RPM can detect a weapon of mass destruction. His full sentence, "That's the best available technology there is in terms of being highly sensitive to be able to detect against even potentially nuclear devices and/or materials that could be used to make nuclear devices,"[28] is true, more or less, but only as far as it goes. Again, RPMs are sensitive enough to detect radioactive material, but they can't distinguish between the harmless kind and the deadly kind. Only radiation isotope identifier devices can.

So, if the key thing is to detect a weapon of mass destruction, and if containers not inspected at a CSI port might or might not be inspected at the U.S. port of entry, it's critical that every CSI port have and use RIIDs, but not every such port has them. In fact, it's unclear whether *any* CSI port has them. All we know is that "CSI has requisitioned radio isotope identifier devices for deployment to operational CSI ports with host country approval."[29] In other words, the only radiation detection devices that are truly effective in detecting the presence of deadly radiation are on order, and they may be deployed to CSI ports only if the host country approves of it.

Indeed, only two CSI ports—Piraeus, Greece, and Rotterdam, The Netherlands—have RPMs,[30] and, as of the summer of 2005, reading between the lines, at least one of those RPMs isn't that effective even at what it's supposed to be able to do—detect the presence of radiation and pinpoint it. GAO reported in March 2005 that the radiation detection equipment installed by our Department of Energy at one foreign port missed the radiation in a container because the quantity of scrap metal in that container was sufficient to shield it from detection.[31]

One would have thought that the Department of Homeland Security could *require* foreign ports to have RIIDs as a condition of their being in the

Container *Security* Initiative, but CBP says that sovereignty concerns and legal prohibitions on endorsing particular brands of equipment have prevented it from setting minimum radiation detection standards that must be met by CSI ports.

Perhaps the *real* reason is that the department is hardly in a position to demand that foreign ports meet a higher standard than American ports do. Our then Customs Commissioner candidly admitted, ". . . we don't have enough funding to totally complete our implementation plan for radiation portal monitors at our own seaports. . . ."[32] The Commissioner emphasized that every CSI port except one (more on this later) has radiation detection equipment that equals or exceeds what we have at our own ports. But he must have meant that all CSI ports have personal radiation detectors, since only two have RPMs, and there's no mention of any having RIIDs.

If so, that's a problem, because, again, personal radiation detectors "are not adequate as search instruments."[33] GAO summed up the security vulnerability in this way: "Although CBP cannot endorse a particular brand of equipment, the bureau could still establish general technical capability requirements for any equipment used under CSI. . . . Because the CSI inspection could be the only inspection of a container before it enters the interior of the United States, it is important that the . . . radiation detection equipment used as part of CSI provide some level of assurance of the likelihood that the equipment could detect the presence of WMD [weapons of mass destruction]."[34]

As for the one unnamed CSI port that even the Department of Homeland Security admits doesn't have adequate inspection equipment, has that port been kicked out of the program? Has it at least been given a deadline by which to upgrade its equipment? The answer to both questions is no, even though the Commissioner declared that ". . . we will not have that port [one that doesn't meet CSI commitments] as a CSI port unless they're meeting their commitments," and even though he acknowledges that the economic benefits that CSI ports derive from participation give us great leverage over those that prove to be recalcitrant.[35]

The Customs and Border Protection bureau in the Department of Homeland Security seems to be eager to expand the CSI program to more and more ports. The program is intended to be up and running in fifty ports by the end of 2006, but it is more important to close the security gaps at each existing port than it is to expand the program to still more ports. Indeed, it is *dangerous* to expand the program before the flaws in it are addressed.

The very fact that a shipment arrives from a CSI port makes it less likely that it will be inspected once it arrives in the United States because of the misimpression that the CSI program is more effective than it really is. The whole point of the program, after all, is to obviate the need for an inspection once a container arrives in the United States. (And, that's not only because there is only so much time and only so many resources to perform inspections here. It's also because if we wait to find a weapon of mass destruction until it's already arrived at one of our ports, it may at that point already be too late.) The more shipments come from CSI ports, the fewer U.S. inspections there will be, and the less assurance we will have that any weapons of mass destruction among them will be found.

To prove the point, consider the case of thirty-two Chinese stowaways found hidden in two cargo containers at the Port of Los Angeles in January 2005. The containers had been loaded at the Chinese port city of Shekou, but the ship then went on to Hong Kong, a top CSI port city, the busiest port in the world, and the one that sends more cargo to the United States than any other. Fortunately, an alert crane operator spotted the men; sophisticated technology did not. It is likely that port officials in Los Angeles made the calculation not to inspect that particular container for stowaways, illegal contraband, weapons of mass destruction, or anything else, precisely because it was arriving from a CSI port where any necessary inspection should already have been conducted.

All this having been said, if the CSI program really were as sound in practice as it seems to be in theory, and we could rest easy that containers leaving CSI ports were free of weapons of mass destruction at the time of departure, what's to stop the container from being tampered with in transit and a weapon of mass destruction inserted somewhere along the journey to America?

As things stand now, there's no way to know for sure whether this is happening to containers en route to the United States. Though the CBP website lists among CSI's features "smarter, tamper-evident containers," this technology has been in various phases of testing since January 2004.[36]

For all the holes in the CSI program, a terrorist would surely calculate that his chances are greater of successfully smuggling into the United States a container with nuclear material if he ships it from a non-CSI port. There are still more non-CSI ports than CSI ports.[37] If a container with deadly radioactive material is either shipped from a CSI port and not inspected there for some reason, or if the container is shipped from a port that is not in the CSI program and, accordingly, it is not expected to be inspected before it arrives in the United States, what is the likelihood of its being inspected here upon arrival? The answer is perilously close to zero, since we established at the beginning of this chapter that no more than 6 percent of incoming maritime cargo is inspected at U.S. seaports. For that 6 percent of cargo that is inspected here, how likely are any weapons of mass destruction to be detected? The answer is that it's more likely than at a foreign port, but only marginally so. The reason for this is that effective radiation detection equipment is in short supply here in the United States, too. As mentioned above, even the then CBP Commissioner, who was not noted for acknowledging shortcomings in Customs' programs and operations, admitted that the department did not have enough money to deploy radiation port monitors at all U.S. seaports.

As of May 2005, fifty-nine large-scale X-ray-type non-intrusive detection machines had been deployed to seaports on the East and West Coasts of the United States and the Caribbean.[38] Nearly 500 radiation portal monitors had been deployed throughout the nation, but CBP is only "initiating the deployment of RPMs in the maritime environment with the ultimate goal of screening 100 percent of all containerized imported cargo for radiation."[39] Again, though, radiation portal monitors can't distinguish between the harmless kind of radiation and the deadly kind. And even if they could, it's unclear how long it will take the department to get from where it is today to screening all cargo for radiation. CBP claims to have deployed more than 10,000 personal radiation devices such that there is 100 percent coverage at the primary point of contact. But again, these devices can only warn the holder that he's being exposed to radiation. They can't tell where exactly the radiation is or what kind of radiation it is. According to the security manager for the Port Authority of New York and New Jersey, *none* of the cargo that moves through the largest ship terminal and *none* of the goods leaving the port by barge or rail are scanned for radiation.[40]

A *New York Times* piece[41] nicely summed up the problems with the various kinds of radiation detection equipment in an account of a visit to the Port Newark Container Terminal in New Jersey.

> Heralded as "highly sophisticated" when they were introduced, the [radiation portal monitors] have proven to be hardly that. The . . . technology has been used for decades by the scrap metal industry. Customs officials at Newark have nicknamed the devices "dumb sensors," because they cannot discern the source of the radiation. That means benign items that naturally emit radioactivity—including cat litter, ceramic tile, granite, porcelain toilets, even bananas—can set off the monitors. Alarms occurred so frequently when the monitors were first installed that customs officials turned down their sensitivity. But that increased the risk that a real threat,

like the highly enriched uranium used in nuclear bombs, could go undetected because it emits only a small amount of radiation or perhaps none if
it is intentionally shielded. "It was certainly a compromise in terms of absolute capacity to detect threats," said [Christopher Y.] Milowic, the customs official [at the port]. The port's follow-up system, handheld devices
that are supposed to determine what set off an alarm, is also seriously
flawed. Tests conducted in 2003 by Los Alamos National Laboratory found
that the handheld machines, designed to be used in labs, produced a false
positive or a false negative more than half the time. The machines were the
least reliable in identifying the most dangerous materials, the tests showed.
The weaknesses of the devices were apparent in Newark one recent morning. A truck, whose records said that it was carrying brakes from Germany,
triggered the portal alarm, but the backup device could not identify the radiation source. Without being inspected, the truck was sent on its way to
Ohio. "We agree that it is not perfect," said Rich O'Brien, a customs supervisor in Newark. But he said his agency needed to move urgently to improve security after the 2001 attacks. "The politics stare you in the face, and
you got to put something out there."

What the department has "put out there" doesn't work. In a May 19,
2005 "information bulletin" to state agencies, the head of the DHS office of
Domestic Preparedness reported that *none* of the four devices currently
used to detect radiation—personal radiation devices (also known as "radiation pagers"), radiation portal monitors, radiation isotope identification devices, and hand-held survey meters—passed all of the tests administered by
the American National Standards Institute, after some ten months of testing.
Manufacturers are working to improve the equipment to meet the standards, but until such ANSI-compliant equipment is available, the department has authorized states and localities to purchase equipment that does
not meet the standard. In other words, the Department of Homeland Security sanctions the purchase of equipment known to be (to varying degrees)
unreliable and ineffective.[42]

The problem isn't just a question of insufficient and inadequate radiation detection equipment. Even if and when equipment is not the issue, the
timing of an inspection can be. Commissioner Bonner admits that containers can sit at a port—including those in high threat cities such as New York
and Los Angeles—for as long as a full week before they're screened for radiation. By the time Customs people get around to inspecting the cargo containers for a weapon of mass destruction, the weapon may have already gone
off.[43]

CUSTOMS TRADE PARTNERSHIP AGAINST TERRORISM

The other Department of Homeland Security program that is intended to serve as a counter to any terrorist attempt to smuggle a weapon of mass destruction into our seaports is called Customs Trade Partnership Against Terrorism, or C-TPAT, which is similar to other Department of Homeland Security programs, such as Known Shipper, Registered Traveler, and Free and Secure Trade (FAST). These programs provide expedited clearance to those who volunteer to undergo a security check and are determined by such a check to be low-risk. The theory is that such programs allow necessarily limited resources to be concentrated on those persons or products that are likeliest to be high-risk.

C-TPAT participants are various members of the global supply chain. According to CBP, members include U.S. importers, customs brokers, terminal operators, carriers, and foreign manufacturers. Members voluntarily agree to take steps to secure their part of the supply chain in exchange for fewer physical inspections and a less extensive document review. While, like CSI, C-TPAT makes sense in theory, there are problems in practice—*big* problems.

One such problem with the program is that its benefits are provided to members *before* CBP validates their claims that they are entitled to them by virtue of the steps they have voluntarily taken to tighten security. At a May 2005 Senate hearing, the Commissioner of Customs testified that there were about 5,000 members of the program, but that only about 10 to 12 percent of them had been validated as having actually put in place the security measures they claimed to have implemented. In its typical "Alice-in-Wonderland" fashion, CBP boasts that only "certified" applicants may participate in the program, pointing out that there were about 9,000 applicants, but only 5,000 of them were accepted.[44] But "certification" does not mean "validation." "Certification" simply means that CBP has reviewed an applicant's application and determined that the paperwork has been satisfactorily completed. Once an applicant's application is certified and that applicant becomes a member of the C-TPAT program, the chances of its shipments being inspected go down significantly. Until complaints were raised about this "trust first, verify later" approach, a member's shipments were six times less likely to be inspected, even if that particular member's security claims were not yet validated. Now, CBP claims to graduate benefits depending upon whether a member's claims are validated. There's an even greater chance of not being inspected if a given member has been validated, but simply for signing up a member still reduces its chances of being inspected by some factor. When pressed on the point, the Commissioner of Customs could not (or, perhaps more accurately, *would* not) specify that factor.[45]

Another big problem is that the few validations that are made by CBP of C-TPAT members' security assertions don't provide much assurance that those assertions are true. That's because CBP doesn't conduct the validations in a thorough, rigorous, and independent fashion. Only some security measures are tested. Furthermore, the only measures tested are those that the member agrees to allow CBP to test! Additionally, record keeping on the results of validations is spotty at best, so there is no assurance that CBP has an accurate accounting in its files as to the adequacy of a given member's security program.[46]

Finally, according to the president of the World Shipping Council, the key players in the global supply chain—manufacturers (other than some from Mexico), and the parties that actually load the containers onto ships—aren't included in the C-TPAT program. So even if adequate security measures were built into the program, it would exclude that part of the supply chain that terrorists would be most likely to try to infiltrate.[47]

It is noteworthy that the carrier ferrying the container from the Port of Shekou, China, through Hong Kong and on to Los Angeles in which the Chinese national stowaways mentioned above secreted themselves was a C-TPAT member. This was not an isolated incident. Three months after this incident, another group of Chinese stowaways was found hidden aboard another C-TPAT carrier traveling the same route. Those stowaways could as easily have been terrorists carrying nuclear weapons.[48]

A sharp Senator, Republican Norm Coleman of Minnesota, put his finger on the problems with C-TPAT, and, indeed, many of the Department of Homeland Security's most touted counterterrorism programs: "In the public's mind, I think certification has some really strong value. . . . Somebody's looked at it, somebody's inspected it, somebody's checked it out and they've made a judgment. And, what we're having here is we've got application, certification really being looking at paperwork. It's looking at paperwork and trusting, this is trust but not verify, that you got what you got. That's a far cry from certification. And then in terms of validation. . . . You're literally looking at one little piece of it that may or may not be representative of the rest of the system. And, you're looking at a piece, by the way, that you've agreed up front to look at. . . . So that's my concern, the phrases here, certification, validation, that I don't think meet the standard definition that most folks would think about. And, again, when we go back to the risks here that they're pretty significant."[49]

All of this raises the question of *why* the department uses terms like "certify," when all it really means is review a C-TPAT applicant's paperwork, or "target," when all that means is determine the risk level of a particular container. Why not use terms in their commonly understood meaning? The inescapable conclusion is that the department is attempting to mislead law-makers and the public alike into thinking that they're doing more than they really are, and that we're safer than we really are.

To make bad matters still worse, the rest of the world is taking steps to replicate CSI and C-TPAT. The Secretary of Homeland Security applauded the move in a press release: "I am pleased by the World Customs Organization's (WCO) decision to adopt a common set of cargo security standards for its 166 member nations. Because of this historic and unanimous vote, virtually all of the world's trade will eventually be screened by standards originally established by the Department of Homeland Security, through the Container Security Initiative and the Customs-Trade Partnership Against Terrorism. These two programs were developed with guidance and expertise from the private sector and they demonstrate that security, when applied correctly, actually facilitates legitimate trade. By harnessing advanced technology and coordinating risk-based security methods, the United States and WCO can further streamline the flow of low-risk trade and greatly enhance global screening capabilities. I am confident that the WCO's decision will ultimately benefit the global business community as much as it will further our common security goals."[50]

It is clear that these programs benefit the global business community. In exchange for using them, businesses reduce their chances of being inspected. Maybe that's what the Secretary means when he talks about security being "applied correctly," but it's much less clear whether (and, if so, how exactly) either of these programs enhances the security of the homeland.

PORT SECURITY

Aside from the problems with CSI and C-TPAT, there's also the issue of the security of ports themselves, not just the cargo that passes through them. The Maritime Transportation Security Act of 2002, among other things, mandated certain improvements in port security. According to Coast Guard testimony,[51] more than 3,000 of the nation's highest-risk port facilities have instituted procedures to ensure that only authorized personnel have access to them and that no deadly devices or substances are brought in.

But we know that the Department of Homeland Security has a history of overselling its security programs, so these claims must be met with some degree of skepticism until they are independently verified by outside investigators. Suffice it to say now that a crucial part of such a program is ensuring that the identity of those who work at ports, especially those who work in sensitive positions, is verified, and that each such person has been thoroughly vetted for terrorist or criminal connections. In this regard, it is troubling that, as noted above, the Transportation Workers Identification Card program has been plagued by delays. The Coast Guard itself has expressed concern about the fact that merchant sailors can access sensitive areas at ports with their identification cards, but that those cards contain no security features to confirm that someone purporting to be a merchant mariner is who he says he is.[52]

To help ports enhance their security programs, the Department of Homeland Security dispenses billions of dollars of grant money through its Port Security Grant Program. Our auditors looked into the issue of exactly how the department was administering this critical counterterrorism program during my time as DHS Inspector General, but the report was not completed until shortly after I departed.[53]

The results of our examination were shocking. More than a half a billion dollars was awarded to over 1,200 proposed projects throughout the nation that were supposed, in one way or another, to improve the security of ports. But rather than funding only projects that were deemed most worthy by evaluators in the field, higher-ups at department headquarters frequently overruled the evaluators' judgment. The result was that several hundred projects of dubious security value were funded, and some projects that would have enhanced security went unfunded. For example, DHS headquarters overruled the field and funded a $180,000 project to install lighting in a port visited by fewer than twenty ships each year. At the same time, headquarters rejected a field recommendation to fund a $250,000-plus project to install gates, fences, cameras, and lighting in a port facility adjacent to a sulfur plant near six other chemical plants, even though the evaluators said that they "*strongly*" recommended approval.

It appeared as though the department was trying to spread the money around to as many parts of the country as possible rather than concentrating on the biggest ports, which are most at risk of terrorist attack. For example, ports in Ketchikan, Alaska and Martinsville, West Virginia got some funding, while a major port, such as the Port of New York and New Jersey, received only 1 percent of the total funds expended.

Finally, even though federal homeland security dollars are limited, the department awarded some of the money to private sector entities that could have afforded to pay for projects on their own. Some of the awards went to projects having nothing to do with homeland security. Others went to projects that businesses were required to undertake anyway in the normal course of affairs. Still more awards provided funding for projects that were intended merely to replace existing security projects.

Since this report was issued, the department has announced another round of port security grants in the amount of $141 million,[54] and it promises that the money will be allocated strictly on the basis of threat, vulnerability, and consequence. But it remains to be seen whether limited port security dollars will be awarded in a way that will most enhance homeland security. The department's track record to date in this regard is *not* encouraging.

In sum, we remain far more vulnerable to a catastrophic attack today by means of a weapon of mass destruction sneaked into one of our nation's ports than we should be. The department has oversold and otherwise misrepresented the programs that are presently in place to guard against this awful possibility, and monies intended to make our ports more secure have all too often been wasted.

As if to illustrate and underscore the fact that the Administration's rhetorical commitment to securing our ports (and, by extension, the homeland as a whole) against terror does not match its record, it came out just a few months before this book was released that a virtually secret interagency group (the Committee on Foreign Investment in the United States, or "CFIUS") chaired by the Treasury Department had approved the acquisition of terminals at six major American seaports (New York, New Jersey, Philadelphia, Baltimore, New Orleans, and Miami) by Dubai Ports World, a company controlled by the government of the United Arab Emirates. This was troubling in the extreme because, at best, the UAE has a mixed record on terror. The nation has generally been supportive of our counterterrorism efforts since 9/11, but the record also shows that: (1) two of the 9/11 hijackers were UAE nationals; (2) much of the financing for the attacks moved through the notably porous UAE financial system; (3) the UAE was one of only three nations in the world that recognized the Taliban regime in Afghanistan that sheltered bin Laden and his Al Qaeda network in the years before 9/11; and (4) Pakistani nuclear scientist A. Q.

Khan shipped some weapons components to Iran, Libya, and North Korea through the UAE.

When the deal become public, a tidal wave of criticism engulfed the White House.[55] How could an Administration that touts itself as tough on terrorism agree to turn over a key element of critical infrastructure like port terminals to a country with ties to terrorism? Since the President was not even informed of the decision, he could have distanced himself from it and insisted on reviewing and then overturning it. Instead, he defiantly embraced it, dared the Congress to file legislation to block it, and vowed to veto any such bill.

In the end, the political pressure on the Administration was so intense that the deal was scuttled. But, I could not help but note a striking contrast in presidential reaction, suggesting that security is not the priority it is claimed to be. When he learned that DHS and State were taking steps to tighten border security by instituting plans to require American citizens to present passports when re-entering the country from elsewhere in the Western Hemisphere, the President expressed surprise and displeasure and the agencies promptly backed off and watered down the measure at issue.[56] When he learned that relatively low-level officials had approved a deal that would weaken security by giving control of key aspects of security at six key ports to a country linked to terrorism, a president who had not cast a single veto in more than five years in office threatened to cast his first one to ensure that the deal would go through.

CHAPTER FIVE

MASS TRANSIT ATTACK

In the summer of 2005 I was among a number of experts asked by the 9/11 Commissioners to testify on the progress made in securing the homeland since their report, and on what remains to be done to make us as secure as possible. Halfway through my remarks, I made the following point, "With regard to mass transit security, despite the attack on a train station in Spain in March of last year—which Europe considers to be its 9/11—relatively little has been done to secure this key transportation sector. Secretary Chertoff's recent announcement of the devotion of $141 million to this task is to be commended, but more urgently must be done."[1] I had no idea that day that my words would soon prove to be prescient.

A little more than a week later terrorists struck the mass transit system in the heart of London. Bombs placed in three subway stations and on one bus killed 52 people and wounded more than 700. It appears as though the terrorists, all four of whom were killed in the attacks, *intended* to blow themselves up with their victims. If so, it would mark the first time in history that suicide bombers have struck in the West.

Exactly two weeks later, a second group of terrorists again struck the heart of London. Again, three subway stations and one bus were targeted, only this time the bombs failed to explode. If there had been any doubt after the first time, the second incident made it clear that London was under attack.

The attacks were additional wake-up calls for us Americans as to the vulnerability of our own mass transit systems to terrorist attack. The Madrid attack, which killed 191 people and wounded 1,400, was preceded by another incident that same year by Chechen terrorists on a Moscow subway. Algerian terrorists bombed the Paris subways in 1995 and 1996. Japanese extremists released deadly sarin gas in the Tokyo subway in 1995. And, of course, Palestinian suicide bombers have repeatedly targeted buses in Israel.

In the immediate aftermath of the first London attack, the threat level for the mass transit sector was raised in the United States from "elevated" to "high." Secretary Chertoff recommended that mass transit systems implement a variety of security measures ranging from increased armed police patrols to the greater use of bomb-sniffing dogs, to surveillance cameras and bomb sensors, to random inspections of passenger bags, and campaigns to encourage the public to report suspicious activity and unattended items.

New York City, New Jersey, and, interestingly, Salt Lake City all instituted random bag inspections. For the first time ever, Washington, D.C., shut down its 106-mile-long subway system for long enough to do a complete security sweep. Cities across the nation implemented one or another of these or other recommended security measures.[2]

It all had the feel of déjà vu. In the immediate aftermath of the Madrid attack, a number of counterterror measures were introduced in the United States that were similar to or identical with those introduced here after the London attacks. The sense of alarm in this country was only heightened when a Spanish newspaper reported that a sketch of Manhattan's iconic Grand Central station was found on a computer disk seized from the home of one of the Madrid suspects. To address the growing fears, then Secretary of Homeland Security Tom Ridge called a news conference to announce that:

> ... we are adding several new layers of security that we believe will help reduce vulnerabilities to our systems and make our commuters and transit riders more secure aboard our nation's trains and subways. The Department of Homeland Security will develop a rapid deployment mass transit canine program to assist state, local and transit authorities in the event of a special explosive threat situation ... the department's Transportation Security Administration will begin to implement a pilot program to test the feasibility of screening luggage and carry-on bags at rail stations and aboard trains ... the Department of Homeland Security will work with

the nation's rail and transit leaders to integrate existing passenger education programs and create new programs to increase passenger, employee
and law enforcement awareness . . . finally . . . one of the best ways to stay
ahead of terrorists is through the development of new homeland security
technologies. The department is working hard to bring the future to bear
on the threats we face today.[3]

As soon as the news of those attacks faded from the headlines, however,
the sense of urgency faded, these measures were relaxed, and the vulnerabilities in America's mass transit system returned.[4]

Despite the Madrid wake-up call and the other wake-up calls before that
one, our guard remained down until the London attacks. While somewhere
between 18 and 20 billion federal dollars were spent in the four years after the
attack on our homeland to secure aviation, only a small fraction of that—$250
million—was spent to secure mass transit systems, even though about 32 million Americans use mass transit each day to go about their daily routine—
more than sixteen times the number of people who take a plane each day.[5]

Indeed, the week after the first London attack, the Senate failed three
times to increase security spending on mass transit. In fact, at one point in
the budget process, the Senate actually voted to *cut* spending in the then
pending 2006 budget by $50 million. In the end, Congress passed, and the
President signed into law, a Homeland Security Department funding bill
that kept mass transit security spending level at $150 million.[6]

When pressed about this vast imbalance between spending on aviation
security and mass transit security, Secretary Chertoff and other Department
of Homeland Security officials counter by pointing to the additional billions
in general homeland security–related federal grants that state and local officials could use for mass transit security purposes. Some $8.6 billion has been
awarded by the department since 2001 through the State Homeland Security
Grant Program and the Urban Areas Security Initiative, but states and localities and their allies in Congress and the lobbying industry counter that the
mass transit sector needs dedicated funds just like the aviation and maritime
sectors do. While the additional billions could, indeed, be used for mass
transit purposes, money drawn down for those purposes is money that state
and localities can't use on equally compelling homeland security needs such
as first-responder preparedness. According to a survey of transit agencies
around the country conducted by the American Public Transportation Association, an additional $6 billion is needed to do everything possible to se-
cure the mass transit sector.[7]

Part of the reason for the reluctance of department leaders to ratchet up federal mass transit security spending to levels similar to that for aviation is a recognition that the mass transit sector is significantly harder to protect than the aviation sector. So many people use subways, commuter rails, and buses each day; so many people are concentrated into such small and confined spaces; there are so many entrances and exits; there are so many different transportation providers and authorities (about 6,000 in all[8]), that it is impossible to reduce the risk of an attack to anything close to zero. Setting up enough checkpoints to screen passengers and their carry-on items for guns, knives, and explosives would be impractical. It would be tremendously costly, and it would slow the already frenetic daily nationwide commute to a screeching halt, bringing our economy to its knees in the process.

Another, less defensible reason is the sense that an attack on mass transit simply couldn't have catastrophic consequences, and that we should concentrate our necessarily limited homeland security resources only on catastrophic threats. Indeed, Secretary Chertoff went so far as to say exactly that shortly after the London attacks: "The truth of the matter is, a fully loaded airplane with jet fuel, a commercial airliner, has the capacity to kill 3,000 people. A bomb in a subway car may kill 30 people. When you start to think about your priorities, you're going to think about making sure you don't have a catastrophic thing first."[9]

Predictably, the Secretary's comments set off a firestorm of criticism, especially from legislators who represent states with high-density populations that are heavily dependent upon mass transit. Even though the Secretary went on to add, "But, it doesn't mean that we only focus on aviation. It means we do aviation, we do other things as well, but we scale our response based on the nature of the architecture,"[10] the political damage was done. The reaction of the senior Senator from New York was typical. Chuck Schumer said that he was "aghast" at the Secretary's remarks, and he went on to wonder whether he (Chertoff) "should continue as Secretary."[11]

The Secretary was certainly right in saying that DHS should focus on those scenarios that, were they to materialize, would cause the most death, injury, and economic damage. But he was wrong to suggest that a mass transit attack could not have devastating consequences. The first London attack killed "only" 52 people (almost double the number that he postulated, incidentally), but a well-timed, well-placed attack in a highly concentrated subway or train station in the Northeast corridor of the United States could easily kill 3,000 people. For the most part, though, the explanation for the department's relatively nonchalant attitude toward mass transit security has to do with the American tendency to fight the last war and to assume that, if there's to be a next time, the next time will be exactly like the last time.

The simple fact of the matter is that we were attacked last time by means of airplanes, not subway cars or commuter trains. Until that attack, aviation security was largely handled by a combination of local authorities and private screening contractors. The system was federalized only *after* the attack. All of the security measures at airports that we tolerate nowadays were thought to be impractical, unduly onerous, disruptive, and prohibitively expensive *before* the attacks took place. To date, there's been no specific, credible intelligence indicating that a mass transit attack is imminent (a reported plot to attack subway stations in New York City in the fall of 2005 turned out to be a hoax), but there was no such intelligence before the London bombings, either. In fact, the British authorities—who are among the best in the world at detecting and foiling terrorist plots—actually *lowered* the threat level in the days immediately before the London attacks.

The fact that there hasn't been an attack on mass transit in this country to date definitely does not mean that one is impossible. Indeed, as noted above, an attack—especially a suicidal attack—is so relatively easy to carry out and so difficult to prevent that it is a wonder that one hasn't already been attempted. But until there is such an attack, it is doubtful that our government will do all it can to reduce the threat to as close to zero as possible. We're simply too reactive.

A little more than a month after the London attacks the Secretary of Homeland Security lowered the alert level for the mass transit sector, citing the absence of "specific, credible intelligence information indicating that an attack in the United States is imminent."[12] Doubtless, another factor in the decision to lower the level was the mounting costs of the higher level of preparedness. The nationwide "Code Orange" alert ordered after the London attacks was costing transit authorities nationwide about $900,000 a day.

This time around, commendably, the department encouraged mass transit authorities to maintain indefinitely some of the measures that they had put in place after the London attacks, and many of them agreed to do so. New York officials said that they planned to continue random searches in subways of passengers' baggage. Washington, D.C., announced that bomb-sniffing dogs and armed police would continue to patrol the subways. The proof will be in the proverbial pudding, though, as the months and then years go by without an attack, or the credible threat of one, on our mass transit systems. The question is whether, absent an attack in this country, the Department of Homeland Security will mandate and help to pay for institutionalizing the various counterterrorism measures it has only fitfully championed as threat levels over time have waxed and waned.

It is certainly true that the mass transit sector is especially hard to secure, but it is precisely that fact that must make it an attractive target to terrorists. Terrorists have demonstrated in other countries that they are aware of the vulnerability; it is only a matter of time before an attack is attempted here in the United States. As the head of the American Public Transportation Authority put it, "How many attacks will it take—successful or failed—before Congress and [DHS] decide that transit security is as important a priority as aviation security?"[13]

While certain measures can't by themselves prevent an attack, they can certainly make it harder for terrorists to succeed in launching a devastating one. More bomb-sniffing dogs, armed police patrols, surveillance cameras, explosive sensors, random searches, and public awareness campaigns on an ongoing basis would have a number of benefits.

Best of all, they might well deter terrorists from even attempting an attack. Terrorists are like water, as I argued earlier; they seek the path of least resistance. If carrying out a terrorist attack on mass transit systems is made notably harder, it's less likely that terrorists will make the effort.

These measures might foil an attack before it kills people. It's certainly possible that an alert attendant monitoring surveillance cameras, who's in communication with patrol cops, could see an attack about to unfold, immediately communicate the danger to the police, and help to catch a terrorist before he's able to strike.

They can certainly help to limit the death, injury, and destruction that an attack can cause. The quicker the response time to an attack, the lesser the consequences in terms of lives lost, wounds inflicted, and destruction caused.

They also can help to catch or, at least, identify perpetrators and accomplices after an attack. The ubiquitous underground surveillance cameras in London were invaluable in identifying and tracking down the terrorists there.

Finally, these measures can reassure a nervous public that the government is vigilant, resolute, and competent enough to protect them against danger. A key goal of terrorists is to strike fear and uncertainty in the hearts and minds of the citizenry. The more people who believe that their government is doing everything possible to protect them, the less likely they are to be terrorized, which, after all, is the purpose of terrorism.

The fact that an attack on mass transit systems is so easy to carry out and so hard to prevent is no excuse for not doing everything within our power to make it harder to carry out and less likely to be attempted. In fact, it's a powerful argument for doing just that.

Just before Christmas 2005, the TSA announced a pilot program to expand air marshals' duties to include teaming with uniformed TSA inspectors, local police officers, and bomb-sniffing dogs to patrol subways, bus terminals, and train stations. Inevitably, there were glitches, mostly because of inadequate DHS consultations and communication with local officials. But the idea beyond the program is unassailable, and the implementation of the program was commendable. TSA is, indeed, the *Transportation* Security Administration, so more must be done to secure other, even more vulnerable transportation modes, such as mass transit. But five years after 9/11 and three years after the creation of the Department of Homeland Security, it is past time to pilot programs that should have been put in place long ago.

CRITICAL INFRASTRUCTURE AND "SOFT" TARGETS

CRITICAL INFRASTRUCTURE

Potential terrorist targets vary in terms of the death, destruction, and economic damage an attack against them could cause. Certain sites and sectors are deemed to be "critical infrastructure" because their continued smooth functioning is so necessary to the security, prosperity, and psyche of the nation that a devastating attack against any of them would be catastrophic for the country as a whole. The Administration has designated the following sectors as critical infrastructure: agriculture and food, water, public health, emergency services, the defense industrial base, telecommunications, energy, transportation, banking and finance, chemicals and hazardous materials, and postal and shipping services.[1] In addition, certain national monuments and icons such as the Washington Monument and the Statue of Liberty, certain government facilities, and certain private buildings are defined as "key assets" because they are likewise critical to the psychic well-being and stability of the nation.

The size and scale of America's critical infrastructure and key assets is so vast that the challenge of adequately securing them all is enormous. There are nearly 2 million farms and some 87,000 food processing plants. There are 1,800 federal reservoirs and 1,600 municipal waste water facilities. There are 5,800 registered hospitals. There are "first responders"—police and fire departments, emergency medical services, and rescue teams—in 87,000 U.S. localities. Some 250,000 firms in more than 200 different industries supply the components, weapons, systems, and other support services that the Pentagon depends upon to defend the United States and our interests around the world. The telecommunications sector runs on some 2 billion miles of cable. There are 2,800 power plants, and 300,000 sites that produce or refine oil and natural gas. There are 5,000 public airports, more than 120,000 miles of railroad, nearly 600,000 highway bridges, 2 million miles of pipelines, 300 inland or coastal ports, and more than 500 operators of mass transit systems. There are more than 27,000 banks and other such financial institutions. There are 66,000 chemical plants. There are 137 million different postal and shipping delivery sites. In terms of key assets, there are nearly 6,000 historic buildings; more than 100 commercial nuclear power plants; 80,000 dams; 3,000 facilities owned and/or operated by the government, and nearly 500 skyscrapers.[2] In the Internet Age, functions, processes, and systems within each such sector, and functions, processes, and systems between and among these sectors are linked to each other by networked computer systems. This connectivity increases efficiency and, therefore, economic productivity, but it makes our key infrastructure and assets easier to penetrate, compromise, and cripple.

To cite just one example of the potentially devastating effect of an attack on a single element of our critical infrastructure, the Environmental Protection Agency has estimated that there are more than 100 chemical plants in the United States that, if attacked under just the right set of circumstances, could expose more than a million people to a toxic gas cloud.[3] The Department of Homeland Security disputes this figure, contending that it overstates the danger.[4] At least, in the scheme of things, carrying out such a deadly attack on a chemical plant is hard to do, but it is so easy to kill millions of Americans by contaminating our food supply that Health and Human Services Secretary Tommy Thompson wondered aloud in his final official press conference why terrorists hadn't already tried to do so.[5] One need only consider the panic and disruption caused by the introduction of tiny quantities of anthrax into the postal system immediately after the September 11 attacks, and the fact that the perpetrator (or perpetrators) has yet to be caught many years later, to understand the potential impact of an attack on critical infrastructure and how difficult it can be to identify and catch those responsible. If terrorists had targeted the levees in New Orleans in the fall of 2005 rather than Hurricane Katrina, the death toll would likewise have approached a thousand; hundreds of thousands of people would likewise have been left homeless, and billions of dollars in economic damage would likewise have been caused.

Adding to the security challenge is the fact that about 85 percent of critical infrastructure assets are owned and/or operated by the private sector. The only way for the federal government to exercise control over them is through legislation or regulation, but both the legislative and regulatory processes are notoriously complex, cumbersome, unpredictable, lengthy, and inefficient.

We know from numerous intelligence reports over the years that terrorists are keenly aware of this rich menu of targets and eager to strike some of them. For example, we now know that terrorists cased the World Bank and the International Monetary Fund in Washington, D.C., the Citigroup buildings and the New York Stock Exchange in New York City, and Prudential Financial in northern New Jersey, prompting the Department of Homeland Security to raise the alert level in the summer of 2004. Iyman Faris was arrested for casing the Brooklyn Bridge in 2003 in apparent preparation for a terrorist attack on that iconic structure. (He was subsequently convicted and sentenced to 20 years in prison.[6])

According to the Director of the FBI:

Poisoning food and water supplies also may be an attractive tactic in the future. Although technologically challenging, a successful attempt might cause thousands of casualties, sow fear among the U.S. population, and undermine public confidence in the food and water supply. . . . Attacks against high-tech businesses would cripple information technology and jeopardize thousands of jobs. The financial sector now depends on telecommunications for most of its transactions. Disruption of critical telecommunications nodes—either physically or through cyber means—would create severe hardships until services could be restored. Failures caused intentionally could persist for longer durations, creating difficult repairs and recovery, and intensifying uncertainty and economic losses . . . there have been a variety of threats suggesting that U.S. energy facilities are being targeted for terrorist attacks . . . Al-Qaeda appears to believe that an attack on oil and gas structures could do great damage to the U.S. economy. The size of major petroleum processing facilities makes them a challenge to secure, but they are also difficult targets given their redundant equipment, robust construction, and inherent design to control accidental explosions. Terrorist planners probably perceive infrastructure such as dams and power lines as having softer defenses than other facilities. Indeed, attacking them could cause major water and energy shortages, drive up transportation costs, and undermine public confidence in the government."[7]

Recognizing the importance of securing critical infrastructure, and the degree to which adequately doing so depends upon access to accurate and timely intelligence, the architects of the Department of Homeland Security wisely set up a separate unit dedicated to this task—the Under Secretariat for Information Analysis and Infrastructure Protection (IAIP). The Office of the Assistant Secretary for Infrastructure Protection was established within this unit, along with that of an Assistant Secretary for Information Analysis. The latter official was to be in charge of accessing, synthesizing, and analyzing intelligence from the Central Intelligence Agency and the rest of the intelligence community concerning threats against the homeland. The IA (Information Analysis) Assistant Secretary was then to share with the chief of Infrastructure Protection that subset of intelligence concerning threats against critical infrastructure and key assets. The IP (Infrastructure Protection) head was then, in turn, to communicate that information as quickly as possible to the owners and operators of those sectors and sites at risk so that such protective steps as might be necessary could be taken.

But after concluding a top-to-bottom review of DHS a few months after taking office in the spring of 2005, Secretary Chertoff took a big step in the wrong direction. He decided to separate the intelligence unit from the infrastructure protection unit.[8] The problem with this was that being in the same unit facilitated the timely sharing of intelligence with those who need it to protect the homeland from a future attack; it also served to help break down the cultural and psychological barrier to information sharing that lay at the heart of the government's failure to prevent the last attack.

Because the size and scope of the nation's critical infrastructure and key assets is so vast, it is simply impossible for the government to ensure that they are all adequately protected. A triage approach must be taken so that its necessarily limited resources are focused on those sectors and sites that are even more "critical" and "key" than the others so designated. In order to take such an approach, there must be a prioritized list of the nation's *most* critical sectors and sites.

Developing such a list was *the* key task given to the Infrastructure Protection unit when the Department of Homeland Security was created in 2003, but lo these many years later, inexcusably, there is still no final list. It took about a year and half to develop a first draft. Members of Congress who saw it dismissed the list as a "joke" and "an exercise in full employment for bureaucrats, rather than a realistic way to make the country safer."[9] Reportedly, the 30,000 or so items on the list included things that, given the core criterion of criticality, clearly shouldn't have been on it, such as garden-variety amusement parks and miniature golf courses, and, reportedly, items that clearly should have been on the list, such as nuclear power plants and chemical facilities, weren't.

Almost a year later, there was still no creditable list of critical infrastructure, and still no final plan in place to protect it. In an October 2005 hearing, the DHS Assistant Secretary for Infrastructure Protection, Robert Stephan, admitted that the interim plan issued earlier in the year gave him a "sinking feeling." He confessed that, "I don't believe (the plan) was accurate; it did not meet President Bush's criteria." Stephan went on to say that he hoped to finalize the plan "*towards*" the first of 2006, conceding that without a final plan "we have no strategic backbone."[10] As of this writing, only a revised draft plan is in place.

Making it even harder to understand why it's taken the department so long to complete this fundamental task is the fact that state governments, private businesses, homeland security enthusiasts, and graduate students have all used information publicly available on the Internet and elsewhere to develop more credible lists. Until the department develops such a list, it is essentially flying blind, as its own top official in this field admits. There is no way for it to determine where it should focus its attention and resources so as to make the most difference in securing the homeland.

As for the private sector, some steps have been taken to increase the security of their respective parts of the nation's critical infrastructure, but for a variety of reasons, commercial businesses have been reluctant to invest the massive amounts of money required to secure themselves.

First of all, there has yet to be an actual terrorist attack on the nation's critical infrastructure. That being so, our national tendency to be reactive rather than proactive when it comes to security leads the commercial sector to conclude that there are more productive ways to spend its necessarily limited capital.

Second, some businesses have been reluctant to work with the Department of Homeland Security to determine the steps that need to be taken to better secure themselves because doing so requires sharing a list of their vulnerabilities, including critical processes, secret formulas, and the like. A number of firms have expressed concerns about whether the department can be trusted to keep such proprietary information confidential. If it were to get into the hands of competitors, businesses' relative market position would be weakened.

Third, some businesses complain that to invest in security measures that their rivals are not required or inclined to invest in would needlessly weaken their competitive position. Only if every business in a given sector makes the same investment does it make sense for any one business to do so, goes the so-called "level playing field" argument.

Finally, the IAIP unit has been plagued by high turnover and a history of strained relations with the private sector. Businesses have complained about micromanagement, insensitivity, poor communication, and ineptitude. For all of these reasons, the nation's most critical sectors and sites are still far more vulnerable to terrorist attacks than they should be. As troubling as it is that the nation as a whole is so vulnerable to another terrorist attack, it is unsettling in the extreme that our critical infrastructure and key assets are likewise still relatively easy to target and penetrate.

Shockingly, illegal aliens have been found to be working at various critical infrastructure sites around the country, demonstrating that businesses fail to do even rudimentary background checks to ensure that those working at such sensitive facilities are American citizens with nothing in their past to indicate that they might pose a terrorist threat. In one sweep alone, the department's Immigration and Customs Enforcement bureau arrested sixty illegal aliens in the spring of 2005 at twelve different critical infrastructure sites, including seven petrochemical plants, three power plants, and a pipeline facility in six different states.[11] There is no evidence to indicate that any of these aliens was a terrorist, thankfully, but any one of them could have been. According to the then head of Immigration and Customs Enforcement bureau (ICE), Michael Garcia, "The aliens arrested in this operation had access to sensitive critical infrastructure locations and therefore pose a serious homeland security threat. Not only are their identities in question, but given their illegal status, these individuals are vulnerable to potential exploitation by terrorist and other criminal organizations."[12] (This was the same Michael Garcia, not incidentally, who thought that I was blowing things out of proportion in my first few months on the job when I launched a criminal investigation after learning that a DHS immigration lawyer had pulled a prank that resulted in the release of an illegal alien convicted of kidnapping.)

In September 2005, three illegal aliens were arrested at a nuclear power plant in Nebraska.[13] Even more incredibly three illegal aliens were arrested the very next month at a *military* base—Fort Bragg in North Carolina. Especially worrisome was that those aliens were not from Mexico or elsewhere in Latin America, but two were from Indonesia and one was from Senegal.[14] As noted earlier in these pages, there are increasing concerns that Mexico in particular, and Latin America in general, are being used by terrorists as transit routes into the United States. It is well established that Indonesia is home to the Al Qaeda-affiliated Jemaah Islamiah, or JI, terror network, and, there are increasing concerns that West Africa, like East Africa before it, is becoming a breeding ground for terrorism.[15] Between April 2004 and September 2005, at least 342 illegal aliens were arrested at 19 sensitive sites around the country.[16]

While some infrastructure owners and operators have taken some steps to protect their respective sectors and sites, it is far too often the case that nothing much has changed. For example, back in 1941, then FBI Director J. Edgar Hoover wrote in the Journal of the American Water Works Association, "It has long been recognized that among public utilities, water supply facilities offer a particularly vulnerable point of attack to the foreign agent,"[17] but nearly sixty-five years later, the Congressional Research Service concluded, "There are no federal standards or agreed upon industry best practices within the water infrastructure sector to govern readiness, response to security incidents, and recovery."[18]

The electric power industry, not having a stockpile of spare transformers, switches, and other critical parts that it would need to restore power if terrorists were to knock out the nation's power grid, is also vulnerable to attack. The good news is that key players such as the North American Electric Reliability Council, the Edison Electric Institute, and more than fifty utilities are working to prepare a database of the necessary inventory and to begin the process of developing a strategic reserve of necessary items, much like the extra stocks of petroleum the government maintains for use in the event of a severe gasoline shortage. The bad news is that the process has only just begun, even though a blackout in the Northeastern United States two summers after the terror attacks demonstrated graphically the vulnerability of the power grid to sabotage.[19]

The effort to develop and stockpile vaccines against bio-terrorism has been hampered by foot-dragging on the part of the department. Project Bioshield was launched in 2004 to encourage the private sector to develop these vaccines by paying drug manufacturers to produce and stockpile them, but the Department of Homeland Security has been slow to determine which among some sixty deadly pathogens are likeliest to interest terrorists, which ones terrorists are likeliest to actually develop, and the number of people who could be infected by any such pathogens that are developed. Absent such determinations, drug manufacturers are loathe to go to the trouble and expense of developing vaccines for which there might not be a market. The upshot of this is that if there were a bio-terror attack, there would be insufficient supplies of vaccines available to public health authorities to treat the infected and to inoculate everyone else.[20]

The nation's vulnerability to cyber attack is well known, yet DHS has consistently given the issue short shrift. A succession of "cyber chiefs" have come and gone at the Department of Homeland Security, with none succeeding in elevating the issue to the top of the nation's security agenda (despite their best efforts to do so). Meanwhile, nearly every month seems to bring another illustration of the peril that we face from an attack launched from cyberspace. To cite one example, due to a flaw in software code, confidential reports of suspected terrorist activity around the country compiled by the Department of Homeland Security were inadvertently posted on the public website of the U.S. Energy Department, available for anyone (including terrorists being surveilled) to see.

To cite another, during my time at the Department of Homeland Security, we looked into whether the department had taken the necessary steps to prevent eavesdropping on its wireless communication devices. Not surprisingly, it had not. Consequently, sensitive cell phone conversations and e-mail messages could be picked up by terrorists. To cite a single sentence from that report, "For example, at the CIS Service Center, we detected wireless signals emanating from the facility in the parking lot, on public roads behind the facility, and the surrounding residences."[21] "CIS" stands for the department's Citizenship and Immigration Services bureau; this sentence means that terrorists positioned near the site could have accessed information from a facility that helps to determine who may reside in this country legally and what benefits they may receive.

It gets worse. Last October, the Inspector General's Office reported that computer systems at both the Customs and Border Protection bureau and the Secret Service are vulnerable to unauthorized penetration.[22] Among other things, the agencies failed to install software that can patch security holes. Of course, CBP is in charge of securing our borders from terrorists and weapons of mass destruction that they might smuggle in to launch a cataclysmic attack. The Secret Service not only protects the President and other senior government leaders from the threat of assassination; it also plays a key role in investigating money laundering and identity theft, two crimes that support terrorist activity.

If the Department of Homeland Security itself is so inept at and lackadaisical about securing its own critical information, how hard can it be for terrorists to gain access to it and to other critical information not in the control of the federal government? According to the FBI Director, "terrorists show a growing understanding of the critical role of information technology in the day-to-day operations of our economy and national security and have expanded their recruitment to include people studying math, computer science, and engineering."[23] According to *Congressional Quarterly*, "Computer systems running dams and pipelines are vulnerable to cyber-attack, and may be the weak leak in the critical infrastructure protection chain."[24]

As noted above, our food supply also remains vulnerable to terrorist attack. While some efforts have been made in the last few years to tighten security, not nearly enough has been done. Indeed, according to the GAO, "agricultural inspections at ports of entry—the first line of defense against the entry of foreign animal and plant diseases—have declined over the past two years at a time when imports have increased."[25] When the Department of Homeland Security was created in 2003, primary responsibility for inspecting agricultural products was transferred to it from the U.S. Department of Agriculture (USDA). There were almost 41 million agricultural inspections at ports of entry in fiscal year 2002 when the Agriculture Department was largely in charge of the process, as compared to 37.5 million two years later under the aegis of the Department of Homeland Security.[26] According to the GAO, foreign animal disease training is not required for USDA-accredited veterinarians, even though they are likely to be called upon to respond if there's a terrorist attack on livestock. Only 26 percent of graduates of U.S. veterinary schools have taken a course on how to spot foreign animal diseases.[27]

In a surprising and dramatic burst of candor, a former high-level White House adviser on homeland security testified before the Senate, "A cleverly designed terrorist attack against a TIH [toxic inhalation hazard] chemical target would be no more difficult to perpetrate than was the simultaneous hijacking of four commercial aircraft by 19 terrorists . . . the loss of life could easily equal that which occurred on September 11, 2001—and might even exceed it by an order of magnitude or more. . . . The voluntary security enhancements implemented by many of the larger chemical firms . . . are a step in the right direction but are insufficient because of their limited scope . . . it is a fallacy to think that profit-maximizing corporations engaged in a trade as inherently dangerous as the manufacture and shipment of TIH chemicals will ever voluntarily provide a level of security that is appropriate given the larger external risk to society as a whole."[28]

It is a step in the right direction—a dangerously belated step—that even the chemical industry and the current leadership of the Department of Homeland Security are beginning to acknowledge that voluntary industry compliance with agreed upon security standards is insufficient in the age of terrorism.

The American Chemistry Council, an industry trade group, developed a "Responsible Care Security Code" in 2002 that was meant to provide voluntary guidelines as to how chemical plants could better secure themselves against a potential terrorist attack. Since the terror attacks, industry members have spent more than $2 billion to implement various protective steps outlined in the code,[29] but according to the Department of Homeland Security's chief infrastructure protection official, "while most companies have been very eager to cooperate with the department, it has become clear that the entirely voluntary efforts and this good faith of these companies alone will not sufficiently address security across the entire sector. . . . Some of them do not allow us the opportunity to do a complete vulnerability assessment while we're there. Some of them let us take a look around, offer some observations, and then move on to the next."[30]

It's troubling enough that not every chemical company in the voluntary program fully cooperates with the Department of Homeland Security. What's even more troubling is that about 20 percent of the chemical plants deemed by the department to be high-risk do not participate in the program at all. In the words of the key DHS official, the owners of these plants "may or may not be taking appropriate precautions, making appropriate investments. There's just no way to determine or gauge the effectiveness of those measures, if they are being taken."[31]

Accordingly, buttressed by the support of the American Chemistry Council, the Department of Homeland Security has concluded that regulations are needed to require that the entire chemical industry take certain security measures.[32] While this development is certainly to be welcomed, it raises the question as to why the department has failed to use the regulatory or legislative processes to impose mandates on the other elements of critical infrastructure. Is it reasonable to believe that voluntary measures and self-assessment work any better in other industries that, if attacked, would likewise result in death, injury, and destruction on a catastrophic scale?

While we wait for the regulatory process to play itself out, at least one in five of the most dangerous chemical plants in America will continue to be dangerously vulnerable to terrorist attack. The security of everything else on the critical infrastructure list will depend upon the "good faith" of companies that, all too often, put a higher premium on profit than security.

⊕

It's one thing for the government to assert its regulatory authority; it's quite another for it to exercise its authority vigorously. The former without the latter is meaningless. If anything, it can be *more* dangerous for the government to have regulatory power that it does not exercise because it can lead policymakers and private citizens alike to think that we're safer than we really are.

To illustrate the point, consider the results of yet another revealing ABC News undercover investigation, this one of security at nuclear research reactors at twenty-five college campuses around the country in October 2005. Unbeknownst to most Americans, I dare say, certain universities—including MIT, the University of Florida, the University of Wisconsin, Texas A&M, Ohio State, and Purdue—have nuclear reactors. Most are left over from the Cold War, and they were built to show that nuclear power could be used for peaceful purposes. At least four of the facilities visited by the news team use highly enriched uranium that can be devastatingly deadly, but even uranium that is not highly enriched can pose a mortal danger if that material makes its way into the wrong hands. Lowly enriched uranium could be mixed with explosives to make a dirty bomb that could endanger crowded urban and suburban areas near those campuses.

Only two of the college facilities had armed guards. Where there were security guards, in one instance a guard appeared to be asleep. None of the facilities had metal detectors. Many facilities permitted vehicles to get close to the reactor buildings without first inspecting them for explosives. At Ohio State, Purdue, and the Universities of Florida and Wisconsin, the undercover team was able to enter secure areas without first undergoing a background check. Nor were the large bags they were carrying inspected beforehand. At the University of Florida, the investigators were given a guided tour by the reactor's director, even though they showed up unannounced, and they were permitted to leave their unsearched bags in an office that was connected to where the nuclear reactor was situated.[33]

Ensuring the security of these facilities is the responsibility of the Nuclear Regulatory Commission, not the Department of Homeland Security, but the point is that unexercised regulatory authority is no regulation at all.

If the Department of Homeland Security took security as seriously as it should, the authority to regulate all critical sectors and sites should lie with it. Diffusing homeland security-related functions throughout the government can create its own problems. After all, the department was born out of the conviction that all such functions should be housed in a Department of Homeland Security.

SOFT TARGETS

For all the vulnerabilities that remain, it is more difficult than ever for terrorists outside the United States to slip in and launch another attack against the homeland by hijacking another airplane, smuggling a weapon of mass destruction into a seaport, blowing up a bus or a subway station, or poisoning our food or water supply. To varying degrees, each of these potential targets has been hardened, and the homeland as a whole is at least somewhat more secure as a result.

The good news stops there. The bad news is that the hardening of these targets has simply increased the appeal of shopping malls, sports arenas, hotels, restaurants, bars and nightclubs, movie theaters, housing complexes, and other "soft" targets that remain relatively unprotected against terror attacks.

To be sure, from what we know of Al-Qaeda's past deeds and future plans, they prefer to carry out spectacular attacks that can kill thousands or even millions of people and cause millions of dollars of collateral economic damage. Not only would the pain and suffering inflicted on us "infidels" be greater, but such attacks have an outsized "shock-and-awe" effect that serves to glorify the terrorists themselves and the cause they serve. Such attacks can galvanize the global terror network and awaken and inspire cells already within the United States and those outside trying to get in to take up the bloodstained jihadist banner here on the soil of their chief enemy. And, carrying out another 9/11-style attack in the United States would put the lie to all the whistling past the graveyard talk that Al-Qaeda is a spent force, the homeland has been secured, and the war on terror here has been all but won.

Terrorists are nothing if not determined, adaptable, and resourceful. If it is harder to strike one kind of target than another, they will eventually strike the easier target. Indeed, it is a marvel that terrorists haven't already struck soft targets in the United States. Such attacks are commonplace throughout the Middle East and South Asia, and they are becoming increasingly routine in parts of Southeast Asia, Russia, and Africa. Periodic intelligence reports raise concerns that terrorists have contemplated carrying out such attacks here and have plotted to do so.

For example, there were reports in October 2004 that American troops in Iraq had discovered a few months earlier two computer disks containing photographs, an evacuation plan, and other crisis management-related information regarding eight school districts in six U.S. states. The districts identified were those in Ft. Myers, Florida; Salem, Oregon; Jones County, Georgia; Rumson and Franklin Township in New Jersey; Birch Run in Michigan; and San Diego, California. (The remaining California district was not identified.)[34] Authorities stressed at the time that no link to terrorism had been found, but alarm bells rang nonetheless, especially because the information surfaced around the time of the deadly siege of a school in Beslan, Russia by Chechen terrorists, in which 340 people (mostly children) were slain. The FBI and the Department of Education have warned schools of terrorist casing and targeting activity.[35] Hundreds of two-way radios for communications between school bus drivers and dispatchers have been stolen in two states, prompting fears that terrorists might be plotting to kidnap and kill schoolchildren.[36] Heightening fears of a potential attack on American schools, Al Qaeda has claimed "the right to kill four million Americans, including one million children"[37] Some 53 million children attend school every day in America, about a fifth of the national population.[38] A poll released in February 2005 found that 92 percent of the school-based police officers who responded to the survey considered schools to be potential terror targets, and 74 percent of them thought that their own school was inadequately prepared for a terrorist attack.[39]

Apartment complexes have been targeted, and synagogues have been threatened.[40] Methods of attack such as suicide bombings, car or truck bombs, and sniper fire have all been thought by intelligence analysts and law enforcement experts to be particularly attractive means of launching attacks against softer targets here at home. FBI Director Robert Mueller has cautioned,

> We must not assume . . . that al-Qaeda will rely only on tried and true methods of attack. As attractive as a large-scale attack that produced mass casualties would be for al-Qaeda, and as important as such an attack is to its credibility among its supporters and sympathizers, target vulnerability and the likelihood of success are increasingly important to the weakened organization. . . . Multiple small-scale attacks against soft targets—such as

banks, shopping malls, supermarkets, apartment buildings, schools and universities, churches and places of recreation and entertainment—would be easier to execute and would minimize the need to communicate with the central leadership, lowering the risks of detection.[41]

While an attack on a soft target is unlikely to cause a huge number of deaths or devastating economic loss, in another sense such an attack could have an even greater impact than one on a traditional, "hard" target. Because there's never been a terrorist attack on a soft target in the United States, the psychological effect would likely be disastrous, even if the casualty toll were relatively low. Especially if the attack were to take place outside a major city that is already considered to be a prime terror target—New York, Washington, D.C., Los Angeles, Chicago, say—the collective national psyche would be traumatized. For the first time, every single American, wherever he or she lived, would feel equally at risk of and vulnerable to terror attacks. A single suicide bomber in a shopping center in Topeka, or a single bomb carrying car rammed into a movie complex in Omaha, could bring the nation to its psychic knees.

Adding to the appeal such scenarios hold for terrorists, precious little can be done to prevent them in a society like ours that rightly values personal liberty so highly. Terror attacks in shopping malls, restaurants, and the like are everyday, fact of life occurrences in Israel, and so the Israelis have come to accept countermeasures like metal detectors, bomb sniffing dogs, armed police patrols, and undercover surveillance teams on the lookout for suspicious looking people and suspicious behavior.

In America, by way of contrast, the few security guards that there are at soft targets tend to be unarmed, untrained, and unmotivated. Camera surveillance systems (when they are in place at all) tend to be monitored only irregularly, and when the cameras are monitored, the security guards tend to focus more on potential thieves and trouble makers than potential terrorists. Absent an actual attack on a soft target here in this country, the American people simply won't tolerate the kinds of draconian countermeasures that Israelis accept without complaint.

The upshot is a deadly double irony. The very fact that there hasn't yet been an attack on a soft target in the United States increases the danger of one. And, the harder we harden hard targets, the more likely an attack on a soft target becomes.

CHAPTER SEVEN

THE FAILURE OF INTELLIGENCE

Thanks to the work of the 9/11 Commission, we now know that there was intelligence available to our analysts before September 11 indicating that an attack on the homeland was imminent. In the chilling and now iconic words of then CIA chief George Tenet, "the system was blinking red"[1] all summer long. Most of the intelligence pointed to an attack on American interests abroad, admittedly, but there were bits and pieces of information here and there indicating Al Qaeda's desire to strike on American soil, *and* an intent to do so by means of airplanes. The attacks are still rightly said to have represented a massive intelligence failure because the proverbial dots weren't connected in time. Had someone somewhere in our government been responsible for putting the bits and pieces of relevant intelligence here and there together, it would have been clear before the terrorists attacked that they were planning to hijack airplanes and fly them into symbolic political and economic targets here in the United States.

A key reason—arguably, *the* key reason—for creating the Department of Homeland Security was to connect the proverbial dots in a timely fashion in the future. With the Department of Homeland Security in place, the next time different government agencies picked up indications of a terrorist plot against the homeland, there would be one government agency with access to everything each relevant agency has and with the mandate and horizon-wide perspective to put it all together into a coherent, actionable whole. With such an overarching radar and early warning system in place, plots could be foiled or, at least, steps could be taken to better protect targets and to limit the deaths, injuries, and economic damage that might be caused if an attack were to occur despite our very best efforts to prevent it.

But in this critical regard, too, the department has failed to live up to its promise. From the very beginning, the Information Analysis (IA) unit of the Department of Homeland Security proved to be a joke, a bad joke. Inattentive, inexpert, and parsimonious Department senior managers refused to allocate a sufficient number of employee slots to IA so that it could hire enough analysts to sift through the massive reams of intelligence information for homeland security-related threats. Many of the slots that were allocated went unfilled for months and months, first because of the lengthy secret clearance process, and eventually because word got around the tight-knit and hyper-status-conscious intelligence community that taking a job at the Department of Homeland Security was *not* a career-enhancing move. There was insufficient office space for the handful of analysts already on board, much less the additional ones needed to get the job done, and there were too few computers with connectivity to the rest of the intelligence community to provide IA analysts with access to the various dots that they were supposed to be connecting. As for hard-copy classified material, there were too few secure safes to store it all, and no one had bothered to establish the policies and procedures necessary for handling and processing it. Even when threat information was already in the public domain—so-called open source information, such as the threat from unexamined cargo in the hold of passenger aircraft—the department's intelligence experts seemed to be unaware of it.

All of this came out in painfully embarrassing detail when the first IA chief Paul Redmond, a storied CIA veteran who played the key role in unmasking Aldrich Ames as a Soviet mole, was grilled by a congressional committee a few months after DHS came into being.

SHAYS: Of the 100 that you hope to staff, how many do you have today?
REDMOND: I believe we have 25 or 26 . . .
SHAYS: Was it your testimony that you didn't hire more because you didn't have space? . . .
REDMOND: We have not hired them, we have not got them aboard because we do not have space for them.

SHAYS: Do you feel that, given the incredible importance of your office,
   that that's a pretty surprising statement to make before this committee?
REDMOND: It's a difficult statement to make . . ."[2]

Difficult, indeed. Shortly after this hearing, Redmond resigned "for health
reasons." Washington insiders diagnosed the malady as the dreaded and
nearly always fatal, "candor" disease.

It is no wonder that the Department of Homeland Security's Information Analysis unit so quickly became a joke. Its effectiveness was undercut
even before it got off the ground when the Administration established yet
another entity—the Terrorist Threat Integration Center (TTIC)—and gave
it, too, the responsibility to access and synthesize the collective intelligence
community's homeland security related threat information.

In a message to Congress transmitting legislation to create the Department of Homeland Security, the President said that, among other things, the
department would "analyze homeland security intelligence from multiple
sources." Among the key arguments in the message for creating the new department was to "improve our homeland security by minimizing duplication of efforts, improving coordination, and combining functions that are
currently fragmented and inefficient. The new Department [will] allow us to
have more security officers in the field working to stop terrorists and fewer
resources in Washington managing duplicative activities that drain critical
homeland security resources."[3]

Yet before the department opened its doors for business on March 1, 2003,
the President announced in his January 28, 2003 State of the Union Address an
intention to create TTIC to ensure "that intelligence information from all
sources is shared, integrated, and analyzed seamlessly—and then acted upon
quickly."[4] Headed by a longtime CIA officer reporting to the Director of the
CIA, the Terrorist Threat Integration Center brought together representatives
from the CIA, the FBI, the Pentagon, and the Information Analysis unit of the
Department of Homeland Security to "fuse and analyze all-source information
related to terrorism."* According to the White House fact sheet announcing the
initiative, TTIC would "optimize use of terrorist-related threat information, expertise, and capabilities to conduct threat analysis and inform collection strate-
gies; create a structure that ensures information sharing across agency lines;

---

* State Department analysts were subsequently added.

integrate terrorist-related information collected domestically and abroad in order to form the most comprehensive possible threat picture; and be responsible and accountable for providing terrorist threat assessments for our national leadership."[5]

Just months after the disastrous Paul Redmond hearing, his successor, retired Marine Corps officer Bill Parish, found himself seated at a congressional hearing with the head of TTIC, CIA veteran John Brennan. In their opening remarks, each served only to confirm the duplication between the Department of Homeland Security's mission and that of the Terrorist Threat Integration Center. The TTIC Director said that, "The officers in TTIC have full access to the information systems and databases of their parent agencies. Their primary responsibility is to analyze all threat information available to the U.S. government, to connect the dots if you will, and make their findings and analysis available to those outside of TTIC who are responsible for preventing and defending against terrorist attacks."[6] To the same effect, the Department of Homeland Security's Assistant Secretary for Information Analysis said, "Our mission is to obtain the intelligence and provide the necessary analysis and assessment to ensure appropriate actions are taken to protect against terrorist attacks directed to the U.S. homeland."[7]

Understandably, this prompted the Congressional panel to probe for substantive differences in the respective roles of IA and TTIC, ultimately to no avail. After hours of probing, the TTIC Director was reduced to incoherence, mouthing words with no real meaning.

> REP. DONNA CHRISTENSEN (D.V.I) (a Congresswoman): . . . I know
> that Mr. Brennan [the then TTIC chief] has been asked in various
> ways over and over again, but I understand the need for the coordina-
> tion that takes place at TTIC. But why is it better outside the Depart-
> ment of Homeland Security, in your opinion? Why shouldn't it be in
> the Department of Homeland Security?
>
> BRENNAN: Because, as I mentioned earlier, that the overwhelming major-
> ity of information about the terrorist threat comes from abroad. To
> understand that information, it takes an understanding of that envi-
> ronment, that overseas environment. That is not the Secretary of
> Homeland Security's responsibility.
>
> CHRISTENSEN: But, why can't the same analysts that are now sitting
> where your office is, coming from all the different agencies to take in
> this information and analyze it, why aren't they sitting in the Depart-
> ment of Homeland Security? The same—the CIA analysts, the FBI an-
> alysts, State Department analysts, why aren't they best seated in the

Department of Homeland Security, which is where the information is going to be acted on?

BRENNAN: Many officers from those agencies are, in fact, sitting in the Department of Homeland Security. But, TTIC has those partner agencies as the TTIC foundation, and so we need to have those different perspectives not just because of different information systems and databases that they bring, but they also bring a number of different perspectives that really help our understanding of the terrorist threat and to connect the dots."[8]

What?

At a minimum, then, TTIC was duplicating the work of the Department of Homeland Security's intelligence unit, even though the President had pledged that creating DHS would "improve our homeland security by minimizing the duplication of efforts, improving coordination, and combining functions that are currently fragmented and inefficient."[9] But, duplication, in and of itself, is the least of the problems.

More important, the danger of having more than one entity responsible for a critical function such as connecting the dots is that a given dot might slip through the cracks in the confusion over which entity is responsible for what, and over the degree to which information can be shared among agencies. We now know from tragic experience that every dot counts, and that even a single dot not connected to the others on a necessarily pointillist canvas might be *the* dot that brings an otherwise opaque terrorist threat picture into sharper focus.

Furthermore, the more diffuse and unclear the lines of authority, the less clear it is who's to be held accountable when things go wrong. This is important because we've learned from bitter experience that unaccountable government is unresponsive government and ineffective government.

Moreover, if any agency is to be given responsibility for assembling, synthesizing, and analyzing all of the nation's intelligence concerning threats against the homeland, shouldn't it be the Department of HOMELAND SECURITY? If not, what's the point of having one? As a practical matter—by virtue of the fact that the Director of TTIC was a CIA officer reporting to the CIA Director—the Central Intelligence Agency was given the lead on the job of connecting the dots so as to prevent future terror attacks. But, after all, it was the CIA that missed the dots last time: What exactly is it that gives anyone confidence that the CIA's analysis is any better today than it was then? Is it that the intelligence community has since been completely reorganized, a whole new Office of Director of National Intelligence (DNI) created, and the CIA Director subordinated to the DNI? Surely not, since the story of the Department of Homeland Security in a nutshell is that reorganizing government in and of itself does not solve problems. Indeed, if anything, reorganizing government is likelier to create still more problems.

Finally, by giving TTIC the lead responsibility for homeland security-related intelligence, and by doing so even before the Department of Homeland Security officially opened its doors, the Administration virtually guaranteed that the department's Information Analysis unit would be a failure.

As if giving the CIA lead responsibility for integrating homeland security-related threat information was not enough to undercut the Department of Homeland Security and its intelligence unit, the Administration compounded the problem by giving the FBI lead responsibility for another critical task that as a matter of law and policy ought to have been performed by the department. One of the key pre-9/11 problems was that there were a dozen different terrorist watch lists in the federal government, and agencies did not freely share their watch lists with each other. The CIA had "watch-listed" two of the nineteen hijackers, but neither the State Department's watch list nor that of the FBI had any of the hijackers' names. Had there been a single, comprehensive, accurate, up-to-date list of all known and suspected terrorists that could be accessed by all relevant U.S. government agencies, the State Department's consular officers abroad would have known to deny at least those hijackers' visa applications, in which case they would never have gotten into the country in the first place. If, nevertheless, the hijackers had somehow managed to get into the country, a master list could have helped the FBI to track them down and arrest, or, at least, monitor them before they could carry out the attacks.

No fewer than six responsibilities spelled out in the Homeland Security Act for the Information Analysis unit strongly implied that the Department of Homeland Security was to take the lead on consolidating the different federal watch lists. For example, IA was to "assess, receive and analyze . . . information . . . and to *integrate* such information to identify, detect, and assess terrorist threats; . . . review, analyze, and make recommendations for improvements in the policies and procedures governing the sharing of homeland security information; and . . . [to] establish and utilize secure communications to disseminate information acquired and analyzed by the Department."[10] While, admittedly, the term "watch list" was not mentioned explicitly, what could be more critical homeland security related "information" than the names of people known or suspected to be terrorists?

Even though the department was given the implicit responsibility by Congress to consolidate the terrorist watch lists, the White House issued a Presidential Directive[11] six months after the department became operational creating a Terrorist Screening Center (TSC) to do the job. Like TTIC (which subsequently was renamed the "National Counterterrorism Center" and housed in a new location off the CIA campus), the TSC was a multi-agency "joint venture," bringing together representatives from the FBI, the CIA, the State Department, and the Homeland Security Department. Unlike TTIC, the Terrorist Screening Center was led by the FBI, with the director of the center reporting to the Director of the FBI.

As Inspector General of the department, I regarded it as my duty to determine whether the Homeland Security Department was living up to its legal responsibilities and, even more important, the expectation that it would be effective in securing the homeland against the possibility of future attack. Accordingly, I asked my Information Technology expert, Frank Deffer, and his staff to examine the terrorist watch list consolidation issue. Not surprisingly, they found that DHS had ceded the field without a fight. Far from contesting the FBI's taking the lead on this issue, the department's senior managers insisted that this was right and proper, and that the Department of Homeland Security had only a subordinate role to play.

First, the department essentially argued that it was incompetent to perform this core homeland security-related function! In the words of the then Under Secretary of Homeland Security for Information Analysis and Infrastructure Protection,

> We agree with the [Office of Inspector General] report in general that effective consolidation of the terrorist watch lists maintained by different government agencies is a critical step in defending the nation against future attacks. However, we strongly disagree with the report's premise that either DHS or IAIP has the lead responsibility within the federal government for consolidating terrorist watch lists. . . . At the time the President was signing HSPD–6, DHS was not even a year old and the IAIP [Information Analysis and Infrastructure Protection] Directorate was still addressing significant resource and staffing challenges associated with the start up of the Department. Given these constraints, and in order to move expeditiously, it was determined at the highest levels of the government that DOJ [the Department of Justice] was in a better position to take on the responsibility for coordinating the federal government's effort in

watch list consolidation. The President, the Secretary and others considered numerous factors. As your report correctly points out, at that time IAIP did not have the personnel or the facility to lead such an important task. Therefore after careful consideration, the White House decided that DOJ should lead this effort."[12]

Second, the department argued that, even if it were capable of leading the terrorist watch list consolidation effort, it lacked the legal authority to do so once the President issued his directive. Tellingly, the department's lawyers refused to give my team and me a legal opinion to this effect. There's a good reason why no lawyer would sign her name to an opinion claiming that the Department of Homeland Security lacked the legal authority to consolidate terrorist watch lists—the department did, indeed, have such authority, notwithstanding the presidential directive. Any first-year law student knows that a statute—a bill passed by both houses of Congress and then signed into law by the President—has more legal weight than a presidential directive or any other kind of Executive Order. So, to the extent that there was any conflict between the presidential directive creating the TSC and the Homeland Security Act, which implicitly gives the job of consolidating terrorist watch lists to the Homeland Security Department, the Homeland Security Act controls.

But, in fact, as we pointed out in our report, there is no conflict between the law and the presidential directive. HSPD–6, by its own terms, makes it clear that it was not intended to undercut the authority of the Department of Homeland Security under the Homeland Security Act. HSPD–6 was "intended only to improve the internal management of the executive branch" and "does not alter existing authorities or responsibilities of department and agency heads. . . ."[13] If he had chosen to, then Secretary Ridge could have insisted on playing a leadership role in the watch list consolidation process, leaving only the mechanics of the process and implementation to the FBI.

Just as Ridge acquiesced in the CIA's takeover of the role of chief homeland security-related intelligence integrator and analyst, he likewise acquiesced in the FBI's takeover of the role of terrorist watch list consolidator. The upshot was that the Department of Homeland Security became at most a bit player in these two core homeland security tasks. The two agencies that were most at fault for failing to detect and foil the last terror attacks were allowed to remain in charge of tasks critical to the prevention of future ones.

As Inspector General, it was my obligation to share our findings and recommendations not only with the department and the Congress, but also with the American people. After all, it is the people's government, and the people have the right to know whether it's working effectively and, if not, to hold government leaders accountable for poor performance. It was my practice, then, to share a draft of any report with the Secretary, the Deputy Secretary, and whichever other senior leaders were in charge of the given program or operation being evaluated, and to give them thirty days to make any comments. If the department could show that we were wrong about something or that there was additional information that we should consider, we would modify the report accordingly before sending a final copy to the applicable congressional committees and then producing a version of the report for public release. We were always careful to write the public version in such a way as to give the American people as much information as possible, without disclosing classified information that might aid terrorists in exploiting the nation's security vulnerabilities.

After receiving the comments of the department's intelligence chief, we were ready to send the full report to Capitol Hill and then, shortly thereafter, to publish a condensed version for the general public, but the Under Secretary for Information Analysis and Infrastructure Protection, retired Marine General Frank Libutti, demanded that I delay public release until a meeting could be arranged between Secretary Ridge and me to discuss the contents.

This was extraordinary and, therefore, suspicious. In nearly two years, the Secretary had never requested a briefing on any of our work. He already had a copy of the full report, so it was unlikely that a briefing could tell him any more about the contents than he could learn simply by reading the document itself. I strongly suspected that the real reason he wanted to meet before a public version of the report was released was to intimidate me into not releasing it.

While suspicious of the motivation, the Secretary being the Secretary, I felt obliged to accommodate his request—at least within reason. I told Libutti that the Secretary was certainly entitled to the courtesy of a briefing if he had so requested, but that I couldn't delay the report unreasonably to accommodate his schedule. I'd have to get an appointment with him within two weeks; otherwise, I'd release the report. If the Secretary was too busy to see me during this time frame, I'd be happy to brief him by phone or to brief, in his stead, the Deputy Secretary or any other designee. I added, though, that if the real motivation was to get me to not release the report at all, the meeting would be a waste of everyone's time.

This frank exchange with the Under Secretary had the desired effect. Within a day, I'd gotten an appointment to see the Secretary, and I asked my investigative team to put together a full briefing. The appointed day arrived,

and we assembled ourselves in the Secretary's cramped, windowless conference room in the non-descript brick office building on the campus of the
World War II–era naval complex that the department used as its Washington
headquarters. The Secretary, accompanied by his General Counsel and another lawyer, arrived promptly and greeted us politely, in his characteristic,
gentlemanly fashion.

I began by thanking him for seeing us, introducing Frank Deffer and the
other members of my team, and asking the lead investigator to start off. A
few minutes into the presentation the Secretary interrupted. "Look, we have
a fundamental disagreement here. You have your lawyers, and I have mine.
And, it's our legal judgment that the department does not have the legal authority to take the lead on consolidating the terrorist watch lists. The President gave that job to the FBI, and that's that."

"Mr. Secretary," I replied respectfully, "we've asked your lawyers to give
us a written opinion to that effect, but they've yet to do so. I think it's clear
why—there's no legal support for that view. You're a lawyer yourself, and
you know, surely, from your first-year studies, that a statute trumps an executive order. The only thing that has more legal weight than a statute is a constitutional provision. So, if there were any conflict between the Homeland
Security Act, which implicitly gives this responsibility to the department's
intelligence shop, and Homeland Security Presidential Directive–6, which
gives the FBI responsibility for setting up the Terrorist Screening Center, the
Homeland Security Act controls. But, as we pointed out in the report and,
orally, to your staff, there is no conflict between the law and the directive. By
its very terms, the directive says it isn't intended to undercut the statute or to
alter existing responsibilities. So, you could take the lead on this if you
wanted to."

"But, you know yourself that IAIP was in no position to handle something this big. We were trying to organize ourselves for a massive new responsibility."

"Agreed, sir," I said, "but this is part of that responsibility. If you didn't
have the resources you needed to get this core homeland security job done,
why not seek them from the Administration and Congress? Why should the
CIA and the FBI be doing jobs that the Department of Homeland Security
was created to do?"

"Are you saying that the President violated the law?" Ridge demanded,
threateningly.

"Look, sir. Nobody's saying the President's violated the law. I'm saying
that you're not carrying out the intent of the law, and you have both the re-

sponsibility and the authority to do so. If you lack the resources to do so, that's a different matter. But, if that's the issue, as I say, it seems to me, respectfully, that you and your team should focus on trying to get them."

It was clear to Ridge that we weren't getting anywhere, so he shifted the discussion to the release of the report, which I'd feared to be the real point of the meeting all along. Somehow, NBC News had gotten a copy of the full report and broadcast a story on it the night before. The segment was brief, but it couldn't have been more dramatic:

> Three years ago, two suspected terrorists known to the U.S. government breezed through security at Dulles Airport [Washington's international airport] and boarded a plane. They had not been put on the government's "no fly" list, and that day, they crashed their plane into the Pentagon. Now in a report obtained by NBC News, a government watchdog warns the problem is still not fixed. . . . The report also criticizes the Department of Homeland Security for "not playing a lead role" in ending turf battles and not forcing agencies to work together on one of the most important post-911 reforms—consolidating all terror watch lists . . . Homeland Security argues the delay in consolidating terrorist watch lists is mostly the responsibility of the FBI. . . . [14]

Needless to say, the leak and the broadcast had only angered Ridge further. "Look, Clark. I'm sure you didn't leak this report, but somebody on the Hill must have. You've been around this town for a while now, so you've got to know that sending a report like this to Congress is tantamount to releasing it to the public. Why do you have to give these reports to the Hill anyway? You know that they're just going to leak them."

"Well, sir, I'm not naïve. You're right. Something explosive like this is bound to be leaked. But there's nothing I can do about that. The applicable congressional oversight committees have a legal right to this information, and I have a legal obligation to provide it to them. I can't ignore my legal obligation simply because somebody up there might leak something before it's time."

"Well, can we at least, to keep this kind of thing from happening in the future, arrange to coordinate our messages, so that your office and our press office characterize these reports the same way?"

"Mr. Secretary," I began, "I'm afraid that I'm not in the 'spin business.' Our reports speak for themselves, and I'm not going to characterize them in any particular way or coordinate them with your press shop. They say what they say. You and your press people can say whatever you want to say about them. That's one reason why we give you copies in advance. You're not blindsided. You know exactly what they're going to say, and you've got time to put the best face on them you can, if that's what you choose to do. But, I won't be a party to that. It's my job to call things as I see them, and, to let the political chips fall where they may."

Predictably, the release of the report created a firestorm. The *Washington Post*'s account was typical:

> The government's effort to consolidate federal agencies' twelve terrorist watch lists into one has all but failed, partly because the Department of Homeland Security has abandoned its responsibility to take the lead on the project, according to a report released yesterday by the department's internal watchdog. . . . The inspector general was blunt in accusing his own department of refusing to take responsibility for the job of consolidating the twelve watch lists, an assignment that he said belonged to the department under the law that established the department two years ago. . . . Homeland Security officials reject the assertion, which has also been made for years by members of Congress, that the department has been too passive in staking out its congressionally mandated role to take the lead in a number of intelligence analysis tasks such as merging watch lists.[15]

Indeed, it is clear that Congress intended for DHS to take the lead on consolidating terrorist watch lists. Congress' own investigative arm, the Government Accountability Office, released a report in April 2003, the month after the department became fully operational, recommending just that. Indeed, according to the GAO, the department's own leaders agreed with the recommendation at the time, and they were taking steps to implement it:

> In his oral comments, DHS's Chief Information Officer stated that the department now has responsibility for watch list consolidation. Additionally, the CIO generally described DHS's plans for watch list consolidation and agreed that our recommendations were consistent with the steps he described. In light of DHS's assumption of responsibility for watch list consolidation, we have modified our recommendations by directing them [from the White House Office of Homeland Security] to the DHS Secretary.[16]

Lacking a central role in the integration and analysis of homeland security-related intelligence, the Department of Homeland Security was left to hope that it was getting all the information it needed from the other intelligence agencies as to threats against the homeland. One slip through the cracks, one failure to share information with DHS, could mean that the agency charged with the responsibility to do everything possible to prevent the next attack would be unaware that another attack was about to come.

In his characteristic, "everything's fine; problems? What problems?" way, Secretary Ridge assured an inquiring television anchor that DHS was right on top of things.

> MARGARET WARNER (NewsHour with Jim Lehrer): You gave a speech this morning in which you talked about the accomplishments of your department. What would you say, if you could tick off two or three, made America measurably safer just in the year since the Department's been created?
>
> RIDGE: Right off the bat, more and better information sharing, not just across the federal level, but down to our state and local partners and into the private sector. . . .
>
> WARNER: Now, your own inspector general had a recent report saying, complaining about the fact that—for instance, just let's take intelligence from abroad, real intelligence—that though HS [the Department of Homeland Security] was supposed to be the central part in this—that in fact now it's being run by the FBI and the CIA and that in his words he said that makes it difficult. He said, "Ensuring that the DHS has access to the intelligence it needs to prevent and/or respond to terrorist threats is under such circumstances an even harder challenge than it otherwise would be."
>
> RIDGE: Well, his conclusion is contrary to our day-to-day experience—of course he's not involved in that. We have analysts working at the threat integration center—we have people at the terrorist screening center. We can go back to the CIA and FBI and give them requirements. All right, you gave us this information, but we'd like to ask you these questions or do you have more information in this regard. So again, I think he is not quite as aware as he should be—not saying he's at fault. But on a day-to-day basis, we interact very well. . . .
>
> WARNER: But in other words you are comfortable with essentially having your department be a consumer of the intelligence produced elsewhere?
>
> RIDGE: That's correct. I mean, I think what the inspector general needs to understand is that we are not empowered to collect independently. What he needs to understand is that we are authorized to go back to the collection agencies, the FBI, the CIA, and others, and ask

questions. But, I don't think the American public wants the Department of Homeland Security collecting information."[17]

This exchange captured it all. The Secretary of Homeland Security was "comfortable" receiving whatever intelligence about threats to the homeland that the FBI and the CIA chose to share with him. If unsatisfied with whatever he was told, the Secretary could ask the FBI and the CIA questions! If you had to boil down to one of all the reasons for establishing a Department of Homeland Security, it would be to make sure that next time we don't miss intelligence that indicates a threat to the homeland. If the department was created for this reason, why should anyone—least of all the Secretary of the department—be "comfortable" depending upon the very agencies that failed to see the signs of the last attack?

The Secretary reacted to our conclusions by disputing something we didn't say, confusing important things in the process. We didn't say that the department should be collecting information; we said that it should take the lead on integrating any and all threat information from any and all sources, and that it should take the lead on consolidating the various terrorist watch lists. But, what he *meant* to say was that the department shouldn't be in the business of spying on Americans, and, while certainly true, no one was suggesting that. The department "collects" information all the time, and rightly so. Every time an airport screener, customs inspector, or Border Patrol Agent spots a suspicious person or a suspicious pattern of behavior, the Department of Homeland Security is collecting information that can protect the homeland from another attack. In ignoring the message and attacking the messenger, the Secretary was demonstrating, again, a fundamental lack of understanding of what intelligence is and what role the Department of Homeland Security should play in obtaining it and using it to protect the nation.

Given the problems that we uncovered in the department's intelligence unit at the very start, the fact that the problems only got worse as time went by, and the leadership's consistent refusal even to acknowledge the problems' existence, it was no surprise to me when I found these words in the report of the bipartisan Silberman-Robb commission the President assembled in the wake of the massive intelligence failure in Iraq to examine the nation's entire intelligence apparatus:

> Since its inception Homeland Security has faced immense challenges in collecting information efficiently, making it available to analysts and users both inside and outside the department, and bringing intelligence support to law

enforcement and first responders who seek to act on such information. . . . Homeland Security faces challenges in all four of the roles it plays in the Intelligence Community—as *collector,* analyst, disseminator, and customer [emphasis added]. The Department of Homeland Security has no shortage of intelligence collectors. With 22 agencies, Homeland Security commands more than 180,000 personnel from the U.S. Coast Guard, Customs and Border Protection, Secret Service, Immigration and Customs Enforcement (ICE), Transportation Security Administration, and Office of Infrastructure Protection. ICE has more than 3,000 employees. ICE collects reams of data on foreigners entering the United States and manages the Student and Exchange Visitor System database, which includes information on foreign students studying in the United States. However, whether agencies like ICE are equipped to make this information available to the Intelligence Community in usable form remains unclear. ICE officials explained that they would not give other agencies unfettered access to their databases (despite those agencies' wishes) because of unspecified legal constraints. We find this September 10th approach to information sharing troubling. . . . A critical Homeland Security function is disseminating threat information to law enforcement and other officials at the federal, state, local, and tribal level. The Department of Homeland Security currently faces many difficulties in this regard. According to one Homeland Security official, local law enforcement are currently "shotgunned" by the information flow coming from a variety of federal sources, and confused as to who has the lead in supporting their information and intelligence needs. Senior officials at Homeland Security emphasize that the process of declassifying information takes too long and frequently prevents the department from quickly sharing concrete, actionable information with law enforcement. Instead, law enforcement officials often receive a steady stream of vague threat reporting, unsupported by adequate sourcing, and incapable of serving as a basis for action. Homeland Security's problems with sharing national security information do not end there. Like many other intelligence organizations, Department of Homeland Security officials expressed concerns about the lack of procedures for sharing intelligence across agencies. As an example, Homeland Security officials have expressed concern that they have no mechanism for getting answers to "hot questions" they pose to the FBI and the National Counterterrorism Center [the successor to the Terrorist Threat Integration Center]. . . . Finally, in a variation on a familiar theme, some law enforcement agents at Homeland Security have expressed unwillingness to share operational information out of concern that other agencies might seek to "steal" their cases.[18]

So, the Department of Homeland Security *is* collecting intelligence; it just doesn't always share it with the people in state and local government and in the private sector, who need it to protect the homeland. In addition, far from getting every relevant piece of intelligence the CIA and the FBI have, the Department of Homeland Security is given only what the CIA and the FBI choose to give it.

In his final appearance before a congressional committee as the intelligence unit's third chief in less than three years, retired General Patrick Hughes candidly acknowledged the problems. Noting that the Administration proposed a $21 million budget cut for his directorate, Hughes pleaded with Congress to be supportive of the troubled intelligence agency. Without identifying the culprits, he admitted that some other intelligence agencies continue to keep information from the department, and he gave the Department of Homeland Security a grade of "between five and six" on a scale of one to ten in terms of effectiveness.[19]

To the same effect, in early appearances before Congress, Hughes' successor, veteran CIA official Charlie Allen, acknowledged that the department's intelligence unit is still very much a work in progress almost three years after its creation. It still lacks adequate facilities to carry out its mission, but in the scheme of things, that is the least of IA's problems. More important, the unit has yet to forge a cohesive and effective whole out of the ten varied and disparate intelligence gathering units among the twenty-two different components that make up the Department of Homeland Security. In Allen's words, "they [the different intelligence units] collect a lot of it, but there's a great amount of information that does not get fully disseminated or used as part of trends and patterns and threat streams." Part of the problem is that there's still no commonly agreed threshold as to what constitutes information that's important enough to constitute "homeland security related intelligence."[20]

There are real-world consequences to this internal dysfunction and continuing confusion about exactly what the department's intelligence role is. For example, in the late fall of 2005, the Department of Homeland Security passed on to local officials reports that terrorists in Iraq were plotting with terrorists already in New York City to bomb subway stations. The mayor and police chief eventually went public with this threat information and implemented a number of protective measures. They did so against the advice of DHS, which questioned the reliability of the information at the same time that it was passing the information on. According to news reports, department officials criticized New York officials off the record for acting on the information. The scare ultimately proved to be a hoax, validating DHS' view of the matter.[21]

The incident had the effect of worsening already strained relations between the department and state and local officials in New York and elsewhere in the nation. If the information was deemed credible enough for DHS to pass on to local officials, why should those officials be criticized for acting on it? Intelligence is never perfect. In the age of terror, it's better to be safe than sorry. The consequences of not acting on available intelligence were made plain for all to see when nearly 3,000 people were killed on September 11.

To make bad matters still worse, two e-mails later surfaced indicating that, at the same time that the department was downplaying this threat information and dissuading city officials from acting on it or going public with it, two DHS officials took the information seriously enough to warn their own family and friends against taking the subway. This disclosure raised not only the issue of confusion *within* the department about homeland security-related intelligence, but also the issue of the department's laxity in handling intelligence information, *and* the issue of the department's using intelligence information only to protect those people lucky enough to be related to or friendly with department officials. When the news media got wind of the e-mails and confronted the department's spokesman, his first reaction was to dismiss it. As the day wore on and the intensity of press inquiries increased, the department reversed course and announced the opening of an internal investigation into the apparent misuse of intelligence.

In retrospect, the department's continuing inability to get intelligence right was foreshadowed at the very beginning by what appeared to me even then to be a failure to take intelligence matters as seriously as they should be. During my time at the State Department, I set aside time each morning to read that day's intelligence traffic, or, at least as much of it as a person at my level in the government was permitted to see (which was a lot). Nothing, and I do mean nothing, was more important to me than reading those documents each day. To my mind, I could hardly evaluate the department's effectiveness in advancing the nation's foreign policy interests without knowing as much as possible about the threats to those interests.

Likewise, at the Department of Homeland Security, I would be in no position to determine whether the department was being effective in countering threats to the homeland if I were unaware of those threats. At DHS I would have to settle for a weekly intelligence briefing, given the department's initial organizational problems and the paucity of briefing officers. I would show up religiously at headquarters each week, at the appointed time, eager to learn the details about, say, the latest warning from bin Laden or the latest evidence of terrorist casing activity. All too often in the department's early days, I would be the *only* DHS official to show up. When I asked the briefer about the whereabouts of everyone else, he'd tell me that they'd pleaded "scheduling conflicts" or "pressing business," prompting me to wonder what could be possibly be more important than finding out the very latest about terrorists' activities, plans, intentions, and capabilities.

The importance of getting homeland security-related intelligence right should now be apparent to all. We had the "dots" before the last attack; it's just that no one connected them in time. The Department of Homeland Security's intelligence unit was supposed to fix that, but even its own leaders give it a grade of no better than five or six on a scale of ten. Given the ability and the determination of terrorists to strike again, can we really afford to have only a 50–50 chance of stopping them?

CHAPTER EIGHT

PREPARING FOR A CATASTROPHIC ATTACK

What if terror were to strike again? There is an infinite number of conceivable scenarios, of course, but according to a secret document inadvertently posted on the web, the Department of Homeland Security thinks that the following ones are most likely.

> *Scenario 1:* Terrorists drive a van loaded with a ten-kiloton nuclear bomb into the central business district of a major city and then detonate the device. Depending upon the circumstances, thousands of people could certainly die, thousands more would be sickened, and the economic impact would run into the hundreds of billions.
>
> *Scenario 2:* Anthrax-making laboratories have been found in Al Qaeda training camps in Afghanistan. Intelligence reporting indicates that terrorists continue to be interested in weaponizing the virus, and, of course, the mystery of the anthrax attacks in the United States shortly after 9/11 remains unsolved to this day. Against that scary real-world backdrop, another scenario is that terrorists spray an aerosolized form of anthrax from a van into three cities, and then two more cities shortly afterwards. Thirteen thousand people would die, and, again, the economic impact would number in the billions.

Scenario 3: Terrorists release pneumonic plague into an airport bathroom, a sports arena, and a train station in a major city and the contagion spreads rapidly. Some 2,500 people would die, and 7,000 people would be injured. The economic impact is estimated to be in the billions.

Scenario 4: Terrorists fly a small aircraft over a packed college football stadium, spraying a chemical blister agent. One hundred fifty people would die; 70,000 would be hospitalized. The economic impact would be half a billion dollars.

Scenario 5: Terrorists attack oil refineries with bombs and grenades. Then, they bomb cargo containers, igniting ships, including one carrying toxic chemicals. Three hundred fifty people would die; 1,000 people would be hospitalized. The economic impact would run in the billions.

Scenario 6: Terrorists release gas into the ventilation systems of three large office buildings in a major city. Six thousand people would die; 350 would be injured. The economic impact would be $300 million.

Scenario 7: Terrorists infiltrate an industrial storage facility and detonate a chlorine gas storage tank, releasing toxic fumes downwind. Seventeen thousand, five hundred people would die; 10,000 would be severely injured; and 100,000 would be hospitalized. The economic impact would be in the millions of dollars.

Scenario 8: Terrorists detonate a "dirty bomb" in three neighboring moderate-to-large cities, contaminating thirty-six city blocks each. There would be 180 dead, 270 injured, and 20,000 contaminated in each city, with an economic impact in the billions.

Scenario 9: Terrorists attack a sports arena or a hospital emergency room using handmade bombs, a large car or truck bomb, and suicide belts. One hundred people would die; 450 would be hospitalized. DHS did not estimate the economic impact, believing that the effects of such an incident would be localized.

Scenario 10: Terrorists infect farm animals at several locations with foot-and-mouth disease, which spreads rapidly as the animals are transported around the country on their way to market. No human casualties were estimated, but the economic impact would run into the hundreds of millions.

Scenario 11: Terrorists launch cyber attacks against several parts of the nation's financial infrastructure over a period of several weeks. There would be no casualties, but the economic impact would be in the millions.[1]

These scenarios all sound plausible to a former homeland security insider like me, but, the casualty and injury figures all seem low, and, likewise, at least some of the economic impact figures. We know from the September 11 attacks that the total costs ran into the billions. And the psychic costs to the nation of another terror attack on the homeland would literally be incalculable. It would show that September 11 was not the end of our terrorist nightmare, but merely the beginning of it.

The happy fact is that there hasn't been another terror attack since September 11. We'd been left to wonder whether, as the Administration claimed, the Department of Homeland Security really had anything to do with that, and whether the department is fully capable of responding to any future attack, as the Administration had likewise claimed.

It was to be only a matter of time before the Fates put those claims to the test. Aside from the obvious question of timing, the only other question was whether the test would come in the form of a man-made disaster caused by an act of terrorism, or a natural disaster caused by an act of God. In the horrific wake of Hurricane Katrina, we now have the answer.

The fact that disaster struck almost four years to the day after the terror attacks, and at the very start of "National Preparedness Month" no less, shows that the Fates have a very dark and ironic sense of timing. It is as if the gods themselves are shouting from the heavens, "You are *still* in grave danger. This is yet another warning. Make haste to prepare yourselves, before it is too late!"

If anything, the slow and bungling DHS response to the hurricane suggested to some that the creation of the department had made bad things even worse. In the immediate aftermath of the disaster a bipartisan consensus quickly began to form around the notion that the problem was essentially structural—the Federal Emergency Management Agency (FEMA) was no longer an independent agency reporting directly to the President. If only, certain political leaders in both parties and FEMA insiders argued, the Homeland Security bureaucracy were reorganized yet again to take FEMA out of the department, all would automatically be well. But this was just Washington being Washington again, confusing reorganizing government with reforming it. The knee-jerk response of politicians and bureaucrats to any problem is invariably to rearrange government in some way, rather than to take the government we have, give it the leadership and resources it needs to be effective, and then hold it to strict account.

If the disaster answered some burning questions, it also raised one. That question, inevitably, was put to the President himself by an intrepid reporter:

REPORTER: Mr. President, given what happened with Katrina, shouldn't Americans be concerned if their government isn't prepared to respond to another disaster or even a terrorist attack?

If the question was predictable, the almost plaintively candid answer was not.

> THE PRESIDENT: Katrina exposed serious problems in our response capability at all levels of government. And, to the extent that the federal government didn't fully do its job right, I take responsibility. I want to know what went right and what went wrong. I want . . . to be able to answer that very question that you asked: are we capable of dealing with a severe attack or another severe storm. And, that's a very important question. And, it's in our national interest that we find out exactly what went on and—so we can be better prepared.[2]

Most of the reaction to this response focused on the President's striking acceptance of responsibility for the federal government's poor performance. But the truly shocking thing about it was the admission that, four years after 9/11 and nearly three years after spending tens of billions of dollars, and reorganizing the whole federal government for this very reason, even the President of the United States was in doubt as to whether we're any better prepared to handle the next attack than we were to handle the last one.

If seeing with our own eyes the chaos and confusion in New Orleans— the thousands of people pinned up like animals for days without sufficient food, water, or medical attention; the throngs of missing men, women, and children, some likely never to be heard from again; the scores of bodies left to drift and decay in the mud and the muck; the total meltdown of government at all levels; and the complete collapse of law and order—was not enough to convince us that our nation remains an open target for terrorists, that one painfully honest answer should have done the trick. The terrorists needed no such convincing, of course; they are as aware of our vulnerabilities as most Americans are ignorant of them. One can only conclude that they must today be emboldened as never before now that our vulnerabilities have been laid bare for all the world to see. In the week following the disaster, *Business Week* put together a pastiche of headlines from papers all around the globe, pithily capturing international schadenfreude. Britain's *Daily Mail* screamed, "Third World America." *Le Figaro* crowed, "The Superpower is forced to call for help." Russia's *Vremya Novostei* harrumphed, "They sank." The most pungent was Mexico's *Reforma* with, "The Day the U.S. Couldn't."[3]

If anything, the flat-footed response to Katrina suggests that we'd be even *less* prepared for a terrorist attack than a natural disaster. After all, there's almost always some warning of a natural disaster. Meteorologists and seismologists can usually predict the timing, location, and severity of hurricanes, floods, tornadoes, and earthquakes with considerable accuracy nowadays.

By way of contrast, intelligence is more of an art than a science, and, as art goes, it's more like a Rauschenberg than a Rembrandt. Intelligence analysts pore over reams of intelligence every day, but the bits and pieces of data are almost always so opaque, so random, and so inconsistent with each other that it's rarely easy for them to tell exactly what they're looking at. Understandably enough, terrorists rarely announce exactly how they're going to strike, when they're going to strike, and where they're going to strike. If they did, they'd be much less terrorizing. Terrorists' aim is to kill and destroy, as many and as much as possible, certainly. But just as important to them is creating in the enemy a vague but real sense of omnipresent danger—a numb but nagging fear of evil as we walk through valley of the shadow of death. The Department of Homeland Security's slow, chaotic, and inept response to the disaster could only have emboldened the terrorists and made them even more determined to strike again.

After all, a hurricane along the Gulf Coast of catastrophic dimension was, contrary to DHS' ex-post facto excuses, not only entirely foreseeable, but actually foreseen, time and again, by people outside and inside the department itself. While Secretary Chertoff claimed that Katrina "exceeded the foresight of the planners, and maybe anybody's foresight," his own FEMA Director had contradicted him just a few days earlier, admitting, "that . . . [the] hurricane caused the same kind of damage we anticipated. So we planned for it two years ago. And, unfortunately, we're implementing it."[4]

More curious, even, than the Secretary's contention, despite copious evidence to the contrary that the disaster was unforeseeable, is that this was *precisely* the kind of catastrophe for which he had famously maintained that the Department of Homeland Security should be in the business of preparing.

Refreshingly, upon taking office, Secretary Chertoff made a point of stressing something that his in-box-driven predecessor had never seemed to grasp—that we have to tackle homeland security *strategically.* Attempting to do a little bit of everything winds up having the effect of doing little or nothing to make us safer.

From the beginning, Chertoff stressed that we can't protect ourselves against every conceivable threat.[5] If we make the mistake of trying to, we'll waste billions of dollars and precious time, with little or nothing to show for it at the end of the day. Even the mightiest nation in the history of the world doesn't have the financial resources and the intellectual capital to imagine every possible way in which terrorists might attack us and to protect ourselves against each such contingency, however remote. Given our finite resources and our finite imagination, we have to set priorities, focusing our prevention and preparedness efforts on only the most likely threats and, then, those likely threats that, if they were to materialize, would have the gravest consequences in terms of death, injury, and economic damage.

Katrina fit this eminently sensible strategic construct perfectly—it was foreseeable *and* catastrophic—and yet the Department of Homeland Security was woefully and manifestly unprepared for it. Indeed, shortly after Chertoff took office, the following story, alluded to earlier, appeared in the *New York Times:* "The Department of Homeland Security, trying to focus antiterrorism spending better nationwide, has identified a dozen possible strikes it views as most plausible or devastating. . . . The document, known simply as the National Planning Scenarios, reads more like a doomsday plan, offering estimates of the probable deaths and economic damage caused by each type of attack."[6] Among the scenarios listed was a Category 5 hurricane with sustained winds of 160 miles per hour and storm surges of twenty feet hitting a major metropolitan area. The projected impact was 1,000 dead, 5,000 hospitalized, and millions of dollars in economic losses, almost exactly the impact that Hurricane Katrina did, in fact, have.

Furthermore, even though the hurricane intervened in deus ex machina fashion to demonstrate the folly of the idea, the Secretary went ahead with his proposal to take FEMA's preparedness responsibilities away, leaving it with only the job of helping the nation recover from catastrophes. Had such a proposal been implemented before the hurricane struck, FEMA would surely have been even less effective. Laying aside the metaphysical question of whether recovery really can be separated from preparedness, it's hard to believe that an agency could be effective at either without being required to do both.

Hurricane Katrina exposed the fact that, for all the planning, training, and exercising federal, state, and local authorities did for four years, America is still dangerously unprepared for disasters of the catastrophic kind. Whether caused by angry gods or angry men, the tools that are needed to respond to and recover from them are basically the same. In either event, potentially huge numbers of people would need to be evacuated from contaminated or otherwise uninhabitable areas to safe and secure places. Those people would need food, water, shelter, and medical attention for prolonged periods of time, and potentially huge numbers of people would be missing. Search-and-rescue teams would have to be dispatched to find and save the living, and to find and recover the dead. There would need to be clear lines of authority so that, whatever the contingency, all would know who was in charge. All relevant agencies would need to be able to communicate with each other in the field, so as to avoid working duplicatively, or, worse still, at cross-purposes.

In a way that no OIG or GAO report, no congressional hearing, and no media investigation could, the hurricane sheared off the façade that had covered up years of drift and neglect. The Department's website boasted that its directorate of Emergency Preparedness and Response "*ensures* that emergency response professionals are prepared for any situation."[7] But then, as if in cosmic mockery, disaster struck, and it was then plain that there was no plan to evacuate people without the means to leave New Orleans on their own. There were no pre-positioned stockpiles of food, water, and medicine waiting to be dispatched to the scene. No shelter was prepared to house huge numbers of people for prolonged periods of time. The living and the dead were stranded for days before search-and-rescue teams were sent in a systematic fashion to find them. Federal, state, and local government officials bickered for weeks as to who was in charge of what. One level of government would say one thing, only to be contradicted by another level of government shortly thereafter. At one point after the worst of the hurricane was over, the mayor of New Orleans invited residents to return, only to succumb later in the same day to federal pressure to order yet another evacuation in the face of yet another threatening oncoming storm. And, just like on 9/11, when an untold number among the thousands who died did so simply because police, fire, and emergency medical personnel could not get in touch with each other, communications all along the Gulf Coast were hampered by the lack of interoperable systems among, between, and within all levels of government.

We have seen what would happen to New Orleans if terrorists were to strike there. If terrorists had targeted the levees rather than the winds and the rains, the results would have been exactly the same. But what about Washington, D.C., or New York, the cities that have already been attacked, and the ones that terrorists freely admit remain their two top targets? The sad truth is that while they would certainly fare far better than New Orleans the anecdotal evidence suggests that neither higher-risk city is as prepared as it should be for an all but certain future attempted attack.

Take Washington, D.C., for example. When a small plane strayed into the restricted airspace around the capital and came within three miles of the

White House a few months before Hurricane Katrina struck, the incident was deemed serious enough by the Secret Service to warrant an evacuation of the White House, and by the Capitol Police to warrant an evacuation of congressional buildings. Local officials, though, had no idea that the city was in any apparent danger, despite having had a representative in the Department of Homeland Security's command center whose job it was to monitor and report back on just such threatening incidents.[8]

When a false-positive test indicated the presence of anthrax in several Pentagon facilities in the capital area a few months before the stray plane incident, the Defense Department treated some 900 of its workers with antibiotics without bothering to alert local health officials. Had this been a real anthrax attack, city authorities would have been in the dark about it and, as a consequence, they would have been totally unprepared to treat potentially thousands of infected citizens.

Just weeks before Katrina hit the Gulf Coast, Washington, D.C., officials tested their evacuation plan on hundreds of thousands of Fourth of July revelers. According to a story in the *Washington Post* on the fourth anniversary of the terror attacks, "the limited test found problems. Traffic signals did not switch to evacuation timing, some Transportation Department radios weren't charged, some officials weren't clear on their responsibilities and didn't communicate well with each other and people in the crowd were confused as to where to go." Noting that the most common and innocuous things routinely snarl traffic in the capital—from rain to snow to football games, the paper concluded, "an emergency evacuation of the entire city— or even part of it—could quickly tie the region into maddening and even dangerous knots."[9]

As for the key issue of communication during a crisis among "first responders," the District of Columbia has a nifty-sounding system—"Alert DC"—that is purportedly capable of calling all 1.5 million land-line-based telephone numbers in the city with a recorded message, and it is advertised as being capable of sending 18,000 text messages each minute. But when the system was tested in the summer of 2004 when the threat level was raised in D.C., New York, and New Jersey because of word that terrorists were casing financial targets in those cities, "no phone calls were made, and the system failed to send residents text messages for more than five hours after the decision [to raise the threat level] was announced. Officials said no phone calls were made because the city was not under attack. The delay in getting out the text message occurred, in part, because the person responsible for writing it and getting it approved had other emergency-related duties."[10]

What about New York City, the only city attacked twice by Al Qaeda? The good news is that in the words of former Deputy CIA chief, John McLaughlin, New York is the "gold standard" as far as terrorism preparedness is concerned,[11] but, although every knowledgeable observer agrees that New York is far better prepared than any other city in the nation for a terror attack, even New York is not as safe as it could be. For all the high-tech communications, for all the planning and drilling, problems remain. According to one media account, police and fire departments would be unable to decontaminate the millions of people who would need it in the event of a "dirty bomb" attack. Lacking the money to prepare, hospitals and the emergency medical services department would likewise be overwhelmed. To make matters worse, nearly one-third of health care workers confessed to pollsters that they'd remain at home and refuse to report for duty. Finally, whatever they were advised to do by authorities, many New York City residents would immediately flee to New Jersey, already the most densely populated state in the nation. While New York is better off than any other place in the country in terms of preparedness, New Jersey is far from prepared to handle throngs of evacuees from the largest city in the nation.[12]

If the low water mark (no pun intended) in terms of preparedness is New Orleans, and the high water mark is New York City and Washington, D.C., and neither of the extremes is adequately prepared, it's a safe bet that the same is true for the vast section of the country in the middle.

The continued and manifest lack of national preparedness prompted the 9/11 Commissioners, in the wake of Katrina and around the anniversary of 9/11, to issue a report card pointing out which of its recommendations have been implemented since the terror attacks and which have not.[13] Among the pending recommendations that, if implemented, could have gone a long way toward improving the government's response to the hurricane, and, by implication, a terrorist attack, were three.

First, scarce homeland security dollars continue to be appropriated by Congress on a "pork barrel" basis. That is to say, funds are not allocated solely on the basis of risk. Even though intelligence and common sense suggest that some areas of the nation are at far greater risk of terrorist attack than others, each state gets some minimum share of homeland security funding.[14] For example, a classic *60 Minutes* segment pointed out that Tiptonville, Tennessee—population 7,900 in an area of 164 square miles—was awarded nearly $200,000 to protect itself from terrorism.[15] The mayor used the money to buy an all-terrain vehicle, defibrillators for use at high school basketball games, and protective suits for the volunteer fire department. In defense of the expenditures, the police chief explained, "Well, if [federal money's] out there, we're going to try to harvest it." Converse, Texas used its homeland security money to transport lawn mowers to the annual lawn-mower races. Columbus, Ohio's fire department used homeland security money to buy bulletproof vests for its "canine corps." Mason County, Washington spent more than $60,000 on a decontamination unit that's been sitting in a warehouse for a year, with no one trained to use it.[16]

While the then chairman of the key House committee on homeland security successfully pushed that body to pass a bill lowering the state minimum, the Republican chairman and top Democrat on the key Senate committee persuaded the Senate to pass a bill with a higher state minimum. It is worth noting that the key House member at the time happened to represent a high-threat state, California, and that the key Senators happened to represent relatively low-threat states, Maine and Connecticut, respectively. Of course, it is impossible to know for sure whether the House member was pushing for a more risk-based formula because of his position as a key congressional leader on homeland security, or because his state would benefit from it. What is clear is that the senators in question (the very senators who, coincidentally, prevented me from being confirmed by their colleagues), were torn between the interests of their states and that of the nation. In the end, notably, they chose to side with the interests of their states.[17]

That said, even high-risk areas have been known to spend homeland security money on things that have, at best, a tenuous connection to making the homeland more secure. When the Mayor of Washington, D.C. was asked to explain the expenditure of $300,000 for a computerized car-towing service, he insisted that this was "absolutely a part of homeland security" because the roadways would have to be cleared quickly in the event of an emergency evacuation. It was proper to spend $100,000 to produce a rap song on emergency preparedness because "a big, big part of the marketing and outreach to kids is through . . . using the rap idiom."[18]

Moreover, even when money is allocated on the basis of risk, and the money is dedicated to homeland security related purposes, jurisdictions can be slow to spend the money. When our auditors looked into the DHS Office of Domestic Preparedness (ODP) program during my time as Inspector General,[19] we found that ODP had done a good job of getting money out to states and localities in a timely fashion. The holdup was largely at the state level. Sometimes, the money was being "drawn down" slowly for good reason, because the states were ensuring that localities weren't submitting duplicative or conflicting requests. But sometimes plain old bureaucratic inefficiency at the state and local levels was causing unnecessary delay in getting sorely needed funds to first responders.

The second outstanding 9/11 Commission recommendation was the need for a unified command structure, so it would be clear in a crisis who's in charge of what. Indeed, the Commission went to so far in its 2004 report as to recommend that first responder funding be contingent upon state and local authorities' agreement to adopt a "unified incident command system." Four years later, the commissioners found that while many police and fire departments have since been trained in unified command procedures, Katrina shows that this is far from true nationwide.

Even the President acknowledged in his post-hurricane address to the nation from waterlogged New Orleans that the federal, state, and local governments have yet to work together optimally. Had Ridge's early promise to set up regional DHS offices around the country been kept, chances are good that there would have been less intragovernmental confusion and quicker dispersal of desperately needed aid to affected communities. I remember vividly sitting in seemingly interminable planning meetings in the late fall of 2002 and early January 2003, as the new Department of Homeland Security was taking shape. On numerous occasions, Ridge and his top management team would stress that setting up a regional structure for the department was job number one, so as to give Homeland Security a visible presence in each community so that officials and ordinary citizens would know whom to turn to in times of crisis. But, according to news reports,[20] the White House repeatedly blocked the plan, and according to Ridge himself,[21] Congress did. Whoever is at fault, the bottom line is that no such DHS regional structure exists to this day.[22]

A third 9/11 outstanding Commission recommendation was designed to ensure that federal, state, and local response teams could communicate with each other in a crisis by increasing the radio spectrum dedicated to public safety purposes. Legislation to address this critical issue has been pending in Congress.[23] Until it is passed and signed into law, lives will continue to be lost needlessly when disaster strikes.

As I sat one day last fall in front of my television set watching the tragedy of Hurricane Katrina unfold before my eyes, I had one of those "aha" moments. "Aha," I thought. That's why I could never get the department to let me observe that TOPOFF exercise. "TOPOFF" stands for "top officials."

There have been three congressionally mandated simulations of terrorist attacks to test how the government would fare the next time we're faced with the real thing. Top-level government officials observe the exercise to evaluate performance, identify problems to be fixed, and determine what needs to be done to fix those problems. Exercises were held in 2001, 2003, and 2005. Having arrived at the department at the beginning of 2003 and having departed at the end of 2004, I could have observed only the exercise in the spring of 2003. But I wasn't invited to observe that simulation, and by the time my staff and I managed to figure out whose office was responsible for holding it, it was too late and TOPOFF II had already come and gone. Did the department have something to hide? Was its performance poorer than it should have been? Were there still problems that should have been fixed? For two years I could only wonder. Now I know. Now we all know.

So, here we are, five years after the terror attacks, and the title of the Council on Foreign Relations' 2003 report on the subject remains an accurate assessment of the state of things today—"Emergency Responders: Drastically Under-funded, Dangerously Unprepared."[24] The President acknowledged as much in his address to the nation, ordering the Homeland Security Department to undertake an "immediate review" of emergency plans in every major American city to ensure that evacuation plans are in order and that food, water, and security can be provided in a timely fashion.[25]

President Bush's candor is both commendable and hopeful, because a huge part of the problem with homeland security to date has been the Administration's failure to acknowledge that it hasn't taken the issue seriously enough, and that creating a Homeland Security department was simply the beginning of the job of securing the homeland, not the end of it.

A little-noticed line in his speech was likewise extraordinarily significant. "It is now clear that a challenge on this scale requires greater federal authority and a broader role for the armed forces—the institution of our government most capable of massive logistical operations on a moment's notice."[26]

Once again another agency, this time the Department of Defense, was being asked to play a central role in a core homeland security-related function—responding to an emergency of catastrophic dimension. As explained in the preceding chapter, the Homeland Security Department is now largely dependent upon the CIA and the FBI to provide it with the intelligence it needs to protect the homeland. Soon, the Homeland Security Department will be even more dependent on the Pentagon than it presently is to help it perform its emergency preparedness and response mission.

So the next time an attack looms, the Department of Homeland Security might not know about it, and the next time an attack comes, the Department of Homeland Security probably will not have all that much to do with responding to it. Given the only fitful progress it has made to date on border and transportation security and on protecting critical infrastructure and soft targets, one might well wonder why it is, exactly, that we still have a Department of Homeland Security!

As the year 2005 drew to a close, the results of the White House's own internal review of the federal response to Hurricane Katrina came in, with "gale force winds." If anything, the president's staff was even harsher than his congenital critics in fixing the lion's share of the blame on Washington, according to congressional staffers privy to the contents of a White House briefing. "Marin [the top Republican staffer on the special House investigative committee] said the briefing had 'surprised' members with the length of the list of errors and mistakes acknowledged by officials. He said members were 'concerned how little progress has been made since Sept 11. If this is the response when we get days and days of notice, I shudder to think what might happen if an event occurred without warning.'"[27] Exactly.

CHAPTER NINE

WASTEFUL
SPENDING AND
SLOPPY ACCOUNTING

"Two areas that DHS needs to get control of early to minimize waste and abuse are the procurement and grant . . . management functions. Getting the right leadership and systems in place for both functions should be made a high priority . . . DHS will be integrating the procurement functions of many constituent programs and missions, some lacking important management controls. . . . Early attention to strong systems and controls for acquisition and related business processes will be critical to ensuring success and maintaining integrity and accountability."[1]

These are the key sentences in a memo that I sent, or, more accurately, that I *tried* to send to the Secretary of the Department of Homeland Security on March 18, 2003, less than three weeks after the department was established. I'm no seer, and I'm no genius, but it did not take much foresight or insight to see that this new agency, with billions of dollars to spend, under tight congressional deadlines and immense political pressure to do something as quickly as possible to make the homeland more secure, would be targeted by rapacious contractors like buzzards homing in on carrion. Unless immediate steps were taken to stop it in its tracks, the department, and the taxpayers who were depending on it to make America safe, would be taken for a very bumpy ride. Among other things, I recommended that DHS "establish a robust and effective contract oversight function," and that it "ensure that contracting officers and contracting officers' representatives are properly warranted, trained, and supervised, and that they maintain proper documentation in the contract files."[2]

The Department of Homeland Security officially opened its doors for business on March 1, 2003. A few days later I ran into Secretary Ridge in the halls of the department's headquarters, and asked for a moment of his time. "Mr. Secretary, I'm really worried about contracts and grants. My top auditor and I were talking about this just the other day, and I said I'd raise it with you at my first opportunity. Needless to say, this is a huge agency, and I don't have to tell you that the contractors are already circling. Before you know it, they're going to swoop down and carry off billions of dollars with little or nothing to show for it, if we're not real careful. I admit that I'm biased, but I've got the best audit chief in the business, and he's putting together the best audit team in the business. If you're willing, we'd be happy to put down on paper some recommendations for you and your management team that, if promptly implemented, we're confident will get the waste and fraud down to as close to zero as humanly possible."

"Why, absolutely, Clark. I'd appreciate that very much. You couldn't be more right about this," the Secretary replied.

"Then, we'll get right on it, sir. Expect something shortly."

I immediately returned to my makeshift offices across town, a few blocks from the White House, and poked my head through Dick Berman's office door. "Dick, I just ran into the Secretary. I told him that we'd get him some recommendations to minimize waste and fraud in the contracting process, if he wanted us to. And, of course, he gladly took us up on the offer. Could you get to work on that memo we talked about the other day?"

Within a day Dick Berman had drafted the memo. I gave it a quick read and made a minor change or two. I then sent it to the Secretary through the department's Executive Secretary, asking that a copy be sent to the Deputy Secretary as well.

At the White House and in every cabinet agency, there's an office that's very powerful but little known outside the relatively small circle of government insiders, the Office of the Executive Secretary.[3] Presidents and Cabinet secretaries are besieged by so many pieces of paper recommending this or that course of action on this or that issue that somebody has to manage the process. In sum, the Executive Secretary keeps track of what goes in to the principal for decision and what comes back out, so that any decisions made are accurately recorded and so that any necessary follow-up action is taken. Just as important, the Executive Secretary is to ensure that, before making a decision, the principal considers all relevant background information and any points of view that differ from that of the official(s) making the recommendation under consideration. Otherwise, the President or the Cabinet member might make an erroneous or otherwise ill-advised decision based on incomplete information or a single person's biased viewpoint. So before sending a decision memo to the principal, the Executive Secretary will "staff it out," meaning simply that he will circulate it to all of the other senior officials with an interest in the subject matter to give them an opportunity to offer up any additional information or contrary viewpoint that, in their judgment, the principal should be advised of and consider before making a decision.

There's one official in the federal government who has the legal right to direct, unfiltered access to the head of an agency, and that's the Inspector General. It is critical that the Inspector General have the right to express his views and to make recommendations, in person or in writing, directly to the agency head without first having to go through the Executive Secretary's vetting process. After all, the job of the Inspector General is to serve as a watchdog over the agency. Accordingly, there will be times when he will have to advise the Secretary that senior officials themselves are mismanaging programs or operations. Sometimes, even, the Inspector General will need to advise the Secretary that senior officials are themselves violating important administrative procedures or, worse yet, engaging in criminal activity. Requiring the Inspector General effectively to tip off his targets so that they can shade the truth, or keep it hidden altogether, disserves the Secretary and the cause of effective, efficient, and economical government.

The Executive Secretary of the Department of Homeland Security was an avuncular, Mister Rogers-type named Ken Hill, who'd served as Executive Secretary of the White House National Security Council. As such, Ken was intimately familiar with the vetting process and with the exceptional oversight role of the Inspector General.

A few weeks after I sent the memo to the Secretary, I was in then Deputy Secretary Gordon England's office on some other business. I mentioned in passing that I was concerned about the potential for abuses in the contracting process, and I hoped that he'd had a chance to look at my memo on the subject. "What memo?," he asked.

"Well, a few weeks ago I sent the Secretary and you a short memo out-lining some steps I thought you needed to take in these early days of the de-partment to keep abuses to a minimum. You didn't get it?"

"No, I've not seen it. You're right that this is a potentially huge problem, and we better get a handle on it before it's too late."

"Well, I'll see what happened immediately," I replied.

I strode down the hall to Ken's office and demanded to know what was going on. "Ken, you know I sent you a memo for the Secretary and Deputy Secretary weeks ago advising them to take some urgent steps to guard against waste and fraud in the contracting process. I was just in the Dep. Sec's office, and he said he didn't know what I was talking about. What's going on? Did you send it?"

"Well, uh, no," he replied, sheepishly.

"Why not?"

"Well, I staffed it out and when Janet [Janet Hale, the Under Secretary for Management] got her copy, she asked me not to send it in yet."

"What?" I said, my voice rising with my indignation. "Ken, you know that no one has the right to hold up Inspector General communications or to keep them from the Secretary."

"Well, Janet said that the controls you're recommending are a good idea, but they're not in place yet. And, she didn't want the Secretary to know that."

"Ken, I know they're not in place yet. That's the point of the memo—to tell the Secretary that, so, if necessary, he can *order* her to put them in place."

Fuming, I stormed out of the building and found the car that was wait-ing to take me back to my office. This very thing—the danger that officials reporting to the Secretary would try to keep him in the dark about their own failure to address a critically important issue—was precisely why the Inspec-tor General's memos were not to be shopped around by the Executive Secre-tariat for review, revision, or supervision. I pulled out my cell phone and called my assistant. "That memo we sent through the Executive Secretary a few weeks ago on contracts and grants, well, it was never sent to the Secre-tary and Deputy Secretary. Janet Hale held it up because she didn't want the Secretary to know that she hadn't done anything yet to get a handle on wasteful spending. So, from now on, please have everything meant for Ridge and England either faxed or hand-delivered, and fax this particular memo over right away."

The Secretary got the memo, but the die had been cast and a pattern had been set. Spending was already getting out of control, and nothing was being done to stop it. My efforts to bring problems to management's attention would be blocked whenever possible, and money that could have gone to protecting the homeland would be misspent. Indeed, unbeknownst to me at the time, money was already flying out the door with little or no effort to get a handle on it. One key department component was *encouraging* one contractor to spend more money than even the contractor wanted to.

In the aftermath of the terror attacks, the government was understandably frantic to take immediate steps to improve aviation security. At the time, the airlines paid private contractors to provide the screener workforce, and the result was a workforce of screeners who were poorly paid, poorly trained, and poorly motivated. The average annual attrition rate was a whopping 105 percent.[4] Scores of government investigations had shown how easy it was to sneak guns, knives, and bombs past checkpoints.

And so, with lightning speed, the President signed into law two months later the Aviation and Transportation Security Act. The law created the Transportation Security Agency (TSA) to oversee transportation security generally and aviation security in particular, and it gave the TSA one year to hire, train, and deploy to all 429 airports in the country federal screeners to replace the contract workforce. To facilitate meeting this extraordinary deadline, the law also exempted TSA from stringent federal contracting guidelines.

Prodded by the Secretary of Transportation, former Democratic Congressman Norm Mineta, and his deputy, Michael Jackson, TSA moved at warp speed to get the job done. Staffers worked seven days a week; sixteen hours a day. Private-sector consultants with expertise deemed relevant to setting up a new agency and completing a complex mission on tight deadlines were brought in, including Kip Hawley, an executive with a California logistics company. The head of the former President Bush's Secret Service protective detail, John Magaw, was brought in as the first head of TSA.

Lacking sufficient staff of its own, TSA was forced, ironically enough, to turn to contractors to perform the bulk of the work. The agency had been created, after all, to take charge of the airport screening function because private companies had failed to do a thorough job. At the end of a competitive bidding process, TSA awarded the contract to a Minnesota-based educational testing firm, NCS Pearson. The charge was to hire 30,000 passenger screeners in thirty-two weeks at a cost of $104 million. Because the firm had done little work in the notoriously Byzantine area of federal human resources management, competitors and other critics questioned whether it was up to the task. One of the factors in NCS Pearson's favor, though, was that it already had 2,500 sites around the country that were in the business of assessing applicants' job qualifications.

The contract was flawed from the start because there was no ceiling on the costs, and the contractor had no incentive to economize. Several decisions were subsequently made that would turn out to make a potentially costly contract extraordinarily costly later.

Three months into the contract, TSA decided to double the number of screeners to be hired, and then to have them screen baggage as well as passengers. On top of having to find an additional 30,000 screeners, NCS Pearson was told to pre-certify an additional 66,000 people who could be hired immediately to fill jobs left open by attrition. Moreover, TSA asked the contractor to hire 2,400 field managers and administrative staffers, and to increase the staff of the call center that had been set up to answer applicants' questions from 25 to more than 2,000 people. The cumulative result of these changes in the scope of the contract was to compress the hiring deadline from an already short thirty-two weeks to an even shorter thirteen, and, of course, to significantly increase the overall cost.[5]

To make bad matters worse, TSA decided not to use NCS Pearson's existing nationwide network of "assessment centers," where applicants were pre-screened to determine their eligibility for the job. Instead, the contractor was ordered to set up temporary centers in hotels throughout the country, near the airports where successful applicants would work. So, after considerable scrambling, NCS Pearson set up shop in some 150 hotels and other meeting facilities throughout the country for weeks at a time. Because the deadlines were so tight and the needs were so great, the contractor in turn hired 168 subcontractors—including call center operators and security teams—to help out with various discrete tasks. The subcontractors, in turn, hired subcontractors of their own. All the while, TSA provided little or no oversight, focusing nearly exclusively on meeting the congressionally mandated deadline. According to the former NCS Pearson employee who ran assessment centers in the Midwest, "The waste was unbelievable because there were little checks and balances. There were Pearson officials and subcontractors who had carte blanche. I never saw any government people. There was [sic] zero government people involved."[6] Indeed, TSA even today denies that keeping an eye out for waste and fraud was its responsibility. In a *Washington Post* interview, the TSA contracting officer said, "I paid the contractor to do that."[7]

Needless to say, costs quickly ballooned. The decision to set up new assessment centers meant hiring office workers and security guards, and renting lots of hotel rooms and meeting facilities. This decision alone added at least $343 million to the cost of the contract, according to NCS Pearson's own estimate. In the end, total contract costs mushroomed to nearly $1 billion, $867 million to be precise. The scale of needless overspending was breathtaking, even by Washington standards.

At every stage in the process, costs were marked up. Kelly Services paid office workers $20 an hour, but billed TSA for more than twice that sum; security guards paid $15-20 an hour were billed out at $30-40 an hour. A travel and event coordination firm was hired without a written contract to book hotels around the country, taking a 10 percent profit on each room it booked. So, the more rooms it booked and the higher the room costs, the greater the firm's take.

There are ordinary hotels, and there are luxury hotels. And luxury hotels were the hotels of choice under this contract. In high-rent Manhattan, relatively high-end hotels like the Waldorf Astoria were booked. TSA was billed $129,621.82 for long-distance phone charges, with no supporting documentation, at two other Manhattan hotels, including almost $3,500 for calls to foreign countries. Pier 94, a Manhattan convention and trade show center, was rented for nearly $700,000, or about $39,000 a day for two weeks. In Boston, a company was hired at a cost of more than a half a million dollars to build a large tent and two smaller ones. The tents flooded when it rained, and it was hotel employees rather than the subcontractor's or Pearson's who had to clean up the mess. Auditors were unable to substantiate the entirety of the claimed $27.4 million in security costs. The president of one firm awarded a no-bid contract to book hotels paid herself a salary of $5.4 million for nine months of work. The firm wasn't even incorporated until it received the subcontract. Auditors were unable to substantiate $15 million of the subcontractor's expenses.

A key TSA contracting official was candid in admitting the agency's responsibility for this total breakdown in the federal contracting system. "We did not properly identify the requirements. There was a real sense of speed on this. That's what led to many of the changes."[8]

While the NCS Pearson contract pre-dated the establishment of the Department of Homeland Security, it would set a dangerous precedent that the department would later follow, despite my office's efforts from day one to prevent it. Notably, two people who played key roles in establishing TSA are now playing an even greater role in the Department of Homeland Security.

Then Deputy Transportation Secretary Michael Jackson is now the Deputy Secretary of the Department of Homeland Security. Kip Hawley, the private contractor who was instrumental in working with Jackson and others to establish TSA, is now the head of TSA. The "anything goes" attitude that led to the egregious NCS Pearson contract is echoed today in the wake of Hurricane Katrina. Already some $60 billion has been appropriated. Even conservative estimates put the eventual cost at a least $100 billion; more liberal ones put the eventual cost at $200 billion. The President has vowed to spend "whatever it takes,"[9] and, at least initially, no-bid contracts are being signed left and right with politically connected companies. In Francophone Louisiana, it was déjà-vu all over again.

Another example of TSA's wasteful spending crossed our radar screen when we learned in a February 2004 news article about a lavish awards ceremony for its employees at the aptly named *Grand* Hyatt Hotel in Washington, D.C.[10] According to the news account, some $200,000 had been spent on an "expensive, high-quality" awards program that included airfare and hotel rooms for a couple of hundred TSA employees and guests. Cash bonuses totaling more than $1 million had been doled out to senior executives.

Our curiosity piqued, we decided to look into the story. What we found was shocking.[11] For once, the media was not exaggerating; in fact, the facts were even more egregious than the initial account had made them out to be. As it turned out, $461,745 had been spent to put on the ceremony, more than twice the figure contained in the news story. In addition to paying employees' travel, hotel, and daily expense account charges, costs were incurred for renting the room where the ceremony was held, food and beverages, photos, plaques, programs, audiovisual services, and a private events planner. While some costs were bid out, hotel costs were not. Transportation expenses alone amounted to $137,148. Plaques and other honorary awards totaled $81,767. The events planning firm charged $85,552. Three cheese displays cost $1,500; each gallon of coffee, $64; and, each soft drink, $3.75.

As troubling as the event costs were, equally troubling to us was the apparent inequity in the treatment of senior and junior employees. TSA doled out $1.45 million to eighty-eight TSA executives. Those eighty-eight executives constituted 76 percent of the executives in TSA eligible for a cash performance award. Government-wide, an average of only 49 percent of eligible executives received a cash award that year. Moreover, the average federal performance award at the time was about $12,000, but TSA paid its executives an average award of a little more than $16,000. And, while the awards were supposed to be for *exceptional* performance, we found that nearly 40 percent of the eighty-eight files we reviewed contained the exact same boilerplate justification language.

While 76 percent of senior executives received a cash award, as near as we could tell only about 3 percent of lower-ranked employees received a cash award, and the non-monetary awards that the lower-ranked employees (who, presumably, had a greater need for cash than their superiors) received had relatively little monetary value. This led us to conclude that "a substantial inequity exists in TSA's performance recognition program between executive and non-executive employees."[12]

Even though TSA was not required by law to bid on the contract for the hotel site (because the initial cost estimate was under the legal threshold), it would have been good business practice for TSA to do so to make sure that the taxpayer's dollar was spent wisely. TSA's use of no-bid contracts, and its tendency to turn a blind eye to perceived conflicts of interest, had become a pattern.

Earlier in the book, I touched on the problems with TSA's contract with Boeing to install and maintain explosive detection equipment at airports throughout the country. It bears going into the issue in more detail here.[13]

The contract, which ultimately grew to be worth $1.2 billion, was supposed to be a standard cost-plus-award fee type of contract. In such contracts, a contractor's approved costs are reimbursed and it receives on top of that some pre-determined amount of money as a reward for its performance. Instead, TSA allowed the contract to become, in effect, a cost-plus-a-percentage-of-cost type of contract. In other words, TSA paid Boeing's costs, and then it paid a percentage of those costs to Boeing as profit. Such contracts are illegal in the federal government for an obvious reason—there's no incentive for the contractor to cut costs, and every incentive to increase them. The higher the costs, the higher the profit.

A plan to determine an award fee based on Boeing's performance was not established until eighteen months after the contract was awarded, and it included cost increases that were unjustified. More than $44 million was paid out to Boeing in award fees before any plan was devised to determine the proper award fee.

Furthermore, my auditors concluded that the profit paid to Boeing was disproportionately high in comparison to what other agencies allow under such contracts, as well as to the degree of risk that the contractor assumed. As near as we can determine, TSA paid Boeing at least $49 million in excess profit.

In terms of risk, Boeing bore little if any. Among other things, it was reimbursed for all of its costs, regardless of its performance. Its only obligation

was to use its "best efforts" to perform under the contract; there was no re-
duction in allowed costs for failure to perform. TSA agreed to reimburse
Boeing for any losses incurred due to terrorist acts that occurred, despite the
installation and maintenance of the explosive detection equipment. TSA,
not Boeing, was responsible for procuring the equipment, and the two subcontractors were responsible for installing and maintaining it. To top it all
off, for the "trouble" of overseeing the contract, Boeing got to make profit on
its costs *and* the subcontractors' costs. Boeing received about $82 million in
profit, or a rate of return of 210 percent, just for being the middleman. Had
TSA contracted directly with the subcontractors, it could have saved us taxpayers the entirety of that $82 million.

As shocking as the contract was, more shocking still was TSA's reaction
to our findings. TSA continued to insist that Boeing had incurred such risk
that the award fee was reasonable. We insisted right back that TSA had, yet,
again, sided with contractors at the expense of taxpayers. "We continue to
disagree with TSA's conclusion that Boeing's risk was high and that the fee
structure was reasonable. While fees on subcontractor costs are permissible,
the practice is not always justified, especially when the general contractor
does not bear the risk of subcontractor non-performance. . . . As the federal
purchasing agency, TSA is responsible for ensuring that profit is reasonable.
We still maintain that TSA has not met its obligation to negotiate a reasonable profit and recommend that TSA carefully evaluate the performance of
Boeing when determining future award fees and consider the reasonableness
of the fee awarded when compared to contractor performance."[14]

And then there was the elaborate "operations center" TSA built to
monitor threats against the transportation sector. Yet again, speed was a key
factor in the breakdown in fundamental contracting practices. With a self-
imposed deadline of ninety days to get the center up and running, senior
managers cut the experienced procurement staff out of the decision-
making process. There was no documentation to support the project's $19
million budget. When the contracting professionals objected to management's cutting corners, they were reprimanded and urged to support the
project manager, who had no training in managing contracts. In our report
on our findings, we concluded, "Senior management's failure to enforce
procurement regulations and policy, as well as the procurement managers'
acquiescence to senior management's pressure, created a culture in which
procurement procedures were abandoned, ethical norms slipped, and fiscal
responsibility was neglected. This environment fostered improper or questionable purchases and construction decisions, as well as disregard for the

ethical duty of impartiality, by the project manager and others involved with the project."[15]

Among the more egregious examples of wasteful and improper expenditures was a total of $500,000 for artwork and silk plants. To make bad matters still worse, these items were not ordered from a gallery, nursery, or furniture store; curiously, they were ordered from a tool company. When the company submitted invoices to TSA for the items, describing them as "enhancements," a TSA manager ordered the company to retract those invoices and issue new ones, deceptively characterizing the items as "equipment and tools." The tool company wound up charging an extra $80,000 to supply the items because the TSA manager insisted on the company's submitting an invoice before final costs were determined. Being a tool company, the vendor had never sold art work and silk plants before. Explaining the mystery of why a tool company would be selected to supply something other than tools, and at an unnecessarily high cost, it turned out that the TSA manager had a prior personal and business relationship with the tool company's owners. The manager eventually resigned from TSA, and, within weeks, took a job as an officer and employee in the tool company, increasing his salary by about $30,000 and obtaining company stock as an added sweetener.

There were other stunning examples of waste under this contract. Forty-five of the fifty-five offices were outfitted with cable television. Seven kitchens were installed with the latest in fixtures, including costly subzero refrigerators. A 4,200-square-foot state-of-the-art fitness center was installed for the center's seventy-nine federal employees, complete with towel service. We pointed out in our report that "there was no documented justification or cost/benefit analysis supporting these expenditures. The real estate contracting officer objected to some of the amenities but was overridden by the project manager."[16] TSA purchase cards were used, against policy, to purchase personal items and furniture. To get around the $2,500 transaction limit, TSA managers conspired with the vendor to split transactions into smaller increments under the threshold.

While TSA in its written comments on our report professed to agree with it, the tone and tenor of the comments suggested otherwise. Indeed, the then head of TSA, Admiral David Stone, suggested that the center was not large enough! "TSA generally concurs with your draft recommendations but does not concur with several significant conclusions of the draft report. In particular, the report does not recognize the absolute criticality of achieving command and control over aviation security incidents as rapidly as possible. . . . According to the Institute for the Analysis of Global Security, the cost of the terrorist attacks of September 11, 2001, was over $100 billion, plus thousands of lives. Accelerating the construction of the [operations center], and the resultant ability to communicate with Federal Security Directors across the country as well as with the Federal Aviation Administration, the Department of Transportation, and other federal agencies in an era of threatened terrorism is worth every dollar spent. . . . In fact, we are becoming concerned that the facility as built is insufficient for future operational and continuity of operations requirements and are planning to increase the space."[17] Further standing reality on its head, the TSA Administrator shifted blame for the contract abuses to lower-level employees. In fact, it was lower-level employees who objected to such practices and were overruled by TSA managers.

In the Alice-in-Wonderland fashion that by then had become typical of the department, Stone concluded his comments on our report as follows: "Shortly, I will be releasing a broadcast message to all TSA employees emphasizing the importance of following sound business practices as well as applicable statutes and regulations. . . . Integrity is one of our core values. . . . I recognize that the overall integrity of our organization depends heavily on the manner in which we execute our acquisition program. As we continue to work to mature the acquisition and procurement function, we will factor this report in our efforts."[18]

Here was the head of TSA on March 25, 2005, almost four years after the agency was created and more than two years after the Department of Homeland Security was created, promising to a send a message to all employees about the importance of following legal and prudent contracting practices "shortly." This was a message that I, on March 18, 2003, had urged the Secretary to send out, almost two years earlier to the day. Rather than invoking the iconic power of September 11 to inspire department employees to spend homeland security money wisely, September 11 was used to justify wasteful spending. Instead of commending lower-level employees for having the guts to challenge their superiors, the TSA Administrator was shifting the blame for the debacle to them. It was yet another reminder, as if I needed another one, that getting along at the Department of Homeland Security required going along with all manner of waste, fraud, and mismanagement.

The problem goes on at TSA. The *Washington Post* reported the following on October 23, 2005:

> Federal auditors say the prime contractor on a $1 billion technology contract to improve the nation's transportation security system overbilled tax-

payers for as much as 171,000 hours' worth of labor and overtime by charging up to $131 an hour for employees who were paid less than half that amount. . . . The project is costing more than double the anticipated amount per month, and the [computer] network is far from complete— nearly half of the nation's airports have yet to be upgraded. Government officials said last week that the initial $1 billion contract ceiling was only a starting point for the project, which they recently said could end up costing $3 billion.[19]

The contractor, Unisys Corp., was awarded a dream contract. Instead of being told exactly what to provide, the contractor was empowered to decide what the department needed in the way of a computer network. It is no wonder, then, that costs quickly spiraled out of control. Instead of putting the remaining four years of the contract out for competitive bidding, the department subsequently granted a $750 million extension.

To be fair to TSA, it is not the only component in the department that is guilty of wasteful spending. For example, we have already discussed the Border Patrol's $280 million Integrated Surveillance Initiative that was so ineffective in using technology to scan the border for illegal aliens that the whole project had to be scratched. But against stiff competition, TSA easily wins the prize for the most "contract-challenged" DHS component.

It would be one thing if we had a significantly more secure homeland to show for the billions we've spent on contractors, but as explained in preceding chapters, security gaps remain in every single sector that can be said to be a likely terror target. A *New York Times* piece summed up the sorry state of affairs two years after the Department of "Homeland Security" opened its doors for business.

> After spending more than $4.5 billion on screening devices to monitor the nation's ports, borders, airports, mail and air, the federal government is moving to replace or alter much of the antiterrorism equipment, concluding that it is ineffective, unreliable or too expensive to operate. . . . In an effort to create a virtual shield around America, the Department of Homeland Security now plans to spend billions of dollars more. Although some changes are now being made because of technology that has occurred in the last couple of years, many of them are planned because devices currently in use have done little to improve the nation's security. . . . [20]

As if wasting money on extravagant contracts were not bad enough, the department has been unable since day one to properly account for the money it has. Indeed, just as department leaders resisted my early efforts to help them get a handle on contracts and grants, they likewise resisted my efforts to enhance their accounting ability.

My audit chief, Dick Berman, approached me in the first few weeks of the department's existence to say that we should convince the leadership to agree to an outside audit of its first-year finances. There was some question as to whether this was legally required of the department in its first year of operation. Conducting an audit would be costly, easily totaling several million dollars, and conducting an audit in the department's first year of operation would be complicated by the fact that it became operational in the middle of the government fiscal year. The government's budgets run from October to October, and the department was formally established in March. So, it would take some doing to separate the year's accounting between the components' legacy agencies for the first five months of the year and DHS for the last seven. Notwithstanding the complications, Dick and I felt strongly that it was important that the department's books be audited in its very first year of operation, if only to provide a baseline against which future progress (or the lack of it) could be measured. Unless the department got a handle on its financial picture early on, it would be hard pressed to correct for weaknesses later on when the stakes would be even higher.

Convinced by Dick that a first-year audit was essential, I went to see Janet Hale, the Under Secretary for Management who'd worked against me in my efforts to get contract costs under control. "Janet, I'm convinced by my top auditor that it's vitally important for the department's books be audited in this first year of operation. I realize that this is an unusual year, and that DHS will have been operational for only a part of it, but unless you have a clear picture of exactly what the status of its financial health is at the beginning, you won't know what problems you have that will need to be fixed in later years when the department is up and running. I realize that this will be very costly, and I'm sure that there will be lots of bugs and kinks. The department was put together so hastily, and so many parts of it have had financial problems for years, that no one in his right mind will expect the department to get a clean bill of health this first year. So, if that's your chief concern, don't worry about it."

"But, Clark. This will be very disruptive to us. People are trying to get the department up and running, and submitting to an audit will take precious time away from that."

"Now that's a legitimate concern, Janet, I admit. But, the auditors are mindful of that, and we'll work with them to make sure that they cause as little disruption as possible. Getting the Department of Homeland Security's finances straight is *also* a matter of homeland security. If the department can't keep track of the money coming in and the money going out, it won't have the resources it needs to secure the nation."

On and on like this it went for weeks, but finally Hale gave in. My team and I considered performing the audits ourselves, but we realized that with only 130 or so auditors, we didn't have the resources to go over the books of such a huge agency. We hired a well-known accounting firm, KPMG, and for the next several months worked hand in glove with the KPMG audit team to give the department's books a good going over.

Not surprisingly, the auditors found problems. Seven of them were major enough to be considered "material" weaknesses because they were serious enough to affect the financial health of the department as a whole.[21] The auditors and Dick's team worked to develop recommendations that, if implemented, would increase the department's chances of getting a better report card from the auditors the following year.

By the end of 2004, however, as my time at DHS was running out, the department's financial picture was actually worsening. We saw it coming. Time and again, we urged Hale and Chief Financial Officer (CFO) Andy Maner, to beef up the CFO's office with more staffers, and ones with the expertise to oversee the hugely complex process of keeping track of the Department of Homeland Security's finances. Getting a "clean" opinion from the auditors would be even more difficult in the second year because the deadline for reporting financial information was moved up by three months, but both Hale and Maner insisted that they had the bodies they needed to get the job done. As predictably as the sun's rising in the east, their optimism proved to be misplaced.

By the end of fiscal year 2004, the number of material weaknesses *increased* from seven to ten. And, worse still, the state of the department's finances was so chaotic that the auditors were unable to render an opinion on *any* of the department's financial statements.[22] While other components had problems, the major problem lay with the bureau of Immigration and Customs Enforcement, or ICE.

The state of finances at ICE was so dire that there was a shortfall at year's end of between $150 and 200 million. In fact, there was a chance that the bureau had violated the law. The Anti-Deficiency Act prohibits government agencies from spending more money than they take in. The records were such a mess that there was no way to tell for sure whether the bureau had run afoul of this law. All of this would be of concern only to accountants and auditors, except for the real-world impact of it. Because the department's finances as a whole were such a mess, it could not keep track of where precious homeland security dollars were going. Without accurate and timely records, the department could not ensure that each dollar was being used efficiently to secure the nation from another terror attack.

As for ICE in particular, its financial problems had a direct impact on its ability to track down illegal aliens, among whom might even be terrorists. Because of its budgetary shortfall, ICE management had to institute a hiring freeze. Agents were told not to use their cell phones. They had trouble filling their official cars with gas. Of course the less money the bureau had, the fewer criminal illegal aliens it could afford to house. So, it is conceivable that a terrorist might have been released onto the streets because ICE could not keep its books straight! It is not as if these problems have been corrected. According to news articles, ICE continues to be an agency "that loses track of millions of dollars a month."[23]

Wasteful spending and chaotic accounting are themselves security gaps. Unless the department can account for every dollar it spends, and every dollar it spends makes the homeland more secure in some way, it is needlessly exposing the nation to additional risk.

CLOSING THE VULNERABILITY GAP

So nearly five years after the September 11 attacks, and more than three years after the establishment of the Department of Homeland Security, the nation is only marginally more secure. There are still numerous gaps in our defenses that make America an open target.

How worried should we be about this? After, all there are lots of dangers out there, and lots of things to be afraid of. In the scheme of things, is the risk of another terror attack really worth obsessing over? Is it the kind of thing that only pointy-headed Ph.D. candidates and chin-pulling think tank theorists (like me) should spend time pondering? With political scandals, a growing deficit, an undereducated population competing in an increasingly knowledge-driven global marketplace, millions of Americans without health insurance, a continued dependence on other nations for the bulk of our energy supplies, growing concerns about global warming, simultaneous nuclear crises with Iran and North Korea, a resurgent Taliban in Afghanistan, and an increasingly Vietnam-like quagmire in Iraq, is the prospect of another 9/11 really worth the full attention of our nation's leaders right now?

After all, as Secretary Chertoff has pointed out in praising his predecessor, there hasn't been another terror attack. While each reader is certainly free to draw his or her own conclusions as to why this is so, I believe that the preceding pages demonstrate that the Department of Homeland Security has had relatively little to do with that. Indeed, after Hurricane Katrina, it's questionable whether the department has had *anything* to do with it. It would be going much too far to say that creating the department has made the prospect of another attack more likely, but it is fair to underscore the point, made earlier, that thinking that the homeland is more secure than it really is simply because there's now a department called "Homeland Security" is dangerous. Overestimating our security has led us to underprepare for a future attack; the less prepared we are, the more vulnerable to attack we are, and, as Defense Secretary Donald Rumsfeld has aptly said, "weakness is provocative."[1]

But how clear and present is the danger of another terror attack on the homeland? The answer is that the danger of another attack is very clear and very present, indeed, and that's what's really scary. There's nothing theoretical or futuristic about it.

If there's any good news about having Al Qaeda as our main enemy nowadays, it's that we know exactly what to expect from them. During the Cold War, our intelligence agencies were chockablock with analysts, psychiatrists, psychologists, and even psychics and other practitioners of the paranormal, who spent decades trying to get inside the heads of the leaders of Soviet Russia and Maoist China. Yes, the Communists talked vaguely of "world domination," but exactly how far they'd go to try to bring it about was always something of a mystery. The only mystery about bin Laden is exactly where he's hiding. As for his intentions, those are all too clear. No, we don't know when, where, or how the next attack will come. But we do know that Osama bin Laden and his followers and imitators remain intent on terrorizing the homeland.

Like Hitler before him—the chief menace to world security in the last century—bin Laden has laid out his objectives in unambiguous detail. The strategic goal is nothing less than to drive the United States and our allies out of the Middle East, to overthrow the secular governments there, and to install a fundamentalist Muslim caliphate in their place. The tactical means to achieve the goal is to inflict so much death, injury, and economic damage on us and our friends—abroad *and* at home—that we literally and figuratively quit the battlefield and give up the fight.

September 11 was not intended to be the end of a struggle, but the beginning of one. In pronouncement after pronouncement, Al Qaeda has made it clear that another attack on the United States is at the tip top of its agenda. In one of his videotaped messages, bin Laden's deputy, Egyptian militant Ayman al-Zawahiri, warned, "As for you, the Americans, what you have seen in New York and Washington, what losses that you see in Afghanistan and Iraq, despite the media blackout, is merely the losses of the initial clashes. If you go on with the same policy of aggression against Muslims, you will see, with God's will, what will make you forget the horrible things in Vietnam and

Afghanistan."[2] Bin Laden himself has urged the American people to "understand the lesson of New York and Washington raids which came in response to some of your previous crimes . . . God is my witness, the youth of Islam are preparing things that will fill your hearts with terror."[3]

Our nation's leaders confirm that these threats should be taken seriously. In his final appearance before a congressional committee before stepping down as the number two man at the Department of Homeland Security, Admiral Jim Loy warned the members of the Senate Select Committee on Intelligence in February 2005:

> We believe that attacking the homeland remains at the top of al-Qaida's operational priority list, despite the fact that more than three years have passed since September 11, 2001. We judge that al-Qaida continues to view the homeland as an attractive target for a variety of reasons, and that the next dramatic attack will attempt to replicate the 9/11 "model" of multiple attacks against geographically distant and symbolic targets that cause unprecedented economic damage, mass casualties, and physical destruction. While al-Qaida and its affiliated elements currently appear more capable of attacking United States interests outside of the homeland, we believe that their intent remains strong for attempting another major operation here. . . . The strategic intent of al-Qaida's remaining leaders and planners to attempt another dramatic homeland attack is clear.[4]

Echoing his Homeland Security Department counterpart, CIA Director Porter Goss stressed at the same hearing that "Al Qaeda is intent on finding ways to circumvent U.S. security enhancements to strike Americans in the homeland."[5]

But wanting to a launch another attack on our homeland is only part of the equation. Even wanting *fervently* to do so something gets you only so far; desire is just one step along the continuum to action. The next step is determination, and so the next question is whether Al Qaeda has the steely resolve it takes to turn a morbid wish into a deadly act.

Sadly for us, the terrorists' determination matches their desire. They are resolved to act on their wish to visit more destruction on the homeland, because, in their minds, to kill Americans in the putative name of Islam is to earn Allah's favor and to win an express ticket to be with him for eternity in Paradise. "Let me be a martyr in the service of jihad," is the prayer constantly on the lips of our enemies. There seems to be no end to the number of young men (and, increasingly, young women) in the Muslim world who are seeking to join their brothers in sowing death and destruction among us.

This bloodlust for death further widens the odds against us in the war on terror at home and abroad. For us, life is an end in itself. For terrorists, death is an end in itself, and life is a means to that end. Therefore, we are far likelier to break under the weight of terror than they are to break under the weight of counterterror. For all the bluster and bravado in Washington today, would it really take more than a couple more 9/11s to persuade us to quit the Middle East and leave the vast majority of Muslims, who no doubt love freedom as much as we do, to the tender mercies of the fanatical fundamentalist fringe? Our retreat from Lebanon in the 1980s and our retreat from Somalia in the 1990s suggests the answer.

Why, then, hasn't there been an attack in five years? Part of the reason, to be fair, is that it's marginally harder to strike the homeland today than it was on September 11.

Part of the reason is the mismatch between our sense of time and theirs. For us, five years is an eternity. If five years have gone by without another terror attack, our internal national clock leads us inexorably to assume that there probably won't be another. Al Qaeda, on the other hand, "operates on a very long timeline."[6] Moreover, paradoxically, the periodic raising of the threat level over the last few years has not served to keep the constant danger of terror uppermost in our minds. That's because none of the alerts has been followed by an actual attack. Of course, that's good news. But, the psychological effect has been to becalm us. Instead of being conscious of danger, afraid of it, and motivated by it, we're skeptical of it. The raising and lowering of the threat level is now only so much extra background noise competing for our attention along with the rest of the cacophony of modern life.

The main reason that there hasn't yet been a follow-up attack is that it takes time to plan and execute spectacular attacks. If the goal were simply to kill a handful of Americans here and there at random, that would be a very short order for Al Qaeda, especially since its foot soldiers are willing to give up their own lives to take others'. But a spectacular attack takes a lot of time and effort to pull off. Al Qaeda is, indeed, "patient, deliberate, and methodical in operational planning for major attacks."[7] Far from being a good news story, that we haven't been attacked in five years probably means that Al Qaeda is working overtime to make the next attack even more horrific than the last one. Indeed, there are indications that this is, in fact, the case.

The CIA, the FBI, and the Homeland Security Department all agree that Al Qaeda desires to attack America with a weapon of mass destruction. The FBI Director allows that the group is "*seeking* weapons of mass destruction, including chemical weapons, so-called dirty bombs or some form of biological agent, such as anthrax."[8] The Homeland Security Department goes further in saying that, "Al Qaeda and affiliated elements currently have the capability to produce small amounts of crude biological toxins and toxic chemical materials, and *may have acquired* small amounts of radioactive materials."[9] The CIA chief went the farthest of all by warning that "it may be only a matter of time before Al Qaeda and other groups *attempt to use* chemical, biological, radiological or nuclear weapons," suggesting that they already have them.[10] We know that bin Laden has declared it a "religious duty" for Muslims to acquire nuclear weapons,[11] and numerous news reports since our invasion of Afghanistan have chronicled the discovery by coalition forces of evidence that Al Qaeda was actively pursuing the acquisition and development of chemical, biological, and nuclear weapons.[12]

This brings us to another element in the calculus as to whether the terror threat is still serious enough to worry about. Terrorists have the desire to strike another devastating blow against the homeland; indeed, they appear intent on striking an even more devastating blow next time. They clearly have the resolve it takes to turn that desire into action. They also appear to be on their way to acquiring the necessary weapons for launching a catastrophic attack; in fact, they may already have them.

However, the reader of any dime-store detective novel can tell you that to make a case against a suspect, you need to establish more than motive and means. You have to show that the suspect had the *opportunity* to commit the crime in question. The bad news is that this is the easiest part of the case to make.

I have shown how easy it remains for terrorists outside the country to sneak in. It's harder for them to do so now than it's ever been before. But, it's still far easier than it should be, and that makes it easy enough. Some unknown number of foreign terrorists is already hiding here among us, and some unknown number of native-born Americans has defected to the terrorists' side.

Once on American soil, a virtual smorgasbord of targets remains open for terrorists to attack. Take the one that you'd think would be the hardest to attack nowadays—aviation. If there's one thing that terrorists shouldn't be able to do five years after the last attack, it is to launch another one in more or less the same way. There are some who say that this is impossible. A former White House adviser on homeland security, Richard Falkenrath, is one of them. In a 2005 hearing, he said that we'd "taken care of" aviation in the years since the last attack.[13]

He, and those who agree with him, should read chapter three. Yes, cockpit doors have been hardened, some pilots are armed, the number of air marshals has been increased, and airport security tends to be tighter nowadays, but it is still just as easy today to sneak guns, knives, and bombs past airport screeners as it was in 2001, even though the federal government has since taken over the screening function and spent billions of dollars to put various enhanced security measures in place. Armed with only box cutters, nineteen hijackers were able to kill nearly 3,000 people, destroy the Twin Towers, seriously damage the Pentagon, and make a beeline for either the White House or the Capitol. Imagine the damage that they could do with guns, knives, and bombs!

Apparently, terrorists *have* imagined this, and apparently, they're not at all deterred by the marginal improvements in security that the Transportation Security Administration has made. The Deputy Secretary of Homeland Security admitted in February 2005 testimony that, despite these improvements, "al-Qaida operatives have received flight training, and . . . al-Qaida continues to consider new and novel methods for planning and conducting attacks against civil aviation in the United States."[14] Months later, in an attempt to bolster the sagging case for the war in Iraq, the President disclosed for the first time that two 9/11-style attacks have been foiled in the last five years, one on the West Coast in 2002 and another on the East Coast in 2003.[15]

Terrorists don't have to go to the trouble of trying to evade the scrutiny of passenger checkpoints. They could bypass the screening process altogether and simply place a bomb in the cargo hold. The loss of life would probably be limited to the occupants of the plane, but *any* attack on aviation would have a devastating impact on the national psyche. It would prove that we are weak at our strongest point.

A nuclear weapon could easily be smuggled into any one of our seaports as well. Ninety-four percent of incoming cargo containers are not inspected; as for the 6 percent that are inspected, there's no assurance that any weapons of mass destruction will be found because (among other things) the department has yet to deploy enough equipment capable of detecting them. Of course, a nuclear attack could exceed the impact of the last attack by several orders of magnitude.

It is easier still to attack mass transit systems, critical infrastructure, and soft targets, and while the Secretary of Homeland Security may think that an attack on mass transit will kill "only" about thirty people, depending upon exactly what is struck, and where, when, and how it's done, the impact of an attack on any of these sectors and sites could easily surpass that of 9/11.[16]

If the CIA or FBI pick up indications that terrorists are plotting to strike the homeland again, will they share this with the department that's supposed to protect the homeland from the attack? Five years after the last attack, that's still a question mark, so terrorists' chances of slipping under the DHS radar screen the next time are better than they should be.

As the disastrous response to Katrina shows, we're still woefully unprepared to deal with the consequences of either a natural disaster or a terrorist attack. Terrorists have surely taken note of this, and, since weakness is indeed provocative, they may well have moved up their timetable for the next strike.

Finally, the Department of Homeland Security has been woefully underfunded from the start. Instead of carefully stewarding its limited resources to get the most bang for each counterterrorism buck, it's wasted millions of dollars and lost track of millions more.

All of these are holes in our security. The terrorists are aware of them, and they are more than capable of slipping through them.

So, we know the terrorists' side of the ledger. They continue to have the intention, the resolve, and the capability to inflict grave harm on us, the creation of the Department of Homeland Security and its subsequent exertions to the contrary notwithstanding.

What about the other side of the ledger? What about our intention, our resolve, and our capability to protect ourselves from terror? If both of sides of the ledger were in equilibrium, there'd be a "balance of terror" again.

But the ledger is not in equilibrium. There isn't a balance of terror. While there were certainly moments of high anxiety during the Cold War, for the most part it was a period of remarkable stability in global affairs. In the age of terror, we can only look back on that anxious period with nostalgia.

Of course, it's not a question of our intent. We don't *want* to be attacked. Yes, the President famously challenged militants by taunting, "bring them on," and that was certainly ill-advised.[17] Hundreds of our fighting men and women have died in Iraq since he uttered those defiant words three years ago. No one can know for sure whether any of those lives were taken in direct response to that specific challenge, but it is never a good idea to encourage attacks on your own forces. The President's remarks were focused on Iraq, and he was merely making the boast that our forces are up to the challenge of defending our interests there. Neither he nor anyone else in his Administration has invited terrorists to attack the homeland again.

What about our *resolve,* then? That's where the scale is dangerously out of whack. On the one side, you have Al Qaeda bound and determined to hit us again, and even harder than last time. On the other side, you have the leaders of the Department of Homeland Security, who, it seemed, spent more time and energy fighting me than fighting the terrorists. Again and again, my words of warning and my pleas for action fell on deaf ears. Our leaders dragged their feet when steps could have been taken to make the homeland more secure.

It's been two years now since I stumbled onto the fact that there are stacks of boxes in our embassy in Saudi Arabia containing the applications of young men who applied for visas to the United States around the same time as the nineteen hijackers, and two years since I pointed this out to the men in charge of securing the homeland. Why hasn't anyone from the Department of Homeland Security bothered to look through them to see whether there might be links between any of those applicants and any of the hijackers? There may or may not be any links, but we'll know for sure only if someone bothers to look through them. If there are any links, each day that goes by without our finding them increases the danger that a sleeper cell plotting and planning a follow-up attack will escape detection until it's too late.

It's been almost three years since we recommended the wide deployment of available technologies that could all but guarantee that any weapons concealed on passengers' bodies or in their carry-on luggage could be detected by airport screeners. Three years later, these technologies are still being piloted or deployed on only a limited basis.

It's been two years since we recommended ways in which Customs inspectors could greatly increase their ability to detect deadly uranium in cargo containers, and, as noted above, those measures have yet to be taken. We've invaded a nation and waged a bloody and costly war to combat a nonexistent nuclear threat overseas; here at home, there's a real nuclear threat and we've left ourselves wide open for it.

In short, our rhetoric to the contrary notwithstanding, our resolve to defeat the terrorist threat here at home does not match the terrorist' resolve to defeat us here at home. This is what makes the vulnerability gap so wide in the terrorists' favor. As long as this imbalance remains, each man, woman, and child in the United States will be in mortal danger.

The good news is that we're more than capable of defending ourselves. That said, let me hasten to make myself absolutely clear. I'm not claiming that we have it in our power to stop terror attacks completely. We can never reduce to zero the chance of another terror strike. Anyone who makes that claim is either woefully ignorant or dangerously demagogic. We can narrow the vulnerability gap, but we can never close it all the way.

The odds favor the terrorists, and it is simply an awful fact of life that this will always be true. This passage from the Introduction is worth repeating here—The Department of Homeland Security inspectors, screeners, and air marshals who guard our borders; the Department of Homeland Security analysts who work with their colleagues in the intelligence community here at home and abroad to detect and analyze threats against the homeland; and the Department of Homeland Security law enforcement personnel who work with their counterparts in other departments in our federal, state, and local governments and with foreign governments to track down known terrorists and to keep track of suspected ones, all have to "get it right" every single moment of the day. One mistake could mean catastrophe. Would-be terrorists, on the other hand, have to succeed just once to kill thousands or even millions, and to devastate our economy and way of life in the process.

To further tip the scales in the terrorists' favor, ours is the most open nation in the world; it's a huge country with a huge number of potential targets, from airports to seaports to train stations to nuclear power plants to shopping malls. If Al Qaeda were ever to settle for small-scale attacks here like the ones it's inflicted on government buildings, places of worship, hotels, restaurants, and nightclubs abroad, the loss of life and the infliction of injury would be relatively small. The psychic impact would be immense, however, and the national economy would likely buckle and sway under the weight of it.

Of course, we are a nation that highly values civil rights and civil liberties. Our Constitution—the legal charter under which we live *and* our collective national "DNA"—prohibits us from imposing the kind of draconian measures on our citizens and residents that other nations do not hesitate to impose when they find themselves to be under siege. Certainly this is as it should be. It would be tragically ironic if, in the process of defending our freedom, we were to sacrifice our liberty. In doing so, furthermore, we will have handed terrorists a signal victory without their firing another shot.

Nor can, or should, we wall ourselves off from the rest of the world by making it all but impossible for foreigners to immigrate to our country legally and to visit for purposes of trade, tourism, and study. Being a welcoming nation is likewise part of our national DNA, and increasingly, it is becoming an economic and security imperative. The demands of the global marketplace are such that we simply must welcome foreign talent to help us compete in the knowledge-driven twenty-first century economy. Because our economy depends upon this international engagement, our national security does, too.

We should do what we can do, though. We should reduce the vulnerability gap to as close to zero as possible. That our leaders haven't done in the last four years what they could have done to secure the homeland is irresponsible and inexcusable, and history will judge them harshly for it. But Lord Keynes was right—in the long run we are all dead; the problem is that we may not have the luxury of waiting for history. We have to get through the "short run" first. Every day is a race against the clock counting down to the next terror attack. Every day we fail to do what we can to secure ourselves against the terror threat is a day the clock wins.

Secretary Rumsfeld's apt admonition that weakness is provocative bears repeating, and this time, it bears noting the context in which he made the remark. He was speaking in reference to the Philippines' decision in the summer of 2004 to pull its forces from Iraq in exchange for the life of a Filipino hostage. "If you want more of something," he chided, "you reward it, and if you want less you penalize it."[18]

I leave to another day the argument over whether capitulating to terrorists' demands is a smart strategy or a dumb one, though I must say that I wholeheartedly agree with the Defense Chief on this one; the issue for this book is the larger point he makes. If you want to discourage something, namely, terrorism, you should make it as hard for terrorists to succeed as you possibly can. If you don't make it as hard as you can, you are only encouraging terrorists to strike again. The import of Rumsfeld's remarks on the war on terror here at home seems to be lost on the Department of Homeland Security.

What, then, specifically, would I have our leaders do? The answer is implicit in the preceding pages, but let me make it explicit here.

BORDER SECURITY

In terms of border security, I'd send a team of investigators to Saudi Arabia to go through those boxes of unexamined visa applications to see whether there might be any links to the fifteen Saudi hijackers. If any such links are found, I would attempt to track down the applicants in question, wherever they may be in the world today.

I would expand the Visa Security Officer program beyond Saudi Arabia and the other handful of countries where it exists today to every one of the other 200 or so countries around the world from which our consular officers issue visas. I would ensure that each DHS officer is trained in fraud detection, interview techniques, and the other tools of the counterterrorism trade. In addition, each such officer should be able to speak the local language and be familiar with local politics, history, culture, and customs. Foreign nationals are, indeed, indispensable to the operation of our diplomatic missions abroad, but they need not and should not be involved in the visa issuance process in any way.

The Terrorist Screening Database should be made as accurate, up-to-date, and comprehensive as possible, and it should be made accessible in real time to those officials who need immediate access to it.

The U.S. VISIT system, including the exit feature, should be installed and operational in *every* port of entry in the United States, and visitors from Mexico and Canada should be subjected to it.

Every foreign visitor to the United States, not just first-time visitors, should be required to submit to having all ten of his fingers scanned so that the scans can be checked against the FBI's extensive database of terrorists and criminals. This process should start immediately.

Fully realizing that this is a very controversial recommendation, I would end the visa waiver program as quickly as possible. I would require every foreigner wishing to visit the United States to submit to the now rather extensive scrutiny of the visa issuance process. This would mean, of course, that we Americans would lose our reciprocal privilege to visit, without a visa, the twenty-seven countries in the program, but this seems to me to be a small price to pay to close a loophole that could permit the next Richard Reid or Zacarias Moussaoui to escape another layer of scrutiny. It is possible to do this without slowing down the flow of trade, tourism, and study upon which the smooth functioning of the United States and, indeed, the international community, depends. It would require, though, the hiring of hundreds more consular officers, but this is a step that I believe to be long overdue anyway.

Doing away with the visa waiver program would have the ancillary benefit of removing the incentive for terrorists to steal passports from countries in the program. If, nevertheless, a passport is found to be a lost or stolen one, the bearer should not, under *any* circumstances, be admitted to the United States, and the document in question should not, under *any* circumstances be returned to him. The bearer should be prosecuted to the full extent of the law for attempting to enter the United States on a passport other than his own. Of course, if there are other criminal law violations, or, worse yet, if the bearer has any terrorist connections, he should be prosecuted on those grounds, too. Any inspector who knowingly admits the bearer of a lost or stolen passport into the United States, and any inspector who fails to check all relevant passport information against the available lost and stolen database, should be fired summarily and prosecuted for recklessly endangering the security of the United States. To the extent we know of people who have already been admitted to the United States on a lost or stolen passport, ICE agents should make every effort to track them down and apprehend them.

As for American passports, the State Department should be required to take fraud much more seriously than it presently does. During my time as Inspector General of the State Department, I would have knock-down, drag-out fights with the Bureau of Diplomatic Security over this. The principal job of "DS," as it is called by State Department insiders, is to guard our embassies and consulates against attack and to protect our diplomats from assassination. A statutory provision also gives DS jurisdiction over investigating passport fraud. The Inspector General of the department is charged by law with investigating any and all kinds of fraud in the programs and operations of the State Department, including passport fraud. Given this concurrent jurisdiction, and the likelihood that DS would focus on physical security issues at the expense of documentary ones, I worked for nearly two years straight to try to reach a compromise to ensure that passport fraud would get the attention it deserved. It was ultimately a losing battle, as DS had much more money, many more agents, and much more clout in the department than the Inspector General. The Consular Affairs bureau continued to refer suspected passport cases to DS as a matter of course, but just as I suspected and feared, after I left the State Department, the GAO issued a report confirming that DS agents give short shrift to investigating passport fraud.[19] To fix the problem, the State Department Office of Inspector General should be given exclusive jurisdiction over passport fraud, and it should be given the money and staffing necessary to pursue the issue as aggressively as homeland security demands.

The diversity visa program should be done away with altogether. Anyone who merits a visa to the United States should apply for it through the normal process.

As for illegal immigration, we cannot end it completely. We cannot and should not close our borders (even if we attempted to, some illegal immigrants would still find a way in), but we can do more to stop the problem than we've done. While there can never be enough agents to man the border, we can and should dramatically increase the number of Border Patrol agents. They must be aided by an intricate network of sensors, alarms, cameras, unmanned aerial vehicles, and robots that is deployed all along the border and that performs at optimal levels at all times.

When we catch illegal aliens, we need to determine whether they have any terrorist connections. Of course, any terrorists among the illegal alien population must be prosecuted. Non-terrorists must be immediately returned to their country of origin. If their country of origin refuses to take them, they must be detained for as long as it takes until their own country or some third country can be persuaded to take them. As an incentive to persuade countries to take back their own citizens who've illegally entered the United States, we should use all of the tools in our diplomatic toolbox to persuade them to do so.

AVIATION

We should immediately deploy backscatter technology to every airport in the country. By means of this X-ray-like device, it is *impossible* to miss any gun or knife concealed on a passenger's body or in his carry-on luggage. To address legitimate privacy concerns, the image of the passenger can be converted into a cartoon-like stick figure. To further mitigate privacy concerns, the person viewing the image can be located at some remove from the checkpoint.

Likewise, multiview X-ray machines should be deployed at airports throughout the United States, so as to enable screeners to automatically view the contents of bags from every conceivable angle. And Threat Image Projection machines, with a regularly updated rotating library of realistic images of deadly weapons, should also be deployed.

Teams of undercover agents from TSA itself, the Office of Inspector General, and the Government Accountability Office should regularly test the screening system to make sure that both screeners and their supervisors are always on alert. Training should be a regular part of each screener's workweek. Screeners who consistently fail to spot suspicious items should be fired, and the same goes for the supervisors who are supposed to supervise them.

Everyone who is to work in and around airports and airplanes should be subjected to an extensive background investigation to determine whether they have any terrorist ties or a serious criminal background. "Everyone" includes vendors, concessionaires, janitors, and maintenance personnel. Only *after* passing such a background check should someone be allowed to work in aviation. Under no circumstances should illegal aliens be allowed to work in airports. The Transportation Worker Identification Card (TWIC) should be rolled out as soon as possible, so that biometrics are used to confirm that those entering sensitive areas are who they claim to be.

Any requirements imposed upon them that compromise the anonymity of air marshals should be jettisoned. Any air marshals found to have engaged in illegal or inappropriate conduct on the job should be immediately fired.

All cargo entering the hold of commercial aircraft should be screened for explosives beforehand. TSA should do this screening, not the airlines. Baggage (as opposed to cargo) should *always* be screened before it is loaded onto flights. *No* "alternative procedures" should be allowed under any circumstances.

The Immigration Advisory Program, by which our customs inspectors are stationed at foreign airports to catch and stop terrorists (and other suspicious people) from boarding airplanes bound for the United States, should be expanded to every country in the world from which such flights depart. According to the Customs and Border Protection chief, foreign governments and airlines have no choice, as a practical matter, but to let these inspectors exercise veto power over who comes into the United States. The program is supposed to pay for itself, and there is precedent for it in other countries. If it takes an agreement on our part likewise to allow a foreign nation's inspectors to be stationed at our airports to check flights bound for their country, so be it.

To prevent mid-air diversions of flights bound for the United States, we should ensure that passenger names are checked against our government's watch lists as much *before* flights depart as possible. If carriers are supportive of transmitting passenger information at the time of check in, and if the technology exists to do this, we should mandate this procedure right away.

PORT SECURITY

The linchpins of Customs' maritime security strategy should be radically overhauled. The Automated Targeting System should be tightened by enacting pending legislation that would, among other things: (1) identify shipments' true port of origin and any and all stops along their way to the United States; (2) determine all the parties who were involved in any way in the shipping process; and (3) confirm the accuracy of the manifest's description of the contents. Electronic anti-tampering devices should be deployed to detect any tampering with a sealed container once it leaves the port of origin.

As for the Container Security Initiative, we should insist on having as many inspectors at foreign ports as we deem necessary properly to oversee the foreign inspection process. "Oversee" should mean to observe with our own eyes that foreign inspectors are carrying out inspections to our satisfaction. All containers bound for the United States must be targeted, and any containers that our inspectors believe should be inspected must be inspected by the foreign inspectors; otherwise, there is no point in our participating in the program. All foreign ports must have and use radiation isotope identifier devices, or RIIDs, the aim being to prevent nuclear bombs from being smuggled into U.S. ports. If foreign ports don't have this one kind of detection device that can detect, pinpoint, and identify deadly radiation, a foreign port inspection will do no good. Of course, inspections here at home must likewise be conducted with the best available nuclear detection technology. Every port must have RIIDs in sufficient numbers so that every container identified in the targeting process as suspicious enough to be inspected is inspected for deadly nuclear material. Finally, both here and abroad, any inspections to be conducted must be conducted promptly. Any delay can constitute another security gap that terrorists can exploit.

As for the Customs Trade Partnership Against Terrorism, or C-TPAT, program, the flaws and holes in it are such that it should be completely abandoned. Even a program that reduces the chance of future inspections *after* an extensive investigation and verification process is risky. In the age of terror, it is far too risky to trust first and verify later.

MASS TRANSIT

It is extraordinarily difficult to prevent attacks on mass transit systems, but we can do more to reduce the risk of them. After the Madrid attacks in the spring of 2004 and the London attacks in the summer of 2005, we took all the right steps. We increased the number of surveillance cameras. Armed police and security guards patrolled subway and rail stations. Bomb-sniffing dogs and sensors were deployed. Passengers were encouraged to report suspicious items and suspicious acting people. After the London at-tacks, New York, New Jersey, and Salt Lake City even went so far as to con-duct random searches of passenger bags. But these measures were quickly ratcheted back or done away with altogether as soon as the danger seemed to pass. All of these measures should be institutionalized; they should be the norm, rather than the exception. Otherwise, terrorists, being observant, clever, and adaptive, will simply wait until heightened security measures are relaxed and then strike us when our guard goes back down.

CRITICAL INFRASTRUCTURE AND SOFT TARGETS

It is inexcusable that the Department of Homeland Security has yet to final-ize and approve a prioritized and credible list of the nation's most critical in-frastructure. It is urgent that the department complete this task so that the necessary plans can be devised and implemented to protect these vitally im-portant sectors and sites from terrorist attack.

As a conservative, I believe that government's regulatory role should be limited. Indeed, regulation (and legislation) should be a tool of last resort, but it's been nearly five years since the attacks, and private industry (in whose hands 85 percent of critical infrastructure lies) has yet to take ade-quate steps to close security gaps that endanger the entire country. It is a good thing that the department now recognizes that regulation of the chem-ical industry is imperative, but the chemical industry isn't the only critical infrastructure sector that has yet to regulate itself adequately, and so it is not the only one in need of government regulation.

Because protecting critical infrastructure is in the national interest, it is entirely appropriate that the federal government share some of the burden of funding security enhancements. Whether that cost sharing takes the form of a direct appropriation or grant, tax incentives, or federally guaranteed loans or bonds is for the Administration and Congress to work out.

Finally, Secretary Chertoff's proposal to separate the department's intelli-gence unit from its infrastructure protection unit could not be more ill ad-vised. Linking intelligence and infrastructure protection was among the more insightful features of the White House strategy upon which the Department of Homeland Security was based. By placing the people in charge of detecting and analyzing threats against the homeland in the same unit as the people in charge of helping the owners and operators of critical infrastructure protect their assets from those threats, the department's founders were making it more likely that threats would be communicated in a timely fashion. Given the tendency of intelligence agencies to keep information close to the vest and given the unfamiliarity of most infrastructure owners and operators with intelligence, linking the two functions serves to inculcate in each a culture of communication, cooperation, and mutual understanding.

In terms of soft targets, there's admittedly little that the government can do to protect us. Soft targets have been attacked so often in Israel that the citizenry is willing to tolerate magnetometers in grocery stores and shopping malls. It is commonplace to find armed guards in restaurants and movie theaters. Absent an attack in this country on a soft target, the American people are unlikely to tolerate security measures like these.

That said, if the department were better at the systematic collection and analysis of intelligence from its employees in the field and its state and local partners, it would be more likely to pick up indications that soft targets are in danger. If there were specific intelligence indicating a threat, the soft target at issue could implement such security measures as might be necessary.

As a general matter, the more iconic the venue, the bigger it is, and the more strategically located it is, the more likely a given soft target is to be attacked. Amusement parks such as Disney World and Disneyland, more adult-focused entertainment venues such as Las Vegas casinos, and office buildings, such as the Empire State building in New York and the Sears Tower in Chicago, come to mind. As it stands today, such potential targets are largely on their own. The department must do a better job of identifying soft targets that are likely to be on terrorists' target wish list and working with those targets to take such steps as are necessary to protect themselves.

INTELLIGENCE

The sine qua non of the department is intelligence. Unless it has immediate access to the best available intelligence as to threats against the homeland, there is little it can do to protect the homeland from another attack.

The department should go back to square one. The drafters of the Homeland Security Act rightly intended for DHS to take the lead on synthesizing and analyzing all intelligence concerning threats against the homeland, and they rightly intended for DHS to take the lead on consolidating the various terrorist watch lists. Accordingly, both the National Counterterrorism Center and the Terrorist Screening Center should be run by the Department of Homeland Security. Any instances of the rest of the intelligence community's keeping homeland security-related information from the department must be brought to the immediate attention of the Director of National Intelligence, or, failing that, the President himself, to resolve in the department's favor.

The department must do a far better job of collating into a cohesive whole the intelligence its various internal components collect. It must also do a better job of ensuring the smooth flow of credible intelligence to *and* from its state and local and private sector partners. The department must be of one mind about intelligence that it passes on: if it's important enough to pass on, state, local, and private sector partners who act on it shouldn't be criticized and undercut for doing so. Finally, under no circumstances should intelligence be passed on to the families and friends of DHS officials before it is shared with the general public.

PREPAREDNESS

It is now clear for all the world to see that the nation is woefully unprepared to respond to another catastrophic disaster. If terrorists had targeted the levees in New Orleans, the government's response would have been no quicker and no more effective than it was to Hurricane Katrina. It is imperative that every major city have a well-thought-out evacuation plan. Contingency plans should be in place as to where people who need shelter for an extended period of time may go. Adequate stockpiles of food, potable water, and medical supplies must be made available. The chain of command must be crystal clear. To facilitate the swift delivery of aid and the establishment of a clear chain of command, the Department of Homeland Security should move at warp speed to open up the regional centers around the country that were promised at its inception. First responders must be able to communicate with each other and with state and federal officials. Drills and exercises must be conducted frequently, they must simulate the chaos of the real world as closely as possible, and any lessons learned must lead to prompt corrective action. One hundred percent of preparedness funds should be allocated on the basis of risk. If pork barrel politics has any place at all in government spending, it should have no place at all when it comes to homeland security spending. Finally, stripping FEMA of its preparedness functions and leaving it with only recovery-related functions should be reversed. It is impossible to separate preparedness from recovery, but if it were possible, the disastrous response to Katrina shows why doing so is ill-advised.

WASTEFUL SPENDING AND SLOPPY ACCOUNTING

Through bitter experience, the following lessons should have been learned by now. If these lessons continue to go unheeded, some of the billions of dollars spent to clean up the Gulf Coast following Hurricanes Katrina and Rita will be misspent.

The Department of Homeland Security has too few experienced procurement professionals. More must be hired on an urgent basis to oversee the billions of dollars that the department spends on contractors. The Chief Procurement Officer should be given the authority to hire, fire, and direct the work of his counterparts at the component level. Otherwise, different department components will continue to have carte blanche to make contracting decisions that may not be in the best interest of the department as a whole.

Under no circumstances should contractors be allowed to police themselves or each other. No-bid contracts should be prohibited. Every contract should be structured so that there is an incentive for the contractor to perform in a prompt, thorough, and cost-efficient manner. Under no circumstances should profits be based on a contractor's costs, and the criteria upon which any awards are based should be established *before* any award fees are actually paid. If the sole function of a contractor is to oversee the work of subcontractors, the department should contract directly with the subcontractors. The department should define contract requirements up front to avoid costly modifications later, and it should not under any circumstances let a contractor determine what its requirements are. And as important as it is to meet deadlines, time pressures should never be allowed to dictate contract costs and performance.

As for accounting matters, likewise, the department has too few accounting professionals. The Chief Financial Officer should be given the authority to hire, fire, and direct the work of the component's CFOs to ensure that each component places the same priority emphasis on accurate, timely, and orderly financial accounting.

In order to implement these recommendations, the department will need three things that it has been sorely lacking to date: more money, competent leadership, and a culture that welcomes and prizes oversight and accountability.

Money

From day one, the department has been underfunded. We cannot "do" homeland security on the cheap. Backscatter machines, multiview X-ray machines, explosive detection systems, explosive trade detection machines, radiation isotope identification devices, and other such technologies all cost money. Placing armed patrols, bomb-sniffing dogs, surveillance cameras, and sensors in subways, at rail stations, and in and around buses on an on-going basis costs money. Protecting chemical plants, nuclear power facilities, financial networks, telecommunication systems, and the food and water supply costs money.

We rightly spare no expense when it comes to defending our interests abroad and defending our nation from a military-style attack by a hostile foreign nation. We should likewise spare no expense to defend our nation here at home, now that we're under a continuous threat of attack on our own soil by hostile foreign groups and individuals.

The Bush Administration has been much criticized for arguing that terrorists are "at war" with us, so we must be at war with them. While I have not hesitated to be critical of other aspects of Administration policy, in my judgment "war" is exactly the right metaphor and organizing principle. Al Qaeda *is* at war with us, and so we had better be at war with them.

But, the problem is that the Administration goes only halfway. There's an offensive aspect to this war, *and* a defensive aspect. The Administration is to be commended for taking the fight to the enemy abroad—the more terrorists we can find, capture, and kill overseas, the better. As the President often says, we are "on the hunt," and we need to stay on the hunt.[20] Indeed, had we stayed on the hunt in Afghanistan and not diverted time, attention, and resources to an exaggerated threat in Iraq, Osama bin Laden might be dead or in custody today, and Iraq might not have become a terrorist training camp and recruiting ground.

But, we've bungled the defensive aspect of homeland security, too. We haven't done everything we can do to make the homeland as safe from terror as possible. A large part of the reason for that is the lack of money. When the department's budget was put together in late 2002, only $125 million was added to the existing budgets of the various component parts. Anyone who knows anything about mergers knows that they are very costly up front. If there are any economies to be achieved by combining businesses, it is usually years down the road that those savings are realized. If you add to the mix that most, if not all, of these components were dysfunctional to start with, even more money was needed at the beginning to try to fix these problems before they compounded themselves and affected the financial and operational performance of the entire organization.

Our priorities are misplaced when the budget of the Department of Defense is almost exactly ten times larger than that of the Department of Homeland Security. As between protecting and advancing our interests abroad, and defending our own soil, the latter is even more important. Defense should be like charity, beginning at home and *then* spreading abroad.

Even the United States of America, the richest nation in the world, can't do everything. We have to make choices. We have to set priorities. We can either add to the deficit, cut government spending, raise taxes, or forego future tax cuts (which the Administration deems to be the same thing). I, for one, believe that it is imperative that we get our fiscal house in order. To my mind, further adding to the deficit is not an option. I'd cut as much waste, pork, and corporate entitlements as possible from the budget and then make up any difference by foregoing tax cuts. For me, raising taxes would be a last resort, but reasonable minds can differ as to what the fiscal choices should be; however, no reasonable person can disagree that choices have to be made. To continue to underfund homeland security is effectively to draw a bull's eye on the nation.

Competent Leadership

We need competent leadership at the Department of Homeland Security, at *every* level of the organization. The establishment of the department represented the largest reorganization of the federal government in more than half a century. It was by far the most complex reorganization in our history. It was at one and the same time a merger, an acquisition, and a start-up, comprising bits and pieces of twenty-two agencies with a total workforce of 180,000 people throughout the nation and abroad. To top it all off, all of this was put together in a few months.

Making a behemoth like this work would test the skills of the most expert business manager. But the first Homeland Security Secretary was a politician, a politician from Central Casting. Like the archetypal politician, Ridge was amiable, charismatic, commanding, and, even inspiring, but also like the archetypal politician, he was a "big-picture guy," long on generalities and short on specifics. He was details-averse, hands-off, and credulous. He lacked business experience, as well as any direct management experience to speak of.

It is telling that the Administration's first choice to succeed him was the ethics-challenged former New York City Police Commissioner Bernie Kerik. It took the press only a few weeks to discover and document what the White House personnel office should have uncovered about Kerik's questionable background before he was nominated. The important point here is that someone like Kerik was nominated in the first place. It's hard to believe that he would have been seriously considered for any other Cabinet position in the national security realm. Yes, he was the head of the largest police force in the nation, and the Homeland Security Secretary has to interact with police chiefs from time to time, but is this enough experience to head what is arguably the most complex and important agency in the federal government?

Secretary Chertoff has been an improvement. He is brilliant, inquisitive, decisive, tough, and detail-oriented. He is certainly no politician, and there is an upside to that.

There is also a downside, and it shows. His offhand comment that greater effort should be focused on protecting airliners, since an attack on one of them could kill 3,000 people, as opposed to a subway bomb, which "may" kill just thirty people, quite predictably got him into hot water. Part of a Homeland Security Secretary's job is to convey the impression that every effort will be made to protect *every* American. It is one thing to say that we have to concentrate necessarily limited resources on the greatest threats and vulnerabilities; it is another thing to suggest that thirty potential deaths are too few to worry about or that the millions who use mass transit are on their own. This is the kind of thing you don't have to explain to a politician.

And, on top of being politically tone deaf, Chertoff has no management experience to speak of, either. That lack of experience certainly showed in the slow, chaotic department response to Katrina.

As I argued in a *New York Times* op-ed as the President considered nominees to succeed Ridge, a Homeland Security Secretary "should have experience in both the business world and in Washington, and be as adept at overseeing mergers and acquisitions as at navigating the federal bureaucracy and Capitol Hill."[21]

If managerial experience and expertise is critical at the top, it's no less critical at other levels in the department. In the wake of Michael Brown's forced resignation as head of FEMA, following Katrina, new attention was focused on the competence of DHS managers. A quiescent Senate Homeland Security Committee that held up my nomination for two years promptly approved Brown's. Stung by Brown's dismal performance when put to the test, the committee briefly held up the nomination of 36-year-old Julie Myers to head the critically important Immigration and Customs Enforcement bureau. Questions were raised as to whether her nomination to head the nation's second largest federal law enforcement agency after the FBI had more to do with her being married to Chertoff's Chief of Staff and her being the niece of the former Chairman of the Joint Chiefs of Staff than her law enforcement credentials.[22]

Brown and Myers are not isolated cases. The department has a history of doing a poor job of vetting people for key positions. In 2004 Laura Callahan, the deputy to the DHS Chief Information Officer, was forced to resign when it came out that her educational degrees were issued by diploma mills.[23] In 2004, my office investigated Faisal Gill, an adviser to the department official in charge of intelligence matters and infrastructure protection, because Gill had omitted on his job application form that he had served as a spokesman for the American Muslim Council. This organization was founded and headed at the time of Gill's employment by Abdurahman Alamoudi, who has since been indicted on two terrorism-related money laundering charges and claimed to have been involved in a Libyan plot to assassinate the then Crown Prince (and now, King) of Saudi Arabia. It turns out, believe it or not, that the law at the time did not require Gill to disclose his ties to this organization or its founder (I recommended that the law be changed in this regard!), but should anyone even remotely connected to terrorism be employed by the Department of Homeland Security in any capacity, especially the ultra-sensitive area of intelligence and infrastructure protection?[24] In the aftermath of Katrina, Secretary Chertoff was right to say that he needs to "replenish [FEMA's] ranks at the senior level with experienced staff,"[25] but, *every* department component should be staffed with experienced people at *every* level.

The Department of Homeland Security is charged with the most important mission in all of the United States government—doing everything possible to protect us from another terrorist attack here on our own soil. Accordingly, the very best and brightest this country has to offer from government, business, academia, and non-governmental organizations should be recruited to staff its ranks. Just as no effort was spared to find the best talent in the country to work on the Manhattan Project or to send a man to the moon, so no stone should go unturned in the search for the best talent in the country today to protect us from a threat of unprecedented gravity. Defending our nation from another terror attack is far too important to be left to insider's in-laws or their college roommates.

Oversight and Accountability

Finally, the department needs to welcome oversight and to hold people accountable for their performance. Time and again we in the office of Inspector General would point out to Ridge and his team that their underlings were selling them a bill of goods with regard to the performance of this program or that. Airport screeners weren't getting better at detecting concealed weapons. Customs inspectors weren't capable of detecting nuclear weapons. The department wasn't getting access to the intelligence it needed from the CIA and the FBI. The proof of this was all there in the black and white of our reports for the Secretary and his managers to see for themselves.

Ridge and his team chose to ignore our warnings and our recommendations. Their subordinates bewitched and befogged them with slick PowerPoint presentations filled with impressive acronyms, matrices, checklists, timelines, and organizational charts. They chose to listen to their spinmeister subordinates, whose jobs and pensions depended on telling their gullible bosses what they wanted to hear.

This denial of reality continues under the present leadership team. Secretary Chertoff dismissed first-hand reports that thousands of desperate people were stranded in the New Orleans convention center during Hurricane Katrina as "rumors" and "anecdotes" because, he later said, his aides were telling him otherwise.[26] A *New York Magazine* columnist scathingly compared him to the notorious and comical "Information" Minister in Saddam Hussein's government, who denied that Americans had entered Baghdad when our troops were plain to see right over the minister's shoulder.[27] We saw before our very eyes that what the Secretary's aides were telling him wasn't true, and yet he continued to defy reality.

It is imperative that the Department of Homeland Security adopt a culture that welcomes independent oversight and outside scrutiny. Only those outside the management chain have the freedom to risk telling the truth about what is and isn't working. Those responsible for homeland security programs should be held accountable for success or failure; to echo Rumsfeld again, only if success is rewarded and failure is punished will we get more success and less failure. While every government agency should follow these principles, it is literally a matter of life and death that the Department of Homeland Security do so.

As I look back on my brief time at the Department of Homeland Security, I remember the day of my Senate confirmation hearing, February 27, 2003, as if it were yesterday. As it happens, another Homeland Security Department nominee was being considered that day along with me, Janet Hale, the Under Secretary for Management-Designate, who I would later consider to be a major antagonist and a major obstacle to progress. As the juniormost member of the Committee, Democratic Senator Mark Pryor of Arkansas got to pose the final question to us.

> I actually do not have any questions, but more of a challenge for both of you . . . you have this tremendous opportunity to have a brand new department . . . everybody in this country gets fed up with bureaucracy and government and some of the seemingly idiotic things or the bad results sometimes government gets itself into when everybody's trying to do the right thing and trying to do good. But, both of you, especially in this department, have a unique opportunity to set the course of this department and set the tone and set up a formula where this department could be the model agency in all of government. I hope that you seize this opportunity and take the chance that history is giving you right now and go out there and do great things for this nation and the world, but also great things for our government so that other agencies, other departments, can look to you about how to do things the right way and things can be done in a government agency under very difficult circumstances, admittedly, but things that can be done there. And, I just want to leave you all with that challenge and hope that you will go to the office every single day trying to establish this agency a model for all of government.[28]

As Inspector General of the Department of Homeland Security, I did my best to live up to this stirring challenge. When I saw a gap in America's defenses, it was my job to point it out and to suggest ways to close it. I did my job, but the department's leaders have not done theirs. As a consequence, America today remains an open target.

NOTES

PROLOGUE

1. Transcript of Hearing before the Senate Governmental Affairs Committee on Homeland Security, Office of Management and Budget Nominations, February 27, 2003, http://homeland.cq.com/hs/display.do?dockey=/cqonline/prod/data/docs/html/transcripts/congressional/108/congressional-transcripts108–000000613509.html@committeesarchive&metapub=CQ-CONGTRANSCRIPTS&seqNum=391&searchIndex=1.
2. "U.S. rejects bin Laden tape's 'truce' offer—CIA: Voice warning Americans believed to be al Qaeda leader's," CNN.com, January 20, 2006, http://www.cnn.com/2006/US/01/19/binladen.tape/index.html.

INTRODUCTION

1. Samantha Levine, "A Job for Superman," *U.S. News and World Report,* June 28, 2004, http://www.usnews.com/usnews/news/articles/040628/28ervin.htm.
2. Edward Abbey (1927–1989), American environmentalist.
3. Statement for the Record of Deputy Homeland Security Secretary James Loy on The World Wide Threat Before the Senate Select Committee on Intelligence, February 16, 2005.
4. The Department of Defense is the largest Cabinet agency, followed by the Department of Veterans Affairs.
5. Statement of Secretary of Homeland Security Michael Chertoff before the House Appropriations Homeland Security Subcommittee, March 2, 2005, http://www.dhs.gov/dhspublic/display?content=4381.
6. Hearing of the Senate Homeland Security and Governmental Affairs Committee on Outlook for Department of Homeland Security, January, 26, 2005, http://homeland.cq.com/hs/display.do?dockey=/cqonline/prod/data/docs/html/transcripts/congressional/109/congressionaltranscripts109–000001501973.html@committees&metapub=CQ-CONGTRANSCRIPTS&seqNum=55&searchIndex=0.
7. White House Press Conference, March 6, 2003, http://www.whitehouse.gov/news/releases/2003/03/20030306–8html.
8. Robert Andrews, "Terrorism will stalk long after bin Laden's gone," *USA Today,* March 2, 2004, http://www.usatoday.com/news/opinion/editorials/2004–03–02-andrews-edit_x.htm.

CHAPTER 1

1. Patrick Yoest, "Some Underwhelmed by Border Patrol Personnel Increases," *CQ Homeland Security News,* October 20, 2005, http://homeland.cq.com/hs/display.do?dockey=/cqonline/prod/data/

docs/html/hsnews/109/hsnews109–000001923012.html@allnews&metapub=HSNEWS&seq Num=41&searchIndex=4.

2. Eric Lipton, "U.S. Borders Vulnerable, Officials Say," *The New York Times,* June 22, 2005, p. A11.
3. Ibid.
4. Government Accountability Office, "Key Cargo Security Programs Can Be Improved," GAO–05–466T, May 26, 2005.
5. Department of Homeland Security Office of Inspector General, "Review of Port Security Grant Program," OIG–05–10, January 2005, p. 27.
6. American Public Transportation Association, "Providing Safe and Secure Transportation; Ensuring America's Emergency Response," 2003, http://www.apta.com/research/info/online/providing_safe. cfm.
7. Sean Madigan, "Union Blasts Senate for Transit Security Cut," *CQ Homeland Security News,* July 15, 2005, http://homeland.cq.com/hs/display.do?dockey=cqonline/prod/data/docs/html/hsnews/109/hsnews109–000001780052.html@allnews&metapub=HSNEWS&seqNUM=26&search.
8. Commission on the Intelligence Capabilities of the United States Regarding Weapons of Mass Destruction, March 31, 2005, pp. 474–5, http://www.wmd.gov/report/wmd_report.pdf.
9. Homeland Security Secretary Michael Chertoff's "Second Stage Review" Remarks, July 13, 2005, http://www.dhs.gov/dhspublic/display?content=4597.
10. Eric Lipton, "U.S. Lists Possible Terror Attacks and Likely Toll," *The New York Times,* March 16, 2005, http:www.nytimes.com/2005/03/16/politics/16home.htm/?el–5090&en=447b6571833ca6bd &ex=1268629200&partner=rssuserland&pagewanted=print&position=.
11. Department of Homeland Security Office of Inspector General, "Evaluation of TSA's Contract for the Installation and Maintenance of Explosive Detection Equipment at United States Airports," OIG–04–44, September 2004.

CHAPTER 2

1. Presidential Address to the Nation on Iraq and the War on Terror, June 28, 2005, http://www.whitehouse.gov/news/releases/2005/06/20050628–7.html.
2. Statement for the Record of Central Intelligence Agency Director Porter Goss before the Senate Select Committee on Intelligence on the Worldwide Threat, February 16, 2005.
3. Statement for the Record of Federal Bureau of Investigation Director Robert Mueller before the Senate Select Intelligence Committee on the Worldwide Threat, February 16, 2005.
4. Presidential Speech on the War on Terror at the National Endowment for Democracy, October 6, 2005, http://www.whitehouse.gov/news/releases/2005/10/2005/20051006–3.html.
5. "U.S. Raises Threat Level at Key Financial Sites: New York City, Washington, and Northern New Jersey Affected," CNN.com, August 2, 2004, http://www.cnn.com/2004/US/08/01/terror.threat/index.html.
6. White House Fact Sheet: "Plots, Casings, and Infiltrations Referenced in President Bush's Remarks on the War on Terror," October 6, 2005, http://www.whitehouse.gov/news/releases/2005/10/20051006–7.html.
7. "U.S. ties smuggler to terror camp trip: Yemeni-American gets 3 years for role in cigarette smuggling ring," CNN.com, July 27, 2005, http://www.cnn.com/2005/LAW/07/27/terrorcamp.sentence.ap/index.html.
8. "California Muslim cleric, son deported," CNN.com, August 17, 2005, http://www.cnn.com/2005/US/08/17/cleric.deportation/.
9. "Appeals court hears accused 'dirty bomb' case," CNN.com, July 19, 2005, http://www.cnn.com/2005/LAW/07/19/padilla/index.html.
10. "Prisoner Abuse Scandal; Al Qaeda in U.S. Prisons," CNN.com, May 6, 2004, http://archives.cnn.com/TRANSCRIPTS/0405/06/ltm.03.html.
11. United States Department of Justice Press Release, "Earnest James Ujaama Sentenced for Conspiring to Supply Goods and Services to the Taliban," February 13, 2004, http://www.usdoj.gov/opa/

pr/2004/February/04_crm_086.htm. See also, William K. Rashbaum and Raymond Bonner, "Suspect in London fatal blasts eluded arrest," *International Herald Tribune,* July 30, 2005, http://www.iht.com/articles/2005/07/29/news/britain.php.

12. Statement for the Record of Federal Bureau of Investigation Director Robert Mueller before the Senate Select on Intelligence on the World Wide Threat, February 16, 2005.

13. "CNN Newsnight with Aaron Brown: Piecing Together Terror Puzzle; Interview with Senator Rick Santorum," CNN.com, July 25, 2005, http://transcripts.cnn.com/TRANSCRIPTS/0507/25/asb.01.html.

14. United States General Accounting Office, "Border Security: Visa Process Should be Strengthened as an Antiterrorism Tool," GAO–03–132NI, October 21, 2002. See also Curt Anderson, "GAO: 105 Terror Suspects Got U.S. Visas," Associated Press, November 26, 2002, http://newsmine.org/archive/9–11/105-terrorists-visas.txt.

15. See Department of Homeland Security Office of Inspector General, "An Evaluation of DHS Activities to Implement Section 428 of the Homeland Security Act of 2002," OIG–04–33, August 2004.

16. The countries participating in the Visa Waiver Program are: Andorra; Austria; Australia; Belgium; Brunei; Denmark; Finland; France; Germany; Iceland; Ireland; Italy; Japan; Liechtenstein; Luxembourg; Monaco; the Netherlands; New Zealand; Norway; Portugal; San Marino; Singapore; Slovenia; Spain; Sweden; Switzerland; and the United Kingdom.

17. United States General Accounting Office, "Tourist Visa Processing Backlogs Persist at U.S. Consulates," GAO/NSIAD–98–69, March 1998.

18. United States General Accounting Office, "Border Security: Visa Process Should be Strengthened as an Antiterrorism Tool," GAO–03–132NI, October 2002, pp. 18 and 84.

19. Edward T. Pound, "The Easy Path to the United States for Three of the 9/11 Hijackers," *U.S. News and World Report,* December 12, 2001, http://www.usnews.com/usnews/news/terror/articles/visa011212.htm.

20. Staff Statement No. 1, National Commission on Terrorist Attacks upon the United States, August 21, 2004, p. 4, http://www.9–11commission.gov/staff_statements/staff_statement_1.pdf.

21. United States Department of State Office of Inspector General, "Review of Nonimmigrant Visa Issuance Policy and Procedures," Memorandum Report ISP–1–03–26, December 2002, p. 18.

22. See "Editorial/Opinion: Pre-9/11 loopholes render U.S. visa process inadequate," *USA Today,* August 4, 2002, http://www.usatoday.com/news/opinion/2002–08–04-edit_x.htm.

23. Section 428(e)(1) of the Homeland Security Act of 2002 (Public Law 107–296).

24. Section 428(i) of the Homeland Security Act of 2002 (Public Law 107–296).

25. "Interview: Homeland Security Secretary Tom Ridge Talks about the Progress his Agency has Made in Keeping our Borders and Ports Safe," *Morning Edition* from National Public Radio News, September 15, 2004.

26. Joel Mowbray, "Open Door for Saudi Terrorists: The Visa Express Scandal," June 14, 2002, National Review Online, http://www.nationalreview.com/comment/comment-mowbray061402.asp.

27. "Welcoming International Students to Community Colleges in the U.S.–the Role of the State Department," Speech by Deputy Assistant Secretary for Visa Services Janice L. Jacobs, NAFSA (National Association of Foreign Student Advisers: Association of International Educators) Annual Conference, Seattle, Washington, June 2, 2005, http://travel.state.gov/law/legal/testimony/testimony_2534.html.

28. Speech by Deputy Assistant Secretary for Visa Services Janice L. Jacobs, 2005 Border Security Summit, June 22, 2005, http://travel.state.gov/law/legal/testimony/testimony_2551.html?css=print.

29. Ibid.

30. Statement by Clark Kent Ervin before the House Government Reform Committee Subcommittee on National Security, Emerging Threats, and International Relations, September 13, 2005.

31. United States Government Accountability Office, "Border Security: Strengthened Visa Process Would Benefit from Additional Management Actions by State and DHS," GAO–05–994T, Testimony before the Subcommittee on National Security, Emerging Threats, and International Relations, Committee on Government Reform, House of Representatives, September 13, 2005, p. 3.

32. United States Department of Justice Office of Inspector General, "Review of the Terrorist Screening Center," Audit Report 05–27, June 2005, p. xi.

33. United States Department of Homeland Security Office of Inspector General, "Review of the Immigration and Customs Enforcement's Compliance Enforcement Unit," OIG–05–50, September 2005.

34. Elisabeth Bumiller, "System Using Fingerprints is Delayed, Report Finds," *The New York Times,* December 30, 2004, www.nytimes.com/2004/12/30/politics/30fingerprint.html?oref=login.

35. Secretary Michael Chertoff, United States Department of Homeland Security, Second Stage Review Remarks, July 13, 2005, http://www.dhs.gov/dhspublic/display?content=4597.

36. United States Department of Homeland Security Office of Inspector General, "An Evaluation of the Security Implications of the Visa Waiver Program," OIG–04–26, April 2004, p. 7.

37. Ibid., p. 8.

38. Under the category—When is what appears to be a "good news story" really a "bad news story?"— the Department of Homeland Security announced in October 2005 that 25 of the 27 Visa Waiver Program countries (France and Italy being the exceptions) had met the October 26, 2005 deadline to produce passports with digital photographs. (See United States Department of Homeland Security Press Release, "Majority of VWP Countries to Meet Digital Photo Deadline," October 26, 2005, http://www.dhs.gov/dhspublic/display?theme=43&content=4907&print=true). To target fraudulent document use, the Enhanced Border Security and Visa Entry Reform Act of 2002 required that any Visa Waiver Program country passport issued after that deadline and used for travel to the United States had to include a biometric identifier. Otherwise, the traveler presenting the passport would have to obtain a visa to be admitted into this country. The problem is that the "biometric identifier" in question is a digital photograph. Digital photographs are certainly better than the traditional kind, in that they are harder to counterfeit and they can be stored electronically for easy access in the future. But, they are not really "biometric." That is to say, unlike fingerprints or iris scans that are highly reliable in confirming identity, digital photographs are no more accurate than traditional photographs in this regard. Had these 25 countries not met the deadline, those of their citizens with passports issued after the deadline would have been required to obtain a visa to enter the United States, with the extra scrutiny that now entails at the issuing U.S. embassy or consulate. And, biometrics taken at the visa issuing post could be compared to those taken at the U.S. port of entry to confirm for a fact that the person presenting himself for entry into the United States is in fact the same person who applied for the visa. Visa Waiver Program countries have an additional year, until October 26, 2006, to produce "e-passports" with an integrated circuit chip capable of storing a digital photograph, biographical information from the data page of a passport, and true biometric identifiers.

39. The department completed the review in November 2005, finding that 25 of the 27 countries were eligible to continue participating in the program. The status of Italy and Portugal are required to be reviewed at a later date.

40. United States Department of Homeland Security Office of Inspector General, "A Review of the Use of Stolen Passports from Visa Waiver Countries to Enter the United States," OIG–05–07, December 2004, p. 8.

41. Ibid., p. 3.

42. Ibid., p. 24.

43. Ibid., p. 20.

44. United States Department of Homeland Security Office of Inspector General, "Implications of the United States Visitor and Immigrant Status Indicator Technology Program at Land Border Ports of Entry," OIG–05–11, February 2005, p. 4.

45. The Intelligence Reform and Terrorism Prevention Act of 2004 required the Secretaries of Homeland Security and State to develop a plan to require U.S. citizens and foreign nationals to present a passport or other appropriate secure identity and citizenship document when entering the United States. Pursuant thereto, the "Western Hemisphere Travel Initiative" was announced, whereby travelers to and from North and South America, the Caribbean, and Bermuda will, by January 1, 2008, need a passport or other accepted document to establish the bearer's identity and nationality to

enter or re-renter the United States. While requiring citizens from Mexico and Canada to present passports to enter the United States and requiring American citizens to present passports when re-entering the United States from elsewhere in the Western Hemisphere would have been steps in the right direction, President Bush himself expressed concern about it, and the Canadian ambassador predicted that no such requirement would be put into effect. See Press Release, United States Department of Homeland Security, "DHS Reminds Public of Deadline for Comments on the Western Hemisphere Travel Initiative," October 28, 2005, http://www.dhs.gov/dhspublic/display?theme=43&content=4911&print=true, and Caitlin Harrington, "United States, Canada Meet on Hemisphere Passport Issue," *CQ Homeland Security News,* June 15, 2005, http://homeland.cq.com/hs/display.do?dockey=cqonline/prod/data/docs/html/hsnews/109/hsnews109-000001726891.html@allnews&metapub=HSNEWS&seqNum=141&searchIndex=0. The Canadian ambassador's prediction proved to be prescient when DHS and the State Department announced in January 2006 that something less than a passport, a "passport card," will be developed to satisfy the law's requirements. See Department of Homeland Security Fact Sheet: "Secure Borders and Open Doors in the Information Age," January 17, 2006, http://www.dhs.gov/dhspublic/display?theme=43&content=5347&print=true.

46. Eric Lipton, "Border Control Takes One Leap Forward," *New York Times,* December 30, 2005, http://www.nytimes.com/2005/12/30/politics/30visit.html.

47. United States Government Accountability Office, "Improvements Needed to Strengthen U.S. Passport Fraud Detection Efforts: A Report to the Committee on Homeland Security and Governmental Affairs, United States Senate," GAO–05–477, May 2005, p. 5.

48. Ibid., p. 2.

49. United States Government Accountability Office, Testimony before the Committee on Homeland Security and Governmental Affairs, U.S. Senate, "State Department: Improvements Needed to Strengthen U.S. Passport Fraud Detection Efforts," GAO–05–853T, June 29, 2005.

50. Transcript of Senate Homeland Security and Governmental Affairs Committee Hearing on Passport Vulnerabilities, June 29, 2005, http://homeland.cq.com/hs/display.do?dockey=/cqonline/prod/data/docs/html/transcripts/congressional/109/congressionaltranscripts109–000001759013.html@committees&metapub=CQ-CONGTRANSCRIPTS&seqNum=6&searchIndex=0, p. 3.

51. Testimony of Howard J. Krongard, Inspector General, United States Department of State and Broadcasting Board of Governors, before the House Committee on the Judiciary Subcommittee on Immigration, Border Security, and Claims, June 15, 2005, http://oig.state.gov/documents/organization/49796.pdf, p. 3.

52. Ibid., p. 3.

53. Transcript of Senate Judiciary Subcommittee on Immigration, Border Security, and Citizenship and Subcommittee on Terrorism, Technology, and Homeland Security Joint Hearing on 9/11 Commission Report on Terrorism Travel, March 14, 2005, http://homeland.cq.com/hs/display.do?dockey=cqonline/prod/data/docs/html/transcripts/congressional/109/congressionaltranscripts109–000001581152.html@commitees&metapub=CQ-CONGTRANSCRIPTS&seqNUM=11&searchIndex=0, p. 25.

54. Statement for the Record of Deputy Homeland Security Secretary James Loy on The World Wide Threat Before the U.S. Senate Select Committee on Intelligence, February 16, 2005, pp. 3–4.

55. Transcript of Hearing of House Appropriations Subcommittee on Science, State, Justice, Commerce and Related Agencies on FY 2006 Appropriations, March 8, 2005, http://homeland.cq.com/hs/display.do?dockey=cqonline/prod/data/docs/html/testimony/109/testimony109–000001561136.html@commitees&metapub=CQ-TESTIMONY&seqNum=5588searchIndex=3, p. 49.

56. Ibid., p. 49.

57. Ibid., pp. 50–51.

58. Ibid., pp. 56.

59. Adam Zagorin, Timothy J. Burger, and Brian Bennett, "Zarqawi Planning U.S. Hit?: Intelligence Officials say Operatives may Infiltrate via Central America to Strike at Soft Targets on American Soil," March 13, 2005, *Time Magazine,* http://www.time.com/archive/preview/0,10987,1037626,00.html.

60. Patrick Yoest, "Some Underwhelmed by Border Patrol Personnel Increases," *CQ Homeland Security News,* October 20, 2005.

61. Zack Phillips, "More Budget '06: High-Tech Border Surveillance Funding Falls Short of Expectations," *CQ Homeland Security News,* February 7, 2005, http://homeland.cq.com/hs/display. do?dockey=/cqonline/prod/data/docs/html/hsnews/109/hsnews109–000001521798.html@allnews &metapub=HSNEWS&seqNum=18searchIndex=1. See also Zack Phillips, "Money Window: DHS to Ask for Help with Border Technology Project," *CQ Homeland Security News,* April 1, 2005, http://homeland.cq.com/hs/display.do?dockey=/cqonline/prod/data/docs/html/hsnews/109/ hsnews109–000001596812.html@allnews&metapub=HSNEWS&seqNum=166&searchIndex=0.

62. Zack Phillips, "Holes in the Border: Massive Technology Overhaul Lapsing," *CQ Homeland Security News,* January 24, 2004, http://homeland.cq.com/hs/display.do?dockey=cqonline/prod/data/docs/ html/hsnews/109/hsnews109–000001498393.html@allnews&metapub=HSNEWS&seqNum=226 &searchIndex=2.

63. See John Mintz, "Probe Faults System for Monitoring U.S. Borders," *The Washington Post,* April 11, 2005, p. A1.

64. Ibid.

65. Zack Phillips, "Holes in the Border: Massive Technology Overhaul Lapsing," *CQ Homeland Security News,* January 24, 2004.

66. Jerry Seper, "Revolving Door at Border," *The Washington Times,* July 21, 2004, http://www.washingtontimes.com/national/20040720–115825–5216r.htm.

67. Patrick Yoest, "Some Underwhelmed by Border Patrol Personnel Increases," *CQ Homeland Security News,* October 20, 2005.

68. See United States Department of Homeland Security Office of Inspector General, "Audit of ICE's Budgetary Status and Other Areas of Concern," OIG–05–32, August 2005. See also Zack Phillips, "ICE Accounting System Flawed, Audit Finds," *CQ Homeland Security News,* September 8, 2005, http://homeland.cq.com/hs/display.do?dockey=cqonline/prod/data/docs/html/hsnews/109/hsnews 109-000001850933.html@allnews&metapub=HSNEWS&seqNum=0.

69. Jerry Seper, "Revolving Door at Border," *The Washington Times,* July 21, 2004, http://www.washingtontimes.com/national/20040720–115825–5216r.htm.

70. Ibid.

71. Testimony of Under Secretary of Border and Transportation Security Asa Hutchinson before Senate Judiciary Committee Subcommittee on Immigration, Border Security, and Citizenship, February 12, 2004, cited by Senator Diane Feinstein (D.-Calif.) in her opening statement in a joint hearing of the Senate Judiciary Subcommittee on Immigration, Border Security, and Citizenship and the Subcommittee on Terrorism, Technology, and Homeland Security on 9/11 Commission Report on Terrorism Travel, March 14, 2005, FDCH Transcripts, p. 9.

72. Opening Statement of Senator Diane Feinstein in aforementioned hearing, ibid.

73. Kris Axtman, "Illegal Entry by Non-Mexicans Rises," *Christian Science Monitor,* July 26, 2005, www.csmonitor.com/2005/0726/p01s01-usfp.html. See also Patrick Yoest, "Non-Mexican Aliens Pose Growing Threat to U.S., Report Says," September 26, 2005, *CQ Homeland Security News,* http://homeland.cq.com/hs/display.do/dockey=/cqonline/prod/data/docs/html/hsnews/109/hsnews 109-000001883513.html@allnews&metapub=HSNEWS&seqNum=102&searchIndex=0.

74. Statement of Homeland Security Secretary Michael Chertoff before the United States Judiciary Committee, October 18, 2005, http://www.dhs.gov/dhspublic/display?content=4890.

CHAPTER 3

1. TSA estimated initially that it would need 30,000 screeners to staff the nation's commercial airports. That number was ultimately increased to 60,000. See Brian Friel, "Security Sweep," GovExec.com, March 15, 2003, http://www.govexec.com/features/0303/0303s4.htm.

2. Argenbright Security, an Atlanta-based firm, became the poster child for the claim that private companies were incapable of putting or unwilling to put security concerns ahead of maximizing

profit. In November 2001, the Massachusetts Port Authority terminated Argenbright's contract at Boston's Logan Airport, one of the airports through which 9/11 hijackers transited on that fateful day, and it announced that Argenbright would cease operations at all Massachusetts airports by the end of the year. As it happens, another contractor provided the screeners for the hijackers' flights, but Argenbright was already on thin ice on account of a series of troubling incidents. In October 2001, for example, a man armed with a knife and stun gun managed to slip past Argenbright screeners at Chicago's O'Hare International Airport. At Logan itself, Argenbright screeners left three checkpoints unattended on two occasions, resulting in the forced re-screening of hundreds of passengers. See "Embattled security firm out at Boston Airport," CNN.com, November 30, 2001, http://archives.cnn.com/2001/US/11/30/rec.logan.argenbright/index.html.

3. Zack Phillips, "See-Through Screeners to Get Privacy Upgrade," *CQ Homeland Security News*, August 9, 2005, http://homeland.cq.com/hs/display.do?dockey=/cqonline/prod/data/docs/html/hsnews/109/hsnews109-000001818273.html@allnews&metapub=HSNEWS&seqNum=95&searchIndex=0.

4. United States Department of Homeland Security Office of Inspector General, "Audit of Passenger and Baggage Screening Procedures at Domestic Airports," OIG–04–37, September 2004.

5. Leslie Miller, "Reports: Airport Screeners Still Do Poorly—AP: Airport Screeners Still Perform Poorly, Reports from Homeland Security and GAO to Reveal," April 15, 2005, http://abcnews.go.com/Politics/wireStory?id=674917.

6. United States Department of Homeland Security Office of Inspector General, "Follow-up Audit of Passenger and Baggage Screening Procedures at Domestic Airports (Unclassified Summary)," OIG–05–16, March 2005.

7. United States Department of Homeland Security Office of Inspector General, "A Review of Background Checks for Federal Passenger and Baggage Screeners at Airports," OIG–04–08, January 2004.

8. "Airports 'Desperate' for Access to Watch Lists to Screen Illegals from Workforce," *CQ Homeland Security News*, April 13, 2005, http://homeland.cq.com/hs/display.do?dockey=/cqonline/prod/data/docs/html/hsnews/109/hsnews109-000001617893.html@allnews&metapub=HSNEWS&seqNum=1&searchIndex=2.

9. Press Release, Immigration and Customs Enforcement Bureau of the United States Department of Homeland Security, "ICE Arrests 14 Illegal Aliens Working at Logan's Airport: Ongoing 'Operation Tarmac' Finds Fugitive Alien Among Illegal Aliens Employed as Temp Workers," March 25, 2005, http://www.ice.gov/graphics/news/newsreleases/articles/Logan032505.htm.

10. Ibid.

11. Caitlin Harrington, "Pilots Blast Airport Security After Discovery of Illegal Aliens in Workforces," *CQ Homeland Security News*, March 31, 2005, http://homeland.cq.com/hs/display.do?dockey=/cqonline/prod/data/docs/html/hsnews/109/hsnews109-000001595232.html@allnews&metapub=HSNEWS&seqNum=1&searchIndex=0.

12. Ibid.

13. Ibid.

14. See Zack Phillips, "TWIC Program Inches Forward," *CQ Homeland Security News*, October 18, 2005, http://homeland.cq.com/hs/display.do?dockey=/cqonline/prod/data/docs/html/hsnews/109/hsnews109-000001917253.html@allnews&metapub=HSNEWS&seqNum=1&searchIndex=0; See also Zack Phillips, "TSA Halts Production of Transportation Worker ID Card In Move to Kentucky," *CQ Homeland Security News*, June 23, 2005, http://homeland.cq.com/hs/display.do?dockey=/cqonline/prod/data/docs/html/hsnews/109/hsnews109-000001744012.html@allnews&metapub=HSNEWS&seqNum=3&searchIndex=1.

15. United States Department of Homeland Security Office of Inspector General, "Evaluation of the Federal Air Marshal Service," OIG–04–32, August 2004.

16. Caitlin Harrington, "Hotel California: Undercover Air Marshals Must Reveal Identity for Room Discounts," *CQ Homeland Security News*, June 20, 2005, http://homeland.cq.com/hs/display.do?dockey=/cqonline/prod/data/docs/html/hsnews/109/hsnews109-000001735974.html@allnews&metapub=HSNEWS&seqNum=8&searchIndex=2.

17. See Press Release, Congressman Christopher Shays, "Markey-Shays Amendments FY '06 Department of Homeland Security Authorization Bill," May 17, 2005, http://www.house.gov/shays/news/2005/may/facts.htm.

18. Caitlin Harrington, "Steamed, Hal Rogers Starts Whacking DHS $100,000 a Day Over Poor Air Cargo Security," *CQ Homeland Security News*, May 5, 2005, http://homeland.cq.com/hs/display.do?dockey=/cqonline/prod/data/docs/html/hsnews/109/hsnews109–000001659797.html@allnews&metapub=HSNEWS&seqNum=6&searchIndex=1.

19. Press Release, Congressman Christopher Shays, "Markey-Shays Amendments FY '06 Department of Homeland Security Authorization Bill," May 17, 2005, http://www.house.gov/shays/news/2005/may/facts.htm.

20. Ibid.

21. Ibid.

22. Customs and Border Protection Commissioner Robert C. Bonner Remarks to the Center for Strategic and International Studies Transnational Threats Audit Conference, February 11, 2004, http://www.cbp.gov/xp/cgov/newsroom/commissioner/speeches_statements/archives/2004/mar03 2004.xml. See also Chris Strohm, "U.S. Wants to Place Immigration Inspectors at Foreign Airports," *Government Executive*, May 5, 2004.

23. Leslie Miller, "Homeland Security is Late with Plane Plan," May 18, 2005, Associated Press, http://www.sfgate.com/cgi-bin/article.cgi?f=/n/a/2005/05/18/national/w150952D63.DTL.

24. Letter from James C. May, President and CEO, Air Transport Association, and Ulrich Schulte-Strathaus, Secretary General, Association of European Airlines, to Homeland Security Secretary Michael Chertoff, May 26, 2005.

25. Ibid.

26. "Homeland Security is Late with Plan to Check Passengers Before Planes Take Off," Associated Press, May 19, 2005, http://officer.com/article/printer.jsp?id=23714&siteSection=8. See also Sara Kehaulani Goo, "U.S. Modifies Air Passenger List Proposal," *The Washington Post*, June 1, 2005, p. D2.

27. United States Department of Homeland Security Office of Inspector General, "Summary of a Review of the Use of Alternative Screening Procedures at an Unnamed Airport," OIG–04–28, April 28, 2004.

28. United States Department of Homeland Security Office of Inspector General, "Review of TSA Screening Practices in Houston, Texas," OIG–04–48, September 2004, pp. 1–2.

29. United States Department of Homeland Security Office of Inspector General, "Transportation Security Administration's Checked Baggage Screener Training and Certification: A Letter Report," ISP–02–03, August 2003.

30. Ibid., pp. 1 and 3.

31. United States Department of Homeland Security Office of Inspector General, "An Evaluation of the Transportation Security Administration's Screener Training and Methods of Testing," OIG–04–045, September 2004.

32. United States Government Accountability Office, "Screener Training and Performance Measurement Strengthened, but More Work Remains," GAO–05–457, May 2005.

33. United States Department of Homeland Security Office of Inspector General, "Audit of Passenger and Baggage Screening Procedures at Domestic Airports," OIG–04–37, September 2004, pg. 3.

34. Mike M. Ahlers, "Report: Airport screeners lack training," CNN.com, May 3, 2005, http://edition.cnn.com/2005/TRAVEL/05/03/airport.screeners/.

35. Statement of Kip Hawley, Assistant Secretary of Transportation Security Administration, before the House Subcommittee on Economic Security, Infrastructure Protection and Cybersecurity Committee on Homeland Security, November 3, 2005, http://www.tsa.gov/interweb/assetlibrary/110305TRAV.pdf.

36. United States Government Accountability Office, Letter to Congressional Committees, "Aviation Security: Transportation Security Administration Did Not Fully Disclose Uses of Personal Information During Secure Flight Program Testing in Initial Privacy Notices, But Has Recently Taken Steps to More Fully Inform the Public," July 22, 2005, GAO–05–864R Aviation Security, http://www.gao.gov/new.items/d05864r.pdf.

37. Statement of Clark Kent Ervin, Inspector General of the United States Department of Homeland Security before the House Committee on Transportation and Infrastructure Subcommittee on Aviation, April 22, 2004, http://www.house.gov/transportation/aviation/04-22-04/ervin.pdf.

38. Lance Williams, "Security Firm Accused of Cheating on SFO Test: Checkpoints were alerted to federal decoys, lawsuit says," *San Francisco Chronicle*, February 22, 2005, http://www.sfgate.com/cgi-bin/article.cgi?file=/c/a/2005/02/22/MNGIJBF3LR1.DTL.

39. The "gateway" airports are: Seattle-Tacoma, Washington; Boston Logan; Houston Hobby; White Plains, New York; LaGuardia, New York; Chicago Midway; Minneapolis/St. Paul; West Palm Beach; San Francisco; Teterboro, New Jersey; Philadelphia; and Lexington, Kentucky. See Press Release, Transportation Security Administration, "TSA Opens Ronald Reagan Washington Airport to General Aviation Operations," October 18, 2005, http://www.tsa.gov/public/display?theme=44&content=090005198017e518.

40. Caitlin Harrington, "Thousands of Airspace Violations Have Occurred Since Sept.11, FAA Reports," *CQ Homeland Security News*, July 20, 2005, http://homeland.cq.com/hs/display.do?dockey=cqonline/prod/data/docs/html/hrnews/109/hsnews109–000001787212.html@allnews&metapub=HSNEWS&seqNum=117&searchIndex=0.

41. Transcript of Hearing on Controlling Restricted Airspace before the House Government Reform Committee, July 21, 2005, *CQ Homeland Security News*, Congressional Transcripts, p. 14, http://homeland.cq.com/hs/display.do?dockey=/cqonline/prod/data/docs/html/transcripts/congressional/109/congressionaltranscripts109–000001793612.html@committees&meteapub=CQ-CONGTRANSCRIPTS&seqNum=3&searchIndex=1.

42. Ibid. at p. 23. See also Angie C. Marek, "A Really Capitol Idea?: The feds are allowing private planes back at Washington's Reagan National Airport. Not everyone's exactly thrilled." *U.S. News and World Report*, August 1, 2005, http:www.usnews.com/usnews/news/articles/050801/1airspace.htm.

43. Caitlin Harrington, "Wilding Blue Yonder: Recent Joy Rides in Private Planes Prompt Queries to Chertoff," *CQ Homeland Security News*, June 30, 2005, http://homeland.cq.com/hs/display.do?dockey=cqonline/prod/data/docs/html/hsnews/109/hsnews109–000001757293.html@allnews&metapub=HSNEWS&seqnum=124&searchIndex=2.

44. Caitlin Harrington, "Guns in Cockpits Program Still Half Cocked, Some Say," *CQ Homeland Security News*, April 27, 2005, http://homeland.cq.com/hs/display.do?dockey=cqonline/prod/data/docs/html/hsnews/109/hsnews109–000001645333.html@allnews&metapub=HSNEWS&seqNum=191&searchIndex=0.

45. Caitlin Harrington, "Federal Screener Workforce to be Reshuffled Under TSA Plan," *CQ Homeland Security News*, July 28, 2005, http://homeland.cq.com/hs/display.do?dockey=cqonline/prod/data/docs/html/hsnews/109/hsnews109–000001802772.html@allnews&metapub=HSNEWS&seqNum103&searchIndex=0. See also, Jeanne Meserve, "Airport screeners to be shuffled," CNN.com, July 28, 2005, http://www.cnn.com/2005/TRAVEL/07/27/airport.screeners/.

CHAPTER 4

1. Transcript of 1st Presidential Debate, October 1, 2004, http://www.foxnews.com/story/0,2933,134152,00.html.

2. Eric Lipton, "Loopholes Seen in U.S. Efforts to Secure Overseas Ports," *The New York Times*, May 25, 2005, p. A6.

3. Transcript of House Homeland Security Committee Subcommittee on Prevention of Nuclear and Biological Attack on Effectiveness of Nuclear Weapons Detection Technology, *CQ Homeland Security News*, June 21, 2005, p. 2, http://homeland.cq.com/hs/display.do?dockey=cqonline/prod/data/docs/html/testimony/109/testimony109–000001736205.html@committees&metapub=CQ-TESTIMONY&seqNum=57&searchIndex=0.

4. Statement of Admiral Thomas H. Collins, Commandant, U.S. Coast Guard/Robert C. Bonner, Commissioner, Customs and Border Protection; Admiral David M. Stone, Acting Administrator, Transportation Security Administration on Maritime Security Status before the United States Sen-

ate Committee on Commerce, Science, and Transportation, March 24, 2004, p. 2, http://www.tsa.gov/interweb/assetlibrary/Maritime03–24–04.pdf.

5. In fact, the Customs and Border Protection bureau of the department almost boasts about this number, contending that its other security measures are so effective that no more inspections are necessary. See Fact Sheet, "Cargo Container Security—U.S. Customs and Border Protection Reality," October 20, 2004, http://www.customs.treas.gov/xp/cgov/newsroom/fact_sheets/2004/factsheet_container_security.xml.

6. Transcript of Senate Homeland Security and Governmental Affairs Subcommittee on Permanent Investigations Hearing on Security of Ocean Shipping Containers, *CQ Homeland Security News,* May 26, 2005, p. 2, http://homeland.cq.com/hs/display.do?dockey=cqonline/prod/data/docs/html/transcripts/congressional/109/congressionaltranscripts109–000001702032.html@committees&metapub=CQ-CONGTRANSCRIPTS&seqNum=5&searchIndex=1.

7. Transcript of House Judiciary Committee Subcommittee on Crime, Terrorism, and Homeland Security Hearing on Seaport and Cargo Security, March 15, 2005, p. 8, http://homeland.cq.com/hs/display.do?dockey=/cqonline/prod/data/docs/html/testimony/109/testimony109–000001573597.html@committees&metapub=CQ-TESTIMONY&seqNum=15&searchIndex=6.

8. United States Department of Homeland Security Office of Inspector General, "Effectiveness of Customs and Border Protection's Procedures to Detect Uranium in Two Smuggling Incidents," OIG–04–40, September 2004.

9. See, for example, Graham Allison, *Nuclear Terrorism: The Ultimate Preventable Catastrophe,* Times Books, 2004. See also Stephen E. Flynn, *America the Vulnerable: How Our Government is Failing to Protect us from Terrorism,* HarperCollins, 2004.

10. United States Government Accountability Office, Report to Congressional Requesters, "Container Security: A Flexible Staffing Model and Minimum Equipment Requirements Would Improve Overseas Targeting and Inspection Efforts," GAO–05–557, April 2005, p. 11.

11. "CBP Reaches International Maritime Security Milestone," August 5, 2005, http://www.cbp.gov/xp/cgov/newsroom/commisssioner/messages/cbp_reaches.xml.

12. See Statement of Clark Kent Ervin, Inspector General of the United States Department of Homeland Security before the Subcommittee on Oversight and Investigations of the House Energy and Commerce Committee, March 31, 2004. See also United States Department of Homeland Security Office of Inspector General, "Audit of Targeting Oceangoing Cargo Containers (Unclassified Summary)," OIG–05–26, July 2005; United States General Accounting Office, Testimony before the Subcommittee on Oversight and Investigations, Committee on Energy and Commerce, House of Representatives, "Homeland Security: Summary of Challenges Faced in Targeting Oceangoing Cargo Containers for Inspection," Statement of Richard M. Stana, Director, Homeland Security and Justice Issues, GAO–04–557T, March 31, 2004.

13. Jeff Stein, "Container Screening Touted, but Senators have their Doubts," *CQ Homeland Security News,* August 4, 2005, http://homeland.cq.com/hs/display.do?dockey=/cqonline/prod/data/docs/html/hsnews/109/hsnews109–000001813612.html@allnews&metapub=HSNEWS&seqNum=2.

14. United States Department of Homeland Security Office of Inspector General, "Audit of Targeting Oceangoing Cargo Containers (Unclassified Summary)," OIG–05–26, July 2005, p. 2.

15. Remarks of Christopher Koch, President and CEO of the World Shipping Council before the American Association of Port Authorities' Annual Spring Conference, April 5, 2005, http://www.secureports.org/speeches/chris_koch_aapa_040505.html.

16. S 1052, the "Transportation Security Improvement Act of 2005." The bill was introduced by Senator Ted Stevens, Republican of Alaska.

17. Remarks by Robert C. Bonner, Maritime Security Lifetime Achievement Award, Third Annual U.S. Marine Security Conference and Expo, New York, New York, September 14, 2004, http://www.cbp.gov/xp/cgov/newsroom/commissioner/speeches_statements/archives/2004/09142004_maritime.xml.

18. Transcript of Senate Homeland Security and Governmental Affairs Subcommittee on Permanent Investigations Hearing on Ocean Shipping Containers, *CQ Homeland Security News,* May 26, 2005, p. 11.

19. United States Government Accountability Office, "Container Security: A Flexible Staffing Model and Minimum Equipment Requirements Would Improve Targeting and Inspection Efforts," GAO–05–557, April 2005, p. 19.

20. Ibid., p. 21.

21. Transcript of Senate Homeland Security and Governmental Affairs Subcommittee on Permanent Investigations Hearing on the Security of Ocean Shipping Containers, *CQ Homeland Security News,* May 26, 2005, p. 36.

22. Ibid., p. 36. United States Government Accountability Office, "Container Security: A Flexible Staffing Model and Minimum Equipment Requirements Would Improve Targeting and Inspection Efforts," GAO–05–557, April 2005, p. 24.

23. Transcript of Senate Homeland Security and Governmental Affairs Subcommittee on Permanent Investigations Hearing on the Security of Ocean Shipping Containers, *CQ Homeland Security News,* May 26, 2005, p. 30.

24. Ibid., pp. 60–61.

25. Transcript of House Homeland Security Committee Subcommittee on Prevention of Nuclear and Biological Attack Hearing on Effectiveness of Nuclear Weapons Detection Technology, *CQ Homeland Security News,* June 21, 2005, pp. 6–7, http://homeland.cq.com/hs/display.do?dockey/=cq online/prod/data/docs/html/testimony/109/testimony109–000001736205.html@commitees& metapub=CQ-TESTIMONY&seqNum=57&searchIndex=0.

26. See Transcript of House Homeland Security Committee Subcommittee on Prevention of Nuclear and Biological Attack Hearing on Effectiveness of Nuclear Weapons Detection Technology, CQ Homeland Security, June 21, 2005, pp. 3, 24–25. See also United States General Accounting Office, Testimony Before the Subcommitee on Oversight and Investigations, Committee on Energy and Commerce, House of Representatives, "Customs Service—Acquisition and Deployment of Radiation Detection Equipment," Statement of Gary L. Jacobs, Director, Natural Resources and Environment, and Laurie E. Ekstrand, Director, Tax Administration and Justice, GAO–03–235T, October 17, 2002, p. 2. See also Press Release, U.S. Customs and Border Protection, "U.S. Customs and Border Protection Radiation Portal Monitor Identifies Smuggling Attempt at Santa Teresa Port of Entry," May 6, 2005, http://www.cbp. gov/xp/cgov/newsroom/press_releases/archives/2005_press_releases/0052005/05122005.xml. Also, I added the following cite to this note, "See also United States General Accounting Office, Testimony Before the Subcommittee on Oversight and Investigations, Committee on Energy and Commerce, House of Representatives, "Customs Service-Acquisition and Deployment of Radiation Detection Equipment," Statement of Gary L. Jacobs, Director, Natural Resources and Environment, and Laurie E. Ekstrand, Director, Tax Administration and Justice, GAO–03–235T, October 17, 2002, p. 2.

27. Transcript of Senate Homeland Security and Governmental Affairs Subcommittee on Permanent Investigations Hearing on the Security of Ocean Shipping Containers, *CQ Homeland Security News,* May 26, 2005, p. 40.

28. Ibid., p. 40.

29. Transcript of House Judiciary Committee Subcommittee on Crime, Terrorism, and Homeland Security Hearing on Seaport and Cargo Security, *CQ Homeland Security News,* March 15, 2005, p. 6.

30. Transcript of Senate Homeland Security and Governmental Affairs Subcommittee on Permanent Investigations Hearing on the Security of Ocean Shipping Containers, *CQ Homeland Security News,* May 26, 2005, p. 33.

31. Transcript of House Homeland Security Subcommittee on Prevention of Nuclear and Biological Attack Hearing on the Effectiveness of Nuclear Weapons Detection Technology, *CQ Homeland Security News,* June 21, 2005, p. 7.

32. Transcript of Senate Homeland Security and Governmental Affairs Subcommittee on Permanent Investigations Hearing on the Security of Ocean Shipping Containers, *CQ Homeland Security News,* May 26, 2005, p. 33.

33. April 2005 United States Government Accountability Office, Report to Congressional Requesters, "Container Security: A Flexible Staffing Model and Minimum Equipment Would Improve Overseas Targeting and Inspection Efforts," April 2005, GAO–05–557, p. 25.

34. Ibid., p. 25.

35. Transcript of Senate Homeland Security and Governmental Affairs Subcommittee on Permanent Investigations Hearing on the Security of Ocean Shipping Containers, *CQ Homeland Security News,* May 26, 2005, pp. 41–42.

36. Transcript of Senate Commerce, Science & Transportation Committee Hearing on Port Security Issues, May 17, 2005, p.13, http://homeland.cq.com/hs/display.do?dockey=/cqonline/prod/data/docs/html/testimony/109/testimony109–000001678549.html@committees&metapub=CQ-TESTIMONY&seqNum=29&searchIndex=2.

37. Transcript of Senate Homeland Security and Governmental Affairs Subcommittee on Permanent Investigations Hearing on the Security of Ocean Shipping Containers, *CQ Homeland Security News,* May 26, 2005, p. 8.

38. Transcript of Senate Commerce, Science & Transportation Committee Hearing on Port Security Issues, May 17, 2005, p. 13.

39. Ibid.

40. Eric Lipton, "U.S. Borders Vulnerable, Officials Say," *The New York Times,* June 22, 2005, p. A11.

41. Eric Lipton, "U.S. to Spend Billions More to Alter Security Systems," *The New York Times,* May 8, 2005, p. A1.

42. United States Department of Homeland Security Office of Domestic Preparedness Information Bulletin No. 168, from Acting Executive Director Matt A. Mayer, May 19, 2005, http://www.ojp.usdoj.gov/odp/docs/info168.pdf.

43. Transcript of Senate Homeland Security and Governmental Affairs Subcommittee on Permanent Investigations Hearing on the Security of Ocean Shipping Containers, *CQ Homeland Security News,* May 26, 2005, p. 32.

44. Ibid., pp. 18–19.

45. Ibid., pp. 22–24.

46. United States Government Accountability Office, Testimony before the Permanent Subcommittee on Investigations, Committee on Homeland Security and Governmental Affairs, United States Senate, "Homeland Security—Key Cargo Security Programs Can Be Improved," Statement of Richard M. Stana, Director, Homeland Security and Justice Issues, May 26, 2005, GAO–05–466T.

47. Transcript of Senate Commerce, Science and Transportation Committee Hearing on Port Security Issues, May 17, 2005, p. 24.

48. Transcript of Senate Homeland Security and Governmental Affairs Subcommittee on Permanent Investigations Hearing on the Security of Ocean Shipping Containers, *CQ Homeland Security News,* May 26, 2005, p. 20.

49. Ibid., p. 66.

50. Statement by Homeland Security Secretary Michael Chertoff on the Unanimous Vote by the World Customs Organization to Implement a Framework of Standards to Secure and Facilitate Global Trade," June 24, 2005, http://www.dhs.gov/dhspublic/display?content=4551.

51. Transcript of Senate Commerce, Science and Transportation Committee Hearing on Port Security Issues, May 17, 2005, p. 8.

52. Ibid.

53. United States Department of Homeland Security Office of Inspector General, "Review of the Port Security Grant Program," OIG–05–10, January 2005.

54. Caitlin Harrington, "Some Ports Feel Pinch of New Port Security Grant Formula," May 13, 2005, http://homeland.cq.com/hs/display.do?dockey=cqonline/prod/data/docs/html/hsnews/109/hsnews109–000001674934.html@allnews&metapub=HSNEWS&seqNum=9&searchIndex=0.

55. Clark Kent Ervin, "Strangers at the Door," *New York Times,* February 23, 2006, p. A27.

56. Caitlin Harrington, "United States, Canada Meet on Hemisphere Passport Issue," *CQ Homeland Security News,* June 15, 2005.

CHAPTER 5

1. Statement of Clark Kent Ervin before the 9/11 Public Discourse Project Hearing, June 28, 2005, http://www.9–11pdp.org/ua/2005–06–28_ervin.pdf.

2. Patrick Yoest, "Some Transit Systems Taking Extra Precautions after London Attacks," *CQ Homeland Security News,* July 22, 2005, http://homeland.cq.com/hs/display.do?dockey=/cqonline/prod/data/docs/html/hsnews/109/hsnews109–000001791972.html@allnews&metapub=HSNEWS&seqNum=68searchIndex=1.

3. Remarks by Secretary of Homeland Security Tom Ridge at a Press Conference on Rail Security, March 22, 2004, http://www.dhs.gov/dhspublic/display?content=3378.

4. Eileen Sullivan, "Threat Level Cut Back Despite FBI Warning," August 12, 2005, http://homeland.cq.com/hs/display.do?dockey=/cqonline/prod/data/docs/html/hsnews/109/hsnews109–000001821873.html@allnews&metapub=HSNEWS&seqNum=86&searchIndex=0.

5. American Public Transportation Association, Public Transportation Safety Funding, Testimony of William W. Millar, President, American Public Transportation Association, before the Subcommittee of Homeland Security of the Senate Committee on Appropriations, April 14, 2005, http://www.apta.com/government_affairs/aptatest/testimony050414.cfm.

6. Sean Madigan, "Union Blasts Senate for Transit Security Cut," July 5, 2005, *CQ Homeland Security News,* http://homeland.cq.com/hs/display.do?dockey=/cqonline/prod/data/docs/html/hsnews/109/hsnews109-00000780052.html@allnews&metapub=HSNEWS&seqNum=22&searchIndex=0.

7. Press Release, "American Public Transportation Association (APTA) Calls on the Senate to Fund Transit Security with Needed Billions of Dollars," July 11, 2005, http://apta.com/media/releases/050711billions_needed.cfm.

8. Transcript of Hearing before the House Homeland Security Committee Subcommittee on Emergency Preparedness, Science and Technology on Training to Respond to Terrorist Attacks in Mass Transit, July 26, 2005, p. 2, http://homeland.cq.com/hs/display.do?dockey=/cqonline/prod/data/docs/html/transcripts/congressional/109/congressionaltranscripts109–000001801333.html@committees&metapub=CQ-CONGTRANSCRIPTS&seqNum=77&searchIndex=1.

9. Lara Jakes Jordan, "Chertoff: States Foot Transit Safety Bill," Associated Press, July 14, 2005, http://www.dailynewspaper.ws/15951-chertoff-states-foot-transit-safety-bill.html.

10. Lara Jakes Jordan, "Chertoff: States foot transit safety bill," Associated Press, July 14, 2005, http://www.boston.com/news/nation/washington/articles/2005/07/14/chertoff_states_foot_transit-safety_bill?mode=PF.

11. Michael McAuliff and James Gordon Meek, "Subway, bus safety? Not *our* problem!," Associated Press, *New York Daily News,* July 15, 2005, http://www.nydailynews.com/news/wn_report/story/328206p–280532c.html.

12. Spencer Hsu & Dan Eggen, "Terrorism Alert Level Lowered for Transit," The Washington Post, August 13, 2005, p. B1.

13. Patrick Yoest, "Some Transit Systems Taking Extra Precautions After London Attacks," *CQ Homeland Security News* July 22, 2005.

CHAPTER 6

1. The National Strategy for the Physical Protection of Critical Infrastructures and Key Assets, February 2003, p. xii, http://www.whitehouse.gov/pcipb/physical_strategy.pdf.

2. Ibid., p. 9.

3. United States Government Accountability Office, Testimony before the Committee on Homeland Security and Governmental Affairs, U.S. Senate, "Homeland Security—Federal and Industry Efforts are Addressing Security Issues at Chemical Facilities, but Additional Action is Needed," Statement of John B. Stephenson, Director, Natural Resources and Environment, April 27, 2005, GAO–05–63IT, p. 3.

4. It should be noted that DHS and EPA have disputed the significance of this claim. GAO, on the other hand, contends that the claim is, if anything, *under*stated. "According to EPA and DHS, the method for calculating these scenarios overstates the potential consequences of a chemical release. However, because the scenarios estimate the effects of an accidental toxic chemical release involving the greatest amount of the toxic chemical hold in a single vessel or pipe, not the entire quantity

on site, an attack that breached multiple chemical vessels simultaneously could result in a larger release with potentially more severe consequences than those outlined in 'worst-case' scenarios." Ibid., p. 3.

5. William Branigin, Mike Allen, John Mintz, "Tommy Thompson Resigns from HHS: Bush Asks Defense Secretary Rumsfeld to Stay," December 3, 2004, http://www.washingtonpost.com/wp-dyn/articles/A31377–2004Dec3.html.

6. "United States Department of Justice Press Release, Iyman Faris Sentenced for Providing Material Support to Al Qaeda," October 28, 2003, http://www.usdoj.gov/opa/pr/2003/October/03_crm_589.htm.

7. Testimony of FBI Director Robert Mueller before the Senate Select Committee on Intelligence Hearing on Worldwide Threats to the Intelligence Community, February 11, 2003, *CQ Homeland Security News* http://homeland.cq.com/hs/display.do?dockey=/cqonline/prod/data/docs/html/transcripts/congressional/108/congressionaltranscripts108–000000595409.html@committeesarchive&metapub=CQ-CONGTRANSCRIPTS&seqNum=11&searchIndex=1.

8. Homeland Security Secretary Michael Chertoff's "Second Stage Review" Remarks, July 13, 2005, http://www.dhs.gov/dhspublic/display?content=4597.

9. Mimi Hall, "Terror Target List Way Behind," *USA Today,* December 8, 2004, http://www.usatoday.com/news/washington/2004–12–08-terror-database_x.htm. See also Tim Starks, "Seriously, Now: Get a Grip on Critical Infrastructure—Before Al Qaeda Does," *CQ Homeland Security News,* January 3, 2005, http://www.homeland.cq.com/hs/display.do?dockey=/cqonline/prod/data/docs/html/hsnews/109/hsnews109–000001472050.html@allnews&metapub=HSNEWS&seqNum=176&searchIndex=2.

10. Benton Ives-Halperin, "Lawmakers Frustrated Over Slow Pace of Infrastructure Plan," *CQ Homeland Security News,* October 20, 2005, http://homeland.cq.com/hs/display.do?dockey=/cqonline/prod/data/docs/html/hsnews/109/hsnews109–000001923015.html@allnews&metapub=HSNEWS&seqNum=68&searchIndex=0.

11. Press Release, "ICE Arrests 60 Illegal Aliens Working at Petrochemical Refineries, Power Plants, and other Critical Infrastructure Facilities in 6 States—ICE Investigation Began with 6 Arrests at Florida Nuclear Power Plant in March," May 20, 2005, http://www.ice.gov/graphics/news/newsreleases/articles/infra052005.htm.

12. "ICE Arrests 60 Illegal Aliens Working at Critical Infrastructure Facilities in 6 States," *Government Technology Magazine,* May 31, 2005, http://www.govtech.net/magazine/channel_story.php/94143.

13. Benton Ives-Halperin, "ICE Presses on with Crackdown at Sensitive Sites," *CQ Homeland Security News,* September 19, 2005, http://homeland.cq.com/hs/display.do?dockey=/cqonline/prod/data/docs/html/hsnews/109/hsnews109–000001870212.html@allnews&metapub=HSNEWS&seqNum=2&searchIndex=0.

14. Caitlin Harrington, "Contract Workers Arrested at Fort Bragg," *CQ Homeland Security News,* October 5, 2005, http://homeland.cq.com/hs/display.do?dockey=/cqonline/prod/data/docs/html/hsnews/109/hsnews109–000001900553.html@allnews&metapub=HSNEWS&seqNum=1&searchIndex=1.

15. Douglas Farah and Richard Shultz, "Al Qaeda's Growing Sanctuary," *The Washington Post,* July 14, 2004, p. A19.

16. Benton Ives-Halperin, "ICE Presses on with Crackdown at Sensitive Sites," *CQ Homeland Security News,* September 19, 2005.

17. J. E. Hoover, "Water Supply Facilities and National Defense," *Journal of the American Water Works Association,* Vol. 33, No. 11 (1941): 1861.

18. Claudia Copeland and Betsy Cody, "Terrorism and Security Issues Facing the Water Infrastructure Sector," *Congressional Research Service Report for Congress,* April 25, 2005, http://www.au.af.mil/au/awc/awcgate/crs/rl32189.pdf.

19. Jeff Stein, "Utilities Bracing for Terrorist Disruption by Hunting for Spare Parts," *CQ Homeland Security News,* August 11, 2005, http://homeland.cq.com/hs/display.do?dockey=/cqonline/prod/data/docs/html/hsnews/109/hsnews109–000001820552.html@allnews&metapub=HSNEWS&seqNum=1&searchIndex=0.

20. Patrick Yoest, "Troubled Bioshield Program Takes More Hits from Congress," *CQ Homeland Security News*, July 28, 2005, http://homeland.cq.com/hs/display.do?dockey=/cqonline/prod/data/docs/html/hsnews/109/hsnews109–000001802812.html@allnews&metapub=HSNEWS&seqNum=90&searchIndex=0.

21. United States Department of Homeland Security Office of Inspector General, "Inadequate Security Controls Increase Risks to DHS Wireless Networks," OIG–04–27, June 2004, p. 11.

22. United States Department of Homeland Security Office of Inspector General, "Improved Security Required for U.S. Customs and Border Protection Networks (Redacted)," OIG–05–39, September 2005, and United States Department of Homeland Security Office of Inspector General, "Improved Security Required for U.S. Secret Service Networks (Redacted)," OIG–05–38, September 2005.

23. United States Government Accountability Office, Report to Congressional Requesters, "Critical Infrastructure Protection—Department of Homeland Security Faces Challenges in Fulfilling Cybersecurity Responsibilities," GAO–05–434, May 2005, p. 6.

24. Benton Ives-Halperin, "Infrastructure Computer Systems Vulnerable to Attack," *CQ Homeland Security News*, October 21, 2005, http://homeland.cq.com/hs/display.do?dockey=/cqonline/prod/data/docs/htmlahsnews/109/hsnews109–000001925293.html@allnews&metapub=HSNEWS&seqNum=451&searchIndex=1.

25. United States Government Accountability Office, Report to Congressional Requesters, "Homeland Security—Much is Being Done to Protect Agriculture from a Terrorist Attack, but Important Challenges Remain," GAO–05–214, March 2005, p. 7.

26. Ibid., p. 7.

27. Ibid., p. 6.

28. Statement of Richard A. Falkenrath before the United States Senate Committee on Homeland Security and Governmental Affairs, April 27, 2005, http://www.globalsecurity.org/security/library/congress/2005_h/050427-falkenrath.pdf.

29. Transcript of Hearing before the House Homeland Security Subcommittee on Economic Security, Infrastructure Protection, and Cybersecurity, "Preventing Terrorist Attacks on America's Chemical Plants," *CQ Homeland Security News*, June 15, 2005, http://homeland.cq.com/hs/display.do?dockey=/cqonline/prod/data/docs/html/testimony/109/testimony109–000001724464.html@committees&metapub=CQ-TESTIMONY&seqNum=27&searchIndex=2. See also Testimony of Martin J. Durbin, Managing Director, Security and Operations, American Chemistry Council, before the Senate Homeland Security and Governmental Affairs Committee, July 13, 2005, http://homeland.cq.com/hs/display.do?dockey=/cqonline/prod/data/docs/html/testimony/109/testimony109–000001772077.html@committees&metapub=CQ-TESTIMONY&seqNum=221&searchIndex=0.

30. Transcript of Hearing before the House Homeland Security Subcommittee on Economic Security, Infrastructure Protection and Cybersecurity on Preventing Terrorist Attacks on America's Chemical Plants, June 15, 2005, http://homeland.cq.com/hs/display.do?dockey=/cqonline/prod/data/docs/html/transcripts/congressional/109/congressionaltranscripts109–000001731515.html@committees&metapub=CQ-CONGTRANSCRIPTS&seqNum=5&searchIndex=1.

31. Ibid., p. 41.

32. Fact Sheet: Protecting America's Critical Infrastructure–Chemical Security," June 15, 2005, http://www.dhs.gov/dhspublic/display?content=4543.

33. Brian Ross, "Exclusive: ABC Investigation Finds Gaping Lapses in Security at Nuclear Reactors: An ABC Investigation Has Found that Nuclear Reactors on 25 College Campuses Lack Security," October 12, 2005, ABCNews.com, http://abcnews.go.com/Primetime/LooseNukes/story?id=1206529&page=1.

34. Kelli Arena, Kevin Bohn, and Jeanne Meserve, "Disks in Iraq hold details about U.S. schools: Military finds computer disks but FBI dismisses terror plot or link, October 8, 2004, http://www.cnn.com/2004/US/10/08/schools.iraq/.

35. Letter from the Deputy Secretary of Education to School Districts, October 6, 2004, http://www.schoolsecurity.org/finalbeslanletter100604.pdf.

36. Pete Baxter, Charles Gauthier, and John Green, "Addressing Security Risks in School Transportation," TR News, March-April 2005, http://trb.org/publications/trnews/trnews237securityrisks.pdf.

37. "Al Qaeda Says It'll Use Chem, Bio Weapons," FoxNews.com, June 10, 2002, http://foxnews.com/story/0,2933,54868,00.html/.

38. "School Safety in the 21st Century: Adapting to New Security Challenges Post 9/11," Report of the Conference, Schools: Prudent Preparation for a Catastrophic Terrorism Incident, October 30–31, 2003, The George Washington University, Washington, D.C., p. 4.

39. "School Safety Left Behind? School Safety Threats Grow as Preparedness Stalls and Funding Decreases, NASPRO 2004, National School-Based Law Enforcement Survey, Final Report on the 4th Annual National Survey of School-Based Police Officers, February 2005, http://www.schoolsecurity.org/resources/nasro_survey_2004.html.

40. "Security Increased Around Jewish Synagogues," CNN.com, February 8, 2003, http://transcripts.cnn.com/TRANSCRIPTS/0302/08/cst.05.html.

41. Testimony of FBI Director Robert Mueller before the Senate Select Committee on Intelligence, February 11, 2003, http://www.fbi.gov/congress/congress03/mueller021103.htm.

CHAPTER 7

1. National Commission on Terrorist Attacks Upon the United States, 9/11 Commission Report, September 2004, p. 254, http://www.9–11commission.gov/report/911Report.pdf.

2. Transcript of Joint Hearing of the House Select Homeland Committee Subcommittee on Intelligence & Counterterrorism and the Subcommittee on Emergency and Preparedness Response on the Ability of Homeland Security Department to Gauge Seriousness of Threats, June 5, 2003, FDCH Transcripts, pp. 45–46.

3. Message to the Congress of the United States from President George W. Bush, June 18, 2002, http://www.whitehouse.gov/news/releases/2002/06/20020618–5.html.

4. White House Fact Sheet, "Strengthening Intelligence to Better Protect America," January 28, 2003, http://www.whitehouse.gov/news/releases/2003/01/20030128–12.html.

5. Ibid.

6. Transcript of Joint Hearing before the Committee on the Judiciary and the Select Committee on Homeland Security, House of Representatives, July 22, 2003, 108th Congress, First Session, Serial No. 64 (Committee on the Judiciary), Serial No. 108–19 (Select Committee on Homeland Security),U.S. Government Printing Office, p. 10.

7. Ibid., p. 15.

8. Ibid., p. 56.

9. White House Fact Sheet, "Strengthening Intelligence to Better Protect America," January 28, 2003.

10. See 6 U.S.C.121(d) (1),(8),(14).

11. HSPD 6, to be precise. For an explanation of presidential directives, see Harold C. Relyea, Congressional Research Service Report for Congress, "Presidential Directives: Background & Overview, January 7, 2005," http://www.fas.org/irp/crs/98–611.pdf, for a discussion of the various kinds of presidential orders and directives.

12. Memorandum from General Frank Libutti, Under Secretary for Information Analysis and Infrastructure Protection, to Clark Kent Ervin, Inspector General, regarding Office of Inspector General Draft Report, "Challenges to Terrorist Watch List Consolidation," OIG-A-IT–04–001; United States Department of Homeland Security Office of Inspector General, "DHS Challenges in Consolidating Terrorist Watch List Information," OIG–04–31, August 2004, p. 41.

13. Homeland Security Presidential Directive–6, "Integration and Use of Screening Information," September 16, 2003.

14. "Terrorist watch lists report: leadership, oversight lacking," MSNBC.com, September 23, 2004, http://msnbc.msn.com/id/6082164/.

15. John Mintz, "DHS Blamed for Failure to Combine Watch Lists," *Washington* Post, October 2, 2004, p. A2.

16. United States Government Accountability Office, "Terrorist Watch List Should be Consolidated to Promote Better Integration and Sharing," GAO–03–322, p. 30.

17. NewsHour with Jim Lehrer, "The State of Security," February 23, 2004, http://www.pbs.org/newshour/bb/fedagencies/jan-june04/ridge_2–23.html.

18. Report to the President, Commission on the Intelligence Capabilities of the United States Regarding Weapons of Mass Destruction," March 31, 2005, http://www.wmd.gov/report/wmd_report.pdf.

19. Tim Starks, "Departing DHS Intelligence Chief Pleads for More Congressional Support," February 16, 2005, http://homeland.cq.com/hs/display.do?dockey=cqonline/prod/data/docs/html/109/hsnews/109–000001537775.html@allnews&metapub=HSNEWS&seqNum=137&searchIndex=0.

20. Shaun Waterman, "DHS Intel chief: 'Some way' to integration," United Press International, October 24, 2005, http://www.upi.com/inc/view.php?StoryID=20051023–081924–5096r.

21. Kelli Arena, "N.Y. officials defend response: Sources: Subway threat tip a hoax," October 11, 2005, http://www.cnn.com/2005/US/10/11/nyc.scare/index.html.

CHAPTER 8

1. Eric Lipton, "U.S. Lists Possible Terror Attacks and Likely Toll," *The New York Times,* March 16, 2005, p. A1.

2. Transcript of Press Conference as President Bush Welcomes President Talabani of Iraq to the White House, September 13, 2005, http://www/whitehouse.gov/news/releases/2005/09/20050913–5.html.

3. Laura Cohn, "A Hurricane of Criticism: For the World, the Debacle Shocks, Surprises, and Reveals," *Business Week,* September 19, 2005, p. 54.

4. "Chertoff: Katrina Scenario did not exist: However, experts for years had warned of threat to New Orleans," CNN.com, September 5, 2005, http://edition.cnn.com/2005/US/09/03/katrina.chertoff/index.html.

5. Secretary Michael Chertoff U.S. Department of Homeland Security, "Second Stage Review" Remarks, July 13, 2005, http://www.dhs.gov/dhspublic/display?content=4597.

6. Eric Lipton, "U.S. Lists Possible Terror Attacks and Likely Toll," *The New York Times,* March 16, 2005, p. A1.

7. "Emergencies & Disasters: Preparing America," http://www.dhs.gov/dhspublic/theme_home2.jsp.

8. Sari Horwitz and Christian Davenport, "Terrorism Could Hurl D.C. Area into Turmoil: Despite Efforts Since 9/11, Response Plans Incomplete," *Washington Post,* September 11, 2005, p. A1.

9. Ibid.

10. Ibid.

11. Transcript of "CNN Late Edition with Wolf Blitzer," CNN.com, September 18, 2005, http://transcripts.cnn.com/TRANSCRIPTS/0509/18/le.01.html.

12. Spencer E. Ante, Amy Barrett, and Paul Magnusson, "New York Takes Another Hit: It has been readying itself for a dirty bomb since 9/11, but . . ." *Business Week,* September 19, 2005, http://www.businessweek.com/magazine/content/05_38/b3951012.htm.

13. Report on the Status of the 9/11 Commission Recommendations, Part I: Homeland Security, Emergency Preparedness & Response, September 14, 2005, http://www.9–11pdp.org/press/2005–09–14_report.pdf.

14. In January 2006, Secretary Chertoff announced that the $765 million in the DHS grant program for urban areas would henceforth be allocated largely on the basis of risk. That is certainly a step in the right direction, but, again, each *state* gets a minimum Department of Homeland Security grant irrespective of its risk. Until 100 percent of scarce homeland security dollars are directed to those states and localities most at risk of and vulnerable to catastrophic attack, the country will be less prepared for another devastating terror strike that it can afford to be.

15. Transcript of *60 Minutes,* CBS.News.com, "Handouts for the Homeland," April 10, 2005, http://www.cbsnews.com/stories/2005/03/31/60minutes/main684349.shtml.

16. Ibid.

17. Tim Starks, "Homeland Spending Bill Would Distribute Responder Funding Based on Risk, Not Population," *CQ Homeland Security News,* September 30, 2005, http://homeland.cq.com/hs/

display.do?dockey=/cqonline/prod/data/docs/html/news/109/news109–000001893452.html@all-news&metapub=CQ-NEWS&seqNum=30&searchIndex=0.

18. Transcript of *60 Minutes*, CBSNews.com, "Handouts for the Homeland," April 10, 2005.

19. United States Department of Homeland Security Office of Inspector General, "An Audit of Distributing and Spending 'First Responder' Grant Funds," OIG–04–15, March 2004.

20. Susan B. Glasser and Michael Grunwald, "Department's Mission Was Undermined from the Start," *Washington Post*, December 22, 2005, p. A1.

21. "Tom Ridge, Measuring Homeland Security," *The Washington Times*, December 13, 2005, http://washingtontimes.com/op-ed/20051212–094443–4940r.htm.

22. "Some Wonder What Happened to Homeland Department's Regional Offices," *CQ Homeland Security News*, September 19, 2005, http://homeland.cq.com/hs/display.do?dockey=/cqonline/prod/data/docs/html/news/109/news109–000001870172.html@allnews&metapub=CQ-NEWS&seqNum=2&searchIndex=0.

23. Tim Starks, "Unpromising Prospects for First Responders," *CQ Homeland Security News*, November 14, 2005, http://homeland.cq.com/hs/display.do?dockey=/cqonline/prod/data/docs/html/weeklyreport/109/weeklyreport109-000001962112.html@allnews&metapub=CQ-WEEKLY-REPORT&seqNum=16&searchIndex=1.

24. "Emergency Responders: Drastically Underfunded, Dangerously Unprepared: Report of an Independent Task Force Sponsored by the Council on Foreign Relations," June 2003, Warren B. Rudman, Chair / Richard A. Clarke, Senior Adviser / Jamie F. Metzl, Project Director, http://www.cfr.org/content/publications/attachments/Responders_TF.pdf.

25. President Discusses Hurricane Relief in Address to the Nation, September 15, 2005, http://www.whitehouse.gov/news/releases/2005/09/20050915–8.html.

26. Ibid.

27. Shaun Waterman, "White House Inquiry Slams Federal Response to Katrina," United Press International, December 22, 2005, http://upi.com/inc/view.php?StoryID=20051218–092744–9353r.

CHAPTER 9

1. United States Department of Homeland Security Office of Inspector General Memorandum dated March 18, 2003, from Clark Kent Ervin, Acting Inspector General, to Secretary Tom Ridge and Deputy Secretary Gordon England.

2. Ibid.

3. The official who performs the Executive Secretary function for the President is called the "Staff Secretary."

4. Brian Friel, "Security Sweep," *Government Executive Magazine*, March 15, 2003, http://www.govexec.com/features/0303/0303s4.htm.

5. Ibid. See also Scott Higham and Robert O'Harrow, Jr., "The High Cost of a Rush to Security: TSA Lost Control of over $300 Million Spent by Contractor to Hire Airport Screeners After 9/11," *The Washington Post*, June 30, 2005, p. A1, and Scott Higham and Robert O'Harrow, Jr., "Contracting Rush for Security Led to Waste, Abuse," *The Washington Post*, May 22, 2005 p. A1.

6. Scott Higham and Robert O'Harrow, Jr., "The High Cost of a Rush to Security: TSA Lost Control of over $300 Million Spent by Contractor to Hire Airport Screeners After 9/11," *The Washington Post*, June 30, 2005, p. A1.

7. Ibid.

8. Scott Higham and Robert O'Harrow, Jr., "Contracting Rush for Security Led to Waste, Abuse," *The Washington Post*, May 22, 2005, p. A1.

9. President Discusses Hurricane Relief in Address to Nation, September 15, 2005, http://www.whitehouse.gov/news/releases/2005/09/20050915–8.html.

10. Martin Edwin Andersen and Jeremy Torobin, "Cash-Strapped TSA Spent $200K on Awards Ceremony," *Congressional Quarterly*, February 11, 2004.

11. See United States Department of Homeland Security Office of Inspector General, "Assessment of Expenditures Related to the First Annual Transportation Security Administration Awards Program and Executive Performance Awards," OIG–04–46, September 2004.

12. Ibid., p. 23.

13. See United States Department of Homeland Security Office of Inspector General, "Evaluation of TSA's Contract for the Installation and Maintenance of Explosive Detection Equipment at United States Airports," OIG–04–44, September 2004.

14. Ibid., p. 14.

15. United States Department of Homeland Security Office of Inspector General, "Irregularities in the Development of the Transportation Security Operations Center," OIG–05–18, March 2005, pp. 5–6.

16. Ibid., p. 7.

17. Ibid., pp. 34–35.

18. Ibid., p. 38.

19. Scott Higham and Robert O'Harrow, Jr. "Contractor Accused of Overbilling U.S.—Technology Company Hired After 9/11 Charged too much for Labor, Audit Says," *The Washington Post,* October 23, 2005, p. A1.

20. Eric Lipton, "U.S. to Spend Billions More to Alter Security Systems," *The New York Times,* May 7, 2005, p. A1.

21. Statement of J. Richard Berman, Assistant Inspector General for Audits, United States Department of Homeland Security, Summary of Material Weaknesses Related to FY 2002 Financial Statements Audit. See also, Department of Homeland Security Office of Inspector General, "Management Letter for the FY 2003 DHS Financial Statement Audit," OIG–04–042, September 2004.

22. See United States Department of Homeland Security Office of Inspector General, "Management Letter for the FY 2004 DHS Financial Statement Audit," OIG–05–33, August 2005.

23. See Zack Phillips, "Losing Track of Millions Monthly, DHS Agency Explores Accounting Options," *CQ Homeland Security News,* August 5, 2005, http://homeland.cq.com/hs/display.do?dockey=/ cqonline/prod/data/docs/html/hsnews/109/hsnews109–000001850933.html@allnews&meta-pub=HSNEWS&seqNum=80&searchIndex=0. See also Zack Phillips, "ICE Accounting System Flawed, Audit Finds," *CQ Homeland Security News,* September 8, 2005.

CONCLUSION

1. "Weakness is provocative, says Rumsfeld on RP pullout," Agence France-Presse, July 22, 2004, http://www.inq7.net/brk/2004/jul/22/text/brkpol_4-1-p.htm.

2. Jenny Booth and Phillipe Naughton, "Al Qaeda No. 2 Warns London of More Destruction," *Times (of London) Online,* August 4, 2005, http://www.timesonline.co.uk/article/0,,22989–1720870,00.html.

3. "Bin Laden threatens more attacks," BBC News, October 6, 2002, http://news.bbc.co.uk/2/hi/ middle_east/2304475.stm.

4. Testimony of Deputy Homeland Security Secretary Admiral James Loy before the Senate Select Committee on Intelligence, February 16, 2005.

5. Testimony of CIA Director Porter Goss before the Senate Select Committee on Intelligence, February 16, 2005.

6. Testimony of Deputy Homeland Security Secretary Admiral James Loy before the Senate Select Committee on Intelligence, February 16, 2005.

7. Ibid.

8. Testimony of FBI Director Robert Mueller before the Senate Select Committee on Intelligence, February 16, 2005.

9. Testimony of Deputy Homeland Security Secretary Admiral James Loy before the Senate Select Committee on Intelligence, February 16, 2005.

10. Testimony of CIA Director Porter Goss before the Senate Select Committee on Intelligence, February 16, 2005.

11. Tony Karon, "The 'Dirty Bomb' Scenario: Talk of radioactive bombs and the safety of nuclear power facilities has raised fears of nuclear terrorism. Just how realistic is it?," *Time Magazine,* June 10, 2002, http://www.time.com/time/nation/article/0,599,182637,00.html

12. Sheila MacVicar, "Al Qaeda documents outline serious weapons program: Terrorist group placed heavy emphasis on developing nuclear device," CNN.com, January 25, 2002, http://archives.cnn.com/2002/US/01/24/inv.al.qaeda.documents/.

13. Transcript of Hearing of the Senate Homeland Security and Governmental Affairs Committee on the Outlook for the Department of Homeland Security, January 26, 2005, http://homeland.cq.com/hs/display.do?dockey=/cqonline/prod/data/docs/html/transcripts/congressional/109/congressionaltranscripts109–000001501973.html@committees&metapub=CQ-CONGTRAN-SCRIPTS&seqNum=55&searchIndex=0.

14. Testimony of Deputy Homeland Security Secretary James Loy before the Senate Select Committee on Intelligence, February 16, 2005.

15. White House Fact Sheet, "Plots, Casings, and Infiltrations Referenced in President Bush's Remarks on the War on Terror," October 6, 2005, http://www.whitehouse.gov/news/releases/2005/10/20051006–7.html.

16. Lara Jakes Jordan, "Chertoff: States foot transit safety bill," Associated Press, http://www.philly.com/mld/philly/news/12131996.htm, July 14, 2005.

17. Text of Comments by President Bush at White House News Conference with Global AIDS Coordinator Randall Tobias, July 2, 2003, http://www.whitehouse.gov/news/releases/2003/07/20030702–3.html.

18. "Weakness is provocative, says Rumsfeld on RP pullout," Agence France-Presse, July 22, 2004, http://www.inq7.net/brk/2004/jul/22/text/brkpol_4-1-p.htm.

19. United States Government Accountability Office, "State Department: Improvements Needed to Strengthen U.S. Passport Fraud Detection Efforts, Report to the Committee on Homeland Security and Governmental Affairs, U.S. Senate," GAO–05–477, May 2005

20. President Addresses Military Families, Discusses War on Terror, August 24, 2005, http://www.whitehouse.gov/news/releases/2005/08/20050824.html.

21. Clark Kent Ervin, "Mission: Difficult, but not Impossible," *New York Times,* December 27, 2004, p. A21.

22. Dan Eggen and Spencer S. Hsu, "Immigration Nominee's Credentials Questioned," *Washington Post,* September 20, 2005, p. A1.The President was ultimately forced to install Myers by means of a recess appointment when Democratic Senator Carl Levin of Michigan held up her nomination on grounds unrelated to her qualifications and refused to budge. See Michael Sandler, "Bush Pick for Immigration Post Given Recess Appointment," *CQ Homeland Security News,* January 5, 2006, http://homeland.cq.com/hs/display.do?dockey=/cqonline/prod/data/docs/html/news/109/news109–000002025160.html@allnews&metapub=CQ-NEWS&seqNum=43&searchIndex=0.

23. Wilson P. Dizard III, "Laura Callahan Resigns from Homeland Security Department," *Government Computer News,* April 5, 2004, http://www.gcn.com/23_7/inbrief/25482–1.html.

24. United States Department of Homeland Security Office of Inspector General, Semiannual Report to the Congress—October 1, 2004–March 31, 2005, http://www.dhs.gov/interweb/assetlibrary/OIG_SAR_Oct04_Mar05.pdf, p. 18. See also Mary Jacoby, "How Secure is the Department of Homeland Security: Senior Homeland Security official Faisal Gill fails to disclose that he worked for an American Muslim leader now in jail on terrorism charges," Salon. com, June 22, 2004, http://www.salon.com/news/feature/2004/06/22/gill/.

25. Statement by Homeland Security Secretary Michael Chertoff before the United States House Select Committee on Hurricane Katrina, October 19, 2005, http://www.dhs.gov/dhspublic/display?content=4896.

26. Interview of Homeland Security Secretary Michael Chertoff by Robert Siegel, *All Things Considered,* National Public Radio, September 1, 2005.

27. Kurt Andersen, "The Imperial City: W's Hurricane—Will Katrina Change What 9/11 Didn't?," *New York Magazine,* September 19, 2005, http://newyorkmetro.com/nymetro/news/columns/imperial-city/14284/.

28. Transcript of Hearing before the Senate Governmental Affairs Committee on Homeland Security, Office of Management and Budget Nominations, February 27, 2003, http://homeland.cq.com/ hs/display.do?dockey=/cqonline/prod/data/docs/html/transcripts/congressional/108/congressional transcripts108–000000613509.html@committeesarchive&metapub=CQ-CONGTRANSCRIPTS &seqNum=391&searchIndex=1.

INDEX